HOPE
and
HISTORY

HOPE
and
HISTORY

Why We Must Share
the Story of the Movement

VINCENT HARDING

ORBIS BOOKS

Maryknoll, New York 10545

Second Printing, October 1990

The Catholic Foreign Mission Society of America (Maryknoll) recruits and trains people for overseas missionary service. Through Orbis Books, Maryknoll aims to foster the international dialogue that is essential to mission. The books published, however, reflect the opinions of their authors and are not meant to represent the official position of the society.

Grateful acknowledgment is made for permission to reprint the following copyrighted material:

Excerpt from "Black Art" by Amiri Baraka. Copyright © 1968. Reprinted courtesy of Amiri Baraka.

Excerpt from "Creation Spell" by Ed Bullins. Copyright © 1969. Reprinted by permission of Ed Bullins.

Excerpts from "Speak the Truth to the People" and "I am a Black Woman" by Mari Evans. Copyright © 1970. Reprinted courtesy of Mari Evans.

Excerpts from poems by Langston Hughes. Excerpts from "Dreams" copyright © 1932 by Alfred A. Knopf Inc., copyright © renewed 1960 by Langston Hughes. "Let America Be America Again" copyright © 1938 by Langston Hughes, copyright © renewed 1965 by Langston Hughes. "Personal" copyright © 1959 by Langston Hughes, copyright © renewed 1987 by George Bass. All poems reprinted by permission of Harold Ober Associates.

Excerpt from "Poem for Mrs. Fannie Lou Hamer" by June Jordan. Copyright © 1989. Reprinted by permission of June Jordan.

Excerpts from *The Voice of the Children*, edited by June Jordan and Terri Bush. Copyright © 1970 by The Voice of the Children, Inc. Reprinted courtesy of The Voice of the Children, Inc.

Excerpt from "A Message All Blackpeople Can Dig" by Haki Madhubuti. Copyright © 1969. Reprinted courtesy of Haki Madhubuti.

Excerpt from "Keep on Pushing" by Curtis Mayfield. Copyright © 1964, Warner Tamerlane Publishing Corp. All Rights Reserved. Used By Permission.

Excerpts from "So Is My Life" from *Song of Protest* by Pablo Neruda, English translation by Miguel Algarin. Copyright © 1976 by Miguel Algarin. Reprinted by permission of William Morrow & Co.

Excerpts from "Malcolm" and "poem at thirty" by Sonia Sanchez. Copyright © 1969. Reprinted courtesy of Broadside Press/Sonia Sanchez.

Excerpt from "Sunrise!!" by Askia Muhammed Toure. Copyright © 1968. Reprinted courtesy of Askia Muhammed Toure.

Excerpt from "For My People" by Margaret Walker. Copyright © 1968. Reprinted courtesy of Margaret Walker.

ORBIS/ISBN 0-88344-664-2

To the Memory of My Father,
Graham Augustine Harding, 1903–1983

Contents

Foreword

Lerone Bennett, Jr.

Before 300,000 could march on Washington, before Martin Luther King, Jr., could climb to the mountaintop, and before John Lewis could cross the Selma bridge, history had to take the form and color of a guerilla band of great teachers who patiently, ploddingly, persistently, all through the thirties, all through the forties—when there was no rain and the laborers were few—prepared the ground for a harvest many of them would never see.

And to understand Thurgood Marshall and *Brown v. Board of Education*, it is necessary, first of all, to understand Charles Hamilton Houston, who taught Marshall and who made the Fourteenth Amendment hop, skip, and dance in his mind.

You understand what I'm saying?

I'm saying that *you can't understand the revolution that desegregated the schools if you don't understand the revolution that a revolutionary teacher made in school.*

And to understand Martin Luther King, Jr., it is necessary, first, to understand the great African-American teacher/preacher, Benjamin Elijah Mays of Morehouse, who saved the dreamer for the dream and for history.

The first point I want to make here, by way of introduction, is that you can't understand *Hope and History* if you don't understand the history and the hope that shaped Vincent Harding and made him one of the legendary teachers of our time.

My brother and teacher and friend says little or nothing about himself in this book, but it was in his classroom at Spelman College that some of the merry mischief and mystery of the

Atlanta revolts was developed. And as I move across this country, I run into men and women everywhere—new men and
women, Black and white—who tell me that it was in his classroom and the classrooms he created in the streets, for he teaches
in airports, offices, sharecroppers' shacks, *everywhere*, that their
minds and spirits first touched the fire.

I say this not to embarrass him, for he is a modest man, but
to emphasize the obvious fact that he speaks here not from
books but from life, that is to say, from history. *Vincent Harding
was there.* He saw the beginning of the new heaven and the new
earth. And in *Hope and History*, a series of interconnected essays
that grew out of his work as a consultant to the TV documentary
Eyes on the Prize, he speaks as a teacher and historian to "teachers of every kind" and students of all ages and colors about
teaching, learning, historicizing, and hope. More concretely, he
calls for the creative use of the Black-led Freedom Movement
of the post–World War II era as an educational tool. In the
process, he calls us back to the 1960s and earlier, to the 1860s,
when education was a total adventure and an authentic teacher
was dangerous to the peace of an unjust society. By implication
anyway, he calls here, as he has called elsewhere (*There is a
River*), for a greater understanding of the relentless flow of history, which is different from discrete biographies, and of the
inexhaustible creativity and genius of the people, who are the
real makers of history and who were the real actors in Montgomery and Birmingham and Watts.

It is important to recognize here at the very beginning that
the Movement (my capital) he recommends was larger, more
inclusive, more revolutionary than the misnamed and misinter-
preted civil rights movement. Contrary to the pablum we read
in media and in textbooks, the Movement was a *national* phenomenon, which anticipated and paved the way for the millions
of people singing "We Shall Overcome" in the freedom movements sweeping through Eastern Europe and Southern Africa.
All Americans, in fact, are indebted to the men, women, and
little children who broke into American history like beneficent
burglars, bringing with them the gifts of vision, passion, and
truth. And a case can be made and ought to be made that the
Movement freed more white people than Black people.

Vincent Harding finds in that great harvest, which transformed the women's movement, the student movement, and the
church, "powerful and humanizing lessons" that could transform
teachers and students and redeem America. He asks teachers —
and he used that dangerous word in a broad sense to include
almost all seekers and givers of light — to "mine the movement
for human treasures" and examples and models — artists, activists, singers, dreamers — who "can draw from students their best
selves, their best strength, their most powerful vision of a more
democratic society." It would also be helpful if teachers, especially minority teachers, would pose the Movement as a *historical*
problem and ask why certain people and movements failed to
catch the eye of the masses and of history. Did they come too
soon or too late? Were the necessary conditions absent, and —
terrible question — had history itself condemned that departure?
These and other questions flow naturally out of a personal representation of the Movement. And to Harding and to an
increasing number of students of the Movement, the great fes-
tival of the sixties is "a continuous classic whose liberating lessons are available to all seers and discoverers, but especially to
those who recognize that the battle is still in their own hands."
In support of this thesis, Dr. Harding marshals evidence from
the Movement and the movies and Motown, delighting and overwhelming the reader with great, rolling Biblical sentences, filled
with concrete images of a vast panorama of Blacks, whites, Hispanics, Asians, Protestants, Catholics, Jews, Buddhists, Hindus,
Muslims, male and female, "chanting songs, beating drums,
watering trees, redeeming a land." One ought to pause and savor
his language. For in Vincent Harding, as in King, as in Howard
Thurman, the Word is *in* and between the words and the
arrangement and rhythm of the words. Like John Coltrane,
whom he salutes, like Bird and Mordecai Johnson and Mahalia,
like all the great shouters and singers of the tradition, he impro-
vises on his basic theme, building layers and layers of sound and
meaning that explore everything and question everything.
What precisely is teaching?
Who teaches? What? To whom? And for what purpose?
Deeper than that, more dangerous than that, is the insistent
question, which comes from everywhere, from Blacks and poor

whites and Native Americans and artists of all colors and persuasions, and Langston Hughes among them, *What, Lord, and
where is the place called America?*

That's the question. And there can be no real teaching or
learning in America until student-teachers and teacher-stu-
dents—and in real education the categories are interchangea-
ble—confront that dangerous question.

Listen!

A teacher who is also a poet—and a dangerous person, like
all great teachers—speaks to us as a teacher and a poet—and a
dangerous man.

"Bring the students close enough to hear, to feel, to tremble. . . ." (And, yes, come close enough yourself.)

I don't know whether they teach trembling at the School of
Education at Harvard University, but they ought to. And they
certainly ought to teach history. "For it is likely," Dr. Harding
says, "that there can be no resurrections by proxy. Each person
and each generation may be called to stand anew—not alone—
at the river."

Wherever they stand and however they stand, it is certain
that they must stand in history. For the first and greatest of all
lessons is that the teacher is historical. Engendered by history,
shaped, molded, and *colored* by history, he or she testifies all
day long and all night long, even in dreams and certainly in
lesson plans, to the choice he or she has made of himself or
herself in history.

Vincent Harding, who has made his choice, asks us to assume
our history not as a spectacle but as a task, not as a *fatum* but
as "a destiny that is still ours to create." That means, if it means
anything, that there is still history to be made. It means that
there is still hope, and we ought to rejoice with our brother and
teacher and friend, who has seen in his lifetime, in broad open
daylight, before klieg lights and TV cameras, crooked places
made straight, and the last made first, in Johannesburg and in
Virginia. Vincent Harding, who speaks here not only for himself
but also for Rosemarie and a long line of witnesses, warriors,
and lovers going back to the pyramids and the slave ships, has
seen troubles, mysteries, and miracles no man or woman who
does not stand with him or very close to him can possibly see,

and he asks us on the following pages to come closer so we can see and tremble and be saved.

Lerone Bennett, Jr.
Chicago, 1990

Introduction

Moving Beyond the Boundaries

*Being a teacher refers less to one who gives answers and
expects conformity ... and more to one who is capable of
providing contexts and stimuli so each learner can discover
for him or herself. Such teachers are skillful intermediaries
and guides in the search for meaning and self-understanding.
Rather than creating followers or imitators, their objective is
to cultivate discoverers and seekers.*

*One of the qualities that seem to characterize great teachers
... is their willingness and capacity to go beyond given and
inherited or conditional boundaries. Part of their genius is to
be able to see things differently and act accordingly.*

—*Ronald L. Massanari*[1]

When I was asked to write these essays for teachers of all
kinds, to explore with them the powerful and humanizing lessons
that are available to us in the story of the post–World War II
stage of the Black freedom movement, I was very pleased and
deeply honored. For this work allowed me to continue repaying
a great debt, one which I owe to all the women and men who
have guided me in schools and churches, in community centers
and on front porches, who taught me faithfully at street corners
in Harlem and in my own living room, and who, even now, still
open new vistas and ventures of the mind and heart for my
continuing growth and development.

Of course, the essays are far more than personal offerings.
They are also meant to send forth words of encouragement,
solidarity, and hope to that far-flung band of patient, wise, often

harassed, but amazingly loving guides who work now with children, young people, and adults in a vast array of teaching and learning situations—from college seminar rooms and religious education programs to public school classrooms, television studios, and prison visiting areas. But let this be heard as well: *Hope and History* is especially dedicated to all those magnificent, often unnamed teachers of democracy, courage, and human compassion who were "able to see things differently and act accordingly" as they sang and spoke to us in words and deeds from the heart of the African-American freedom movement that swept across this land not long ago. Now we know that they offered great gifts to this nation and to the world, inspiring a revival of hope in ourselves, in the most humane possibilities of our nation, and in the best dreams of democracy. Now we know, and we are grateful.

Emerging out of gratitude, these essays focus on that freedom movement and on our continuing need to understand, to experience, and to share the humanizing power inherent in its dramatic story. But there is simply no way to re-visit and re-vision the Black-shaped epic that burst out of the 1950s without some minimal recollection of the tumultuous moments of global history that now surround us and began seriously to demand our attention in 1989. (Indeed, it often seems that our best teaching requires such a passage from the present to the past, in order to gain some firmer grasp on the possible futures that await our creation.) In January 1990 one of our most gifted guides to the building of democracy, Richard J. Barnet, stated briefly what so many of us were experiencing in the midst of the creative tumult which spread across the world. Writing in the pages of *The New Yorker*, Barnet observed, "As the decade draws to a close, the globe seems to be spinning faster than at any time in forty years, blurring long-familiar landscapes."[2]

On one level, I felt that the image was accurate, resonant with some of my own deepest perceptions, but as I reflected on Barnet's description I knew that something else of great importance was also moving me. For at the center of all the whirling movement, at various points in the portentous year I had caught a glimpse of familiar ground, rising firm and shimmering, reminding me of other times and places in our own nation, suggesting fascinating lessons to be learned and taught. Indeed, as I pondered these remembrances of things past, it seemed to me that both the spinning globe and the quiet, focused points of memory were important contributions to those of us who teach, whatever our settings, whoever our students may be, especially if we see our teaching as part of "the search for meaning and self-understanding" to which Ronald Massanari challenged us. But first let me share more specifically what I saw and felt in the spinning globe.

The initial engagement with the past occurred for me as I watched with the world the events in Beijing's Tiananmen Square. There, before the soldiers came, I was struck by the powerful and committed simplicity of the students' call for democracy, and I relived many decades and saw many images when some of them built their goddess and defined the democracy they sought as "government of the people, by the people, for the people." But the images that almost took my breath away on first sight were the great banners in the square, announcing, "We Shall Overcome," and the T-shirts painted with the same familiar words of our African-American freedom movement anthem, T-shirts soon to be soaked in blood. Nor will I soon forget the voice and face of one of the fasting students, firmly declaring, "We are willing to starve for democracy." For in addition to its own integrity it immediately brought to my mind the filmic image of C. T. Vivian, one of the nonviolent heroes of the African-American freedom movement, rising from the sidewalk in Selma, Alabama, in 1965, facing the sheriff who had knocked him down, and with blood streaming from his face, declaring, "We are willing to be beaten for democracy. And you misuse democracy in the streets. You beat people blind in order that they will not have the privilege to vote."

The overwhelming shock of recognition came again as I watched the television images of a nighttime march in Leipzig, East Germany. In that forgotten city hundreds of thousands of citizens, so long declared faceless and powerless by propaganda agencies both here and there, were marching, armed with candles and courage. By those lights from within and without, I could not miss the familiar human longings for freedom and justice etched in their faces. Nor could I miss the familiar song.

Once again, half a world away from our own fields of struggle for the expansion of American democracy, the theme song of our movement had helped to embolden and empower other men and women in search of freedom: "We Shall Overcome."

Then, at the top of the Berlin Wall, as the past exploded in our midst, there was yet another encounter with a profoundly remembered history, mediated by that power of music which transcends so many of humanity's external and internal barriers. I was listening to a public radio portrayal of the hours when citizens from both sides first scaled the wall and began physically and symbolically to work at tearing it down. At one point, as they labored to open a new day, they were singing a song whose words simply repeated, "The wall is coming down." But the tune they sang was wrapped up in generations of shared memory, for it was music created in the struggles of slavery, music made popular by Fannie Lou Hamer, the great singing soldier of the modern African-American freedom movement. The tune was "Go Tell It on the Mountain," and I was on familiar ground again, remembering Mrs. Hamer's version: "Go tell it on the mountain . . . to let my people go."

The last evocative moment that I want to share from the heart of this spinning globe was located in Romania. It was just a brief commentary from one of the freedom movement participants there. Speaking not long after the massacre in Timisoara, and reflecting on the rising determination of the people to transform themselves and their society, he said, "The people have broken through their fears. We cannot turn back." How many times had I heard those words and seen them embodied, as a Black people who were supposedly cowed, dispirited, and adapted to injustice, rose up with power from the very places where their foreparents had been lynched, burned, and exploited, to break through their fears and give costly leadership to the on-going creation of American democracy?

Of course, I had also seen, heard, and felt many such direct connections in all the personal and televised reports from South Africa over the years. But perhaps I had taken those ties between the struggles of the children of Africa for granted. I knew that at their most profound levels these were connections based not on "civil rights," but on the quest for freedom, justice, democracy, and the creation of a new society. Even when the Sandinistas told of taking King's *Strength to Love* into the mountains in their struggle against Somoza, and the Vietnamese testified to the encouragement they received from the spirit of the Black freedom movement, and disciples of Martin Luther King worked among the people of the Philippines to be prepared for their nonviolent revolution, I was still surprised by what came out of China, Germany, and Eastern Europe. But now we know more about what our movement meant to others and can therefore gain a greater sense of what it really means to us.

In other words, what I had seen in Barnet's imagery was a vital center of opportunity. This in no way denies the great and blurring history-making movements, but I am suggesting there is more. Somewhere at the heart of this spinning globe there is a fascinating common ground on which we and our students may stand to shape past and present into a vector of hope and responsibility. For when they wonder aloud in schools and synagogues, in churches, summer camps, and prisons about the meaning of "We Shall Overcome" in Tiananmen Square or Leipzig, when they ask about the trajectory that took a song of enslaved Africans in America to the top of the besieged and broken Berlin Wall, when they question us about the connections between the freedom struggles here and in South Africa, we have great resources to share with those women, men, and children who wish to "see things differently" from the conventional wisdom, and who seek to let their vision shape their actions.

The essays that follow are reflections on the many humanizing resources deeply embedded in the story of the freedom movement that emerged out of the African-American community in the decades following the end of World War II. To a large degree they are also reflections on the magnificent documentary television series *Eyes on the Prize* and *Eyes on the Prize II*, a project with which my wife, Rosemarie Freeney Harding, and I served as advisers. In spite of (or because of?) my own involvement in the process, I think I can still say that there is no richer, more powerful visual recording of the post–World War II freedom movement than one finds in the fourteen one-hour films in this series. As a matter of fact, this is probably the best place to recognize and honor another set of dedicated and gifted teachers. For though they are primarily known to the world as filmmakers, I saw the members of the two *Eyes* production teams, led by the gifted Henry Hampton, develop into a group of invaluable guides to that process of personal and collective discovery that Ronald Massanari rightly identified as the heart of teaching and learning. So, while the essays in this book are not limited to the crucial base provided by that film series, it should be clear to all of us who teach that *Eyes* is a great gift to our work.

(By the way, it is important to note that in the development of these essays I have not assumed that most of us already have an extensive knowledge of the story of the African-American freedom movement. Rather, what the work assumes is that many of us will want to learn and teach from the treasures of that epic. So the essays are not written for specialists — though specialists are welcome to read them.)

Reflecting on those empowering images, remembering many of the persons Rosemarie and I met in our own years of participation in the freedom movement, I have positioned one central assumption at the heart of all that I have written here: The conventional term *civil rights movement* is too narrow a description for the great, Black-led eruption that shook the anti-democratic, white-supremacist foundations of this nation not long ago. Indeed, when we look back now from the vantage point of Beijing and Prague, from Berlin and Soweto, we realize that the post–World War II African-American freedom movement was our own seminal contribution to the massive pro-democracy struggles that have set the globe spinning in these times. At its deepest and best levels, what we so often call the civil rights movement was in fact a powerful outcropping of the continuing struggle for the expansion of democracy in the United States, a struggle in which African-Americans have always been integrally engaged, but one in which we provided major leadership from the mid-1950s at least to the 1970s.

Properly located in the context of humankind's best movements for personal and social transformation (rather than exiled into some corner called "civil rights for our colored folks"), the Black-led freedom movement provides great opportunities for creative and healing teaching. From the largest perspective, it demonstrates the ways of human solidarity in the face of oppression, the common hope which empowers people everywhere, the deep yearning for a democratic experience that is far more than periodic voting, but which searches diligently for the best possibilities—rather than the worst tendencies—within us all. The ties between Birmingham and Beijing, between Fannie Lou Hamer and the Berlin Wall, are central to that sense of the common ground on which our humanity is built.

When seen as far more than a contest for legal rights, when understood as a Black-led, multiracial quest for democracy in America, for the healing of the nation, for the freeing of all our spirits, then the story belongs to every one of us in this country— just as the students in Tiananmen Square and the marchers, organizers, and martyrs in Eastern Europe and South Africa realized it belongs to them. Once we can begin to help our students lay claim to this common, living history, this ongoing task, then its powerful possibilities and its awesome responsibilities may be opened up to us all, and we may begin to grasp the meaning of Henry Thoreau's statement from another time:

It is the province of the historian [and the teacher?] to find out, not what was, but what is. Where a battle has been fought, you will find nothing but the bones of men and beasts; where a battle is being fought, there are hearts beating.[3]

The essays in this book search for beating hearts, seek out those elements of the freedom movement story that may contribute to the healing of our wounded nation. For instance, the emphasis on the development of democratic possibilities allows us to avoid the limited vision of civil rights as a package that can be finished off, wrapped up, and delivered at some point in time. It calls us away from the divisive idea that the freedom movement was only for Black people, and that other, non-Black peoples are threatened by the problem of "a diminishing pie." Rather, when we envision the need for a continuing, creative national movement for the expansion of American democracy, new conversations may begin about the essential nature of democracy, about its economic, military, educational, and cultural implications, about its profound personal and collective costs. In such a context of exploration and hope, we will be able to make far better connections than we have so far with the heart of the unfolding pro-democracy movements across the world, connections that will surely take us beyond our simplistic "victory of capitalism" approaches. We will discover a vivid new beginning rather than an end of history.

When we compare the experiences of these struggles for democracy and note the people who stand at the heart of the movements, we are given another powerful opportunity for teaching and inspiring. For everywhere we turn the central role of young people is obvious, and we are certainly compelled to ask important questions about why young people in Nashville, Birmingham, Atlanta, and later in Prague and Leipzig took such responsibility for the future of their people, their nations. Of course, such reflection leads naturally to explorations about young people today, about possibilities for their own development that may take them beyond consumerism, limited horizons, and random rebelliousness to a higher level of responsibility and hope. And we need to be prepared to offer our own personal responses when they raise their calls for living models, humane guides on the path of responsible commitment to the expansion of democracy.

Remembering the Black-led freedom movement and the courageous white allies who joined the struggle, we are also empowered to ask significant questions about the basis for the Black-white solidarity that developed at critical points in the earlier movement. We are challenged to look carefully at the factors which led to the breakdown and re-casting of that common commitment. Those are critical questions for our own racially fractured times.

Closely related to such provocative issues is the matter of how we search for cultural and personal identity in a pluralistic society. A clear-headed revisitation of Black Power, Black nationalism, and the rise of the Black studies movement, for instance, will provide valuable assistance in our contemporary attempts to create on these shores a new nation (as well as individual schools, communities, and other institutions) made up of all the peoples of the globe and all their formative stories. In such a context, the creative contributions of artists and other cultural worker/teachers are central. So one of the essays, "Poets, Musicians, and Magicians: Prophetic Black Artists of the New Creation," seeks especially to focus our attention on the explosive Black renaissance that was a natural concomitant of and contribution to the struggle for humane and democratic truth.

Although we often forget it, the work of the artists reminds us that the transformation of human societies toward their best possibilities is not primarily a job for political technicians, but a task requiring significant creative genius. Such creativity was one of the hallmarks of the Black-led freedom movement in our land, and the search for nonviolent approaches to the systemic problems of American democracy was one of its best manifestations. Those of us who mine the post–World War II movement for its human treasures must certainly move beyond historical clichés and stereotypes to explore the experiments with heroic nonviolence that opened so many unexpected human possibilities. For one of the stirring results of the spinning globe and the welcome cessation of the Cold War is the growing recognition of our need for new visions of human unity, new understandings of the paths toward resolving human conflicts, new peace brigades to help us solve the great problems and meet the great challenges common to humankind. So even though the commitment to nonviolent struggle was not uniformly accepted in the African-American freedom movement, it is certainly one of the elements most urgently needed in our time.

In the light of those needs and opportunities of the contemporary moment, it becomes apparent that our teaching is granted a great gift when we are able to explore and reflect on a freedom movement in which many leaders and thousands of other participants committed themselves to the ways of nonviolent life and struggle. Indeed, a movement overflowing with the lives and testimonies of women and men who had broken through their fears, who transcended their weaknesses, who sang "We are not afraid" even as their knees were quivering, who were willing to live and die for more than a private agenda — such a movement and such persons are perhaps the greatest gifts of all to those of us who teach about the life of the human community. For here was a greatness of heart and spirit that had nothing to do with celebrity status and bank accounts. Here are countless models for authentic life and work which may help us to reclaim and restate the old saying into words like, "The lives of great women and men teach us that all of us may tap the magnificent powers of divine creativity which now lie dormant within us and use those powers for the development of our own lives and the most humane life of our society."[4]

Indeed, these are models of women and men who were not satisfied with the transformation of their own lives, the breaking of their own fears, but saw their own renewal as a call to participate in the rebuilding of their people and their nation—and in that process they found even more powerful sources of personal renewal than they dreamed. If nothing else comes forth from the exploration and sharing of the epic story of our own struggle for democracy in the United States of America, such an insight would be reward enough. And if the insight helps us to guide desperately searching—or desperately trapped—individuals to discover and claim their own best possibilities, our teaching will have leaped beyond the sharing of information to the sharing of life.

The essays in this book are meant for those who seek to leap, who recognize their teaching as both gift and calling, as opportunity and mandate to work for the advancement of humanity's best hopes, beginning in very specific beating hearts. For I am convinced that the story of the Black-led struggle to expand American democracy is a grand opportunity for us to learn and teach what we have already known at levels far beyond words: When we search deeply enough into the struggles for truth, justice, and hope of any human community, moving with disciplined compassion and vision, we emerge from the exploration with lessons that were meant for us all. In other words, when approaching the movement from this perspective, what we realize is that the story of the African-American struggle for freedom, democracy, and transformation is a great continuing human classic whose liberating lessons are available to all seekers and discoverers, but especially to those who understand that the battle is still in their own hands and hearts.

That is why we sing common songs of determination and hope across decades and continents. That is why the nineteenth-century-based cries and melodies of enslaved Africans in America echo off a wall in the center of Europe today. That is why we can hear and see Gandhi's teachings on the essential unity between democratic politics and soulful religion and at the same time recognize the voices and lives of Fred Shuttlesworth, Abraham Heschel, Diane Nash, Clarence Jordan, and many other inspired weavers of faith and work in this land. (Given the growing interest in the subject, what better way to teach religion — in any setting — than through the experiences of those persons whose lives have been deeply moved by the power of the divine and who have allowed that movement to expand their hearts and draw them into the struggle for a more just, compassionate, and democratic society?)

These are some of the major themes of this book, always pressing us beyond history, toward the future, by way of the transformative demands of our present time. Because I have always believed that the African-American struggle for the expansion of democracy in our land is a liberating gift for us all, I have also assumed that if we enter and teach it with creativity and hope to all of our nation's citizens, we will eventually find a critical mass who are prepared to continue to seek for what a Chinese student demanded of us — "more advanced ideas about democracy." Nor have I ever forgotten the fact that in both South and North, wherever the freedom movement was active and compelling, the Black crime rate dropped dramatically in that community. So I look forward to the re-emergence of our large-scale struggle for democracy, encouraged by teachers of wisdom and compassion, filled with participants of many colors, offering creative alternatives for the lives of us all. What a magnificent way to "fight crime." (How else shall we "fight the power"?)

As we continue "to see things differently and act accordingly," we may eventually claim both the vision and the hope of one of our nation's greatest teachers and workers for democracy, W.E.B. Du Bois. In his early nineties, after many decades of fighting for freedom and justice at home and abroad — often at great cost — Du Bois was able to write,

This is a beautiful world; this is a wonderful America, which the founding fathers dreamed until their sons drowned it in the blood of slavery and devoured it in greed. Our children must rebuild it.[5]

Of course, he knew what we all know. The task is not really our children's if it is not ours. For we are the teachers. Thoreau's beating hearts belong to us all, connect us to the heartbeats of the world. So our final introductory lesson must come from Langston Hughes, our poet/teacher who saw what was needed and said, "We, the people, must redeem our land . . . And make America again."

What does it mean to redeem a land, to remake a nation? Who are "the people" who must do it? And who are the teachers, and what is the curriculum that will prepare us for such a task? These are the issues which often burned at the center of the movement, which today demand the attention of democratic movements everywhere. These are the questions that inform the heart of my work. *Hope and History* is an invitation to other seekers, a search for companions in the rediscovery and re-creation of our nation, fellow-travelers beyond the boundaries, passionate dancers possessed by a vision of the divine possibilities of our humanity. Welcome.

1

Signs . . . Signs . . . Turn Visible Again

The Transformative Uses of Biography

One summer night not long ago my family and I found ourselves in the midst of a powerful and unusual learning situation. We had been invited for supper and conversation to a small townhouse apartment in Dorchester, one of the Boston area's most troubled and, in some ways, dangerous communities. There we sat together with some of the new, unsung heroes of the continuing movement for compassionate liberation and hope in this country—a group of Afro-American young men and women in their twenties and early thirties. Most of them were either students at or recent graduates of some of the elite colleges and universities of the Boston/Cambridge area, and, according to the prevailing wisdom of our time, they should have been somewhere else—preferably on a fast, one-way shuttle toward the pleasures of an upwardly mobile Black middle-class life.

Instead, inspired by profound religious convictions and a politically informed social vision, this group of a dozen or so attractive and highly skilled Black young people had decided to turn their lives toward the broken beauty of the Dorchester and Roxbury communities. While continuing their schooling or earning a living with their considerable talents, they have recently formed a community of hope and commitment, dedicated to

13

working in solidarity with their neighbors, especially the young people of the area. They are seeking to find and offer alternatives to the explosive hopelessness or the money-driven fantasies of material success built on drugs, violence, and other superheated expressions of mainstream American values. The townhouse, with its smashed and boarded front window to maintain our sense of perspective, was the home of two of the leading members of this courageous group of urban organizers, who call themselves the African People's Pentecostal Church. It was they who had invited their young friends from the neighborhood to come in and meet us, as well as to share a meal prepared by some of the extended family of concern.

Just the day before our visit a neighborhood teenager had been killed simply because she had stood unwittingly in the line of fire between young men whose drug-dealing arguments had erupted into a shootout, again. So for a time that all-too-common incident formed the center of our conversation. Then, as we all squeezed into the small living room, occupying its spare, basic furniture and spreading out on the floor, I was especially drawn to a young man who was something of a hero to his younger companions on the block. Built like a football tight-end, Darryl was tall, dark-complexioned, and very articulate. At the age of twenty-two he was also a major drug runner in the area, supervising at least a dozen younger boys who held him in awe at least as much for his charismatic personality as for the expensive cars he drove.

For a while Darryl and I spoke only to each other, and the conversation between the two of us moved quickly to the subject of what it means to grow up and survive in such a community. Very soon it became clear to me that I was talking to a person of impressive intellectual capacities who was also the possessor of a lively conscience. Although he had not gone beyond high school in his formal education, Darryl had obviously exposed himself to the worlds of history, religion, science, psychology, and a variety of "New Age" philosophies. As we talked I could easily see him one day teaching in a classroom, sharing the unconventional wisdom that he had already gathered from his dangerous and ultimately destructive occupation. At every moment, though, he persistently broke in on my dreams of him to talk about his present realities, especially about what it meant to be a caring and compassionate person on the streets, "where caring and compassion don't mean nothing, where they can get you killed."

Darryl was obviously talking about his own experiences in those words and he expressed great appreciation for the fact that young Black people like the members of the African People's Pentecostal Church had decided to move in among his friends, to share their struggles, to embody other alternatives for their lives. For when I asked him why the young men and women on his streets found themselves so deeply enmeshed in the traps and deadly values of such a world, he became even more serious than before, and in an accent that mixed West Indian and southern Black rhythms, he said something like this: "You know, doc, out on those streets it's like being on a dark, dark country road at midnight, with no moon and no lights to guide you; and you can't see any signposts at all. So they're lost, don't know where to go, and they can be pulled down into any hole."

Then our articulate guide paused and looked around at the college- and university-educated sisters and brothers who both accepted him and challenged him to move beyond his own darkness. Finally, he gestured toward some of his young drug-runners and hangers-on who were moving in and out of the open door of the house, and he said, of them, of himself, "What we need are signposts to help us find the way. I don't mean no regular signposts," he added. "I mean like live, human signposts, people—people we can look at, be with, listen to, people like Gene and these folks here. That's what we need. Signposts."

I have never forgotten those words, or the sound of Darryl's voice, or the slightly defiant, desperate, and guarded look in his eyes as he honored me by sharing so deep a part of his hunger. (Nor have I forgotten my dreams and hopes for him as strong, stalwart teacher, as signpost, one day running a longer, more life-giving race. And I hear variations on the song within me: "Guide his feet, while he runs this race.")

Months after I met Darryl, his words took on even larger meaning when I heard the Talking Heads on their *Naked* album crying out, "Signs/Signs are lost/Signs disappear/Turn invisible."

Obviously the darkness and the need for directed lives were not confined to Dorchester and Roxbury, could not be limited to the Black communities of this nation. No, as always, because of our sensitivity, our vulnerability, we are emblems of a larger, more extensive hunger, one shared by many kinds of young people, and others, across the land. And though this ubiquitous plea for life-shepherding signs to become visible is masked by a thousand off-putting poses, and often covered with the wildest screams, or silences, every teacher with a modicum of compassion recognizes its presence in every imaginable educational setting.

Listening to Darryl and his moonless generation, catching the cries of the millions of youth and adults for whom the Talking Heads speak, we are able to sense one of the great privileges of our vocation (for teaching at its best is surely better described as a calling than as a profession — unless, of course, we allow the original Middle English religious meaning of that latter word to guide us). These songs and confessions seem to ask us not only to be signposts, but to introduce our students to other living signs who may be able to help them find the way. For though their declared, official heroes may often be pop music stars, athletes, and other millionaire entertainers, the voices are telling us that they really need something more than such glittering reflections of their own limited dreams. They need to see and know the lives of women and men who provide intimations of our human grandeur, who open doors beyond darkness and invite us all toward the magnificent light of our own best possibilities, as mature, compassionate, evolving human beings.

When we look carefully and with insight, it soon becomes evident that few bodies of knowledge are more filled with such living signs of hope than the story of the Black freedom movement in the United States. (Indeed, human struggles for liberation and resurrection, wherever they occur, are often rich in such lively, translucent testimonies, personified in men and women of amazing possibilities.) Interestingly enough, our students seem to have already intuited something of the power of this biographical treasure. For not long ago they provided an important surprise to some educational experts when, in the course of a national assessment of historical knowledge among

high school seniors, their response revealed that one of the fig-
ures in American history who was best known among the students was Harriet Tubman, the indomitable heroine of the
Underground Railroad and the Civil War, who later became a
pioneer in the postwar care for the aged.[1]

The scholars who reported the strength of the Tubman/
Underground Railroad image in the minds of our students were
not sure why it was so real. They suggested that the "inherent
drama and conflict" of the subject matter might help account
for its presence, as well as the fact that the testing had been
done shortly after a national television treatment of the topic.
These, of course, are likely enough factors, but at a deeper level
it may well be that the students caught the essence of the "drama
and conflict," recognizing that in the case of Tubman and others
like her they were being confronted by powerful, authentic per-
sonalities, rooted in a great human determination to overcome
the forces of darkness within and the systems of domination and
destruction all around them.

When we turn to Harriet Tubman's great-grandchildren, to
the lives that flowered in the Black-led freedom movement of
the post–World War II period, we are flooded with opportunities to provide our students with access to authentic signposts
whose biographies may challenge, illuminate, and inspire young
people and adults—across lines of race, class, gender, and
nationality. There are literally hundreds of well-documented
examples and thousands more still waiting for their compelling
life stories to receive the documentation that groups of curious
and committed students and teachers could provide. The potential subjects of such explorations are living and dead, Black and
white, urban and rural, poor and not-so-poor, people of varied
religious and nonreligious persuasions, a marvelous cross-
section of hope. Each provides us with a vivid opportunity to
use biographical study as a teaching tool, to allow the life stories
of significant women and men to draw students into their light,
and to make it possible for all of us to reassess our own understandings of what makes for a "significant" life.

So we could begin, for instance, with Fannie Lou Hamer,
allowing students to hear her magnificent voice on tape and see
her in a documentary such as *Eyes on the Prize*, while beginning

to ask themselves what it was like to grow up Black (or white) in Mississippi in the 1920s and 1930s. To understand why Mrs. Hamer never went beyond fourth grade, to sense what kind of prison the institution of sharecropping could be, and how a woman in her forties could finally break through the past to become one of the activist-philosopher heroines of the southern freedom movement—these could be compelling tasks for a group of students. But it is likely that nothing would be more challenging than to be asked to respond to June Jordan's "Poem for Mrs. Fannie Lou Hamer," perhaps to write lines of their own in response to the mourning beauty of Jordan's final song for this friend, this

> one full Black lily
> luminescent
> in a homemade field
> of love[2]

If we continued with the strange light of the Magnolia State, we could turn to Michael (Mickey) Schwerner and his wife, Rita, and ask why a young professional Jewish couple from New York City would want to come to Mississippi and risk their lives working in a Black-led movement for freedom, justice, and the renewal of both the state and the nation. In the light of the tensions that periodically surface between Black people and members of the Jewish communities of America, in the light of this nation's historic and contemporary tendencies toward anti-semitism, there are some important questions to ask and answer here, questions that the film *Mississippi Burning* essentially ignored.

Keeping some of the fascinating historical lines intact, we might turn our students toward Bernice Johnson Reagon, who grew up as a Black minister's child in Albany, Georgia, and helped organize the Freedom Singers as part of the movement's rich cultural life in that city. Bernice then traveled with the group across the country, raising funds for the movement, telling its story in words and music, finally singing and testifying in New York City, where Mickey and Rita heard the group and were so deeply moved that they decided to give a period of their lives to the southern struggle. Bernice is now the leading spirit of Sweet Honey in the Rock, one of the best-known women's singing groups in the world. At the same time, she is also Dr. Bernice Reagon, musicologist and ethnographer, on the staff of the Smithsonian Institution in the nation's capital, and a recipient of one of the prestigious MacArthur Fellowships. So she stands as a luminous signpost who can be seen, heard, and touched right here and now.

Actually, the list is long enough for years of teaching. Students know something of Martin Luther King, Jr., but often not enough to help them see the richness, strength, and costliness of the life he led. They have usually not been guided to consider the motivations that take a person from a relatively comfortable middle-class existence to the place where finally he was sharply challenging the dominant values, structures, and leadership of a nation he loved so dearly. Perhaps, then, it would be good to let our students see King through the eyes of younger people, like Martin King III, or Bernice "Bunny" King, the youngest child, who has decided to be both lawyer and minister, or through the life of Yolanda ("Yoki"), oldest child, who went to jail for the first time when she was in her thirties, seeking a just American policy toward South Africa and the freedom movement there.

Of course, even (or especially) as we deal with such relatively young lives, it will be good to be prepared for issues that take us beneath the surface of social and political activism. For Martin III needs to be allowed to recollect the time of his father's assassination and to say, "All through that period . . . I was hurt. I couldn't understand why a man who loves and tried to love so many could be brutally assassinated for no apparent reason."[3] All our students, of all ages, surely need to feel free to go with Marty, probing that ancient question for their own lives, raising their own questions with and about martyred heroes of our times, always in search of their own signs.

On the other hand, we and our students tend to know almost nothing of Malcolm X (many ask, "Who was Malcolm the Tenth?"). Here was one of the greatest signposts of this century, planted originally in the heart of darkness. Here was life so powerful in its self-destruction and then in its redemptive force that its authenticity grasps all who approach him. Here was De-Troit Red, self-hating denizen of criminal depths who rose to become "much more than there was time for him to be,"[4] first Malcolm X, then El-Hajj Malik El-Shabazz. Which students will we assign to learn the meaning of his X and of his new names, to help us and themselves understand the power and meaning of new names in the lives of those humans who seek to become new people? Perhaps they will want to hear from Malcolm's widow, Betty Shabazz, or from his oldest daughter, Attalah Shabazz, women who help carry the life of Malcolm's signs, women who have themselves become powerful signposts.

There are, of course, names that our students may never have heard, like that of Ella Baker, one of the wisest, most courageous, and most influential shapers of the modern freedom movement. Let them meet her—if only through books, films, and the memories of those who knew her—and ask their questions. Let them wonder aloud what she meant when toward the end of her life Miss Baker (as she was called by so many in the movement) kept saying that her autobiography should be titled *Making a Life, Instead of Making a Living.*

Let them uncover the name of June Johnson of Greenwood, Mississippi, who joined the freedom movement there when she was thirteen. Let them reflect on the fact that June was not too young to be brutally beaten in prison the next year as she joined Mrs. Hamer and their fellow movement worker Annelle Ponder in an impromptu challenge to segregation and attempted police intimidation at an interstate bus stop. June continues to work, to speak. Let them hear her.

And perhaps in a different way they will also see and hear Viola Liuzzo, white activist housewife from Detroit, who drove down to Selma, Alabama, in 1965 to work in solidarity with those who were determined to cross the Edmund Pettus Bridge, marching, working for justice. Let them imagine why she left four children to come south. Perhaps they should be asked to re-enact that night in March, to feel what it was like on that dark highway, to remember how she kept driving her car and humming a freedom song as the Klan members drove up alongside and fired their bullets into her head, because she loved freedom more than life. What signs will become visible on that road?

Of course, students also need to meet the unknown numbers of Klan members who changed their lives, like the one who approached Jesse Jackson during the 1988 presidential primary campaign and confessed that he had been "on the wrong side" in Selma. But now he came to get his picture taken with Jackson, just to reaffirm his resolve never to be on the wrong side of the quest for justice again. To consider how men and women change, to discover that such a change is indeed possible—that is certainly signpost material, especially when the pondering seems to begin with the minds and hearts of students themselves. (Sometimes I ask myself how we can get this word, this message of the possibility of change, of Malcolm's change, of the Klan man's change, to the nineteen-year-old Black drug dealer in Cleveland I heard saying, "It's too late for me. I've already chosen my lifestyle. I can't start over again. It's too late." Where are the teachers for him?)

To help them reach such deep places, let them meet Black poets like Sonia Sanchez and Amiri Baraka (LeRoi Jones), who have sung, written, chanted, organized, and suffered in the cause of humanizing change for three decades or more. Introduce them to Angela Davis and let them ask why this brilliant Black woman who was born in Birmingham, Alabama, whose young friends were killed in a church bombing, eventually became one of the leading members of the Communist Party of the United States. Let them explore the events that made her one of the world's best-known fugitives (was Harriet anyplace near?) and now one of the nation's most articulate advocates and teachers for justice. Diane Nash, who grew up Black in Chicago and then emerged to embody some of the southern movement's most powerful manifestations of nonviolent courage, resistance, and creativity, is still available to our students. Her story is rich, filled with insights concerning the power of spirituality in the transformation of her life. Perhaps she will also tell our students about her continuing determination to organize a "nonviolent army" in America. Will we encourage them to explore such a path? Are there better armies they could join?

Facing that question, it would be good for young people to

be introduced to conscientious objectors such as Bayard Rustin, now dead, and James Farmer, still living, but almost without the use of his eyes. The lives of such men convey powerful stories of what it means to be willing to spend years in prison rather than join their lives to the destructive mission of the military. They would help us to see the relationship between such beliefs and the organizing of freedom rides. They would tell us what it meant to have to hide in a coffin to escape a mob, or what it's like to spend almost half a century living and working in the cause of freedom, justice, and hope. Surely such veterans of the struggle for democracy in America would know something and could help us all to understand what it means to be afraid in the midst of danger and yet not submit to the power of fear. That is one of the issues most often raised in one form or another wherever Rosemarie and I have introduced contemporary students of every age to Reverend C. T. Vivian, one of the most persistent of the long-distance runners for freedom and democracy. Especially if they've seen him in films of the Selma movement, courageously confronting armed law officers and being clubbed to the ground, they want to know how you get up again. How you keep coming back. Why you neither run away nor strike back, but keep moving forward, like C.T., right into the 1990s. Let them explore.

In the same way, let James and Grace Lee Boggs (one a Black native of Alabama, the other a first-generation Chinese-American) open the treasures of their half-century of work for human rights and responsibilities, for the humane transformation of our society. Perhaps their story of life in Detroit over the past four decades will also provide signposts, suggestions for creating outposts of hope in very tough spaces.

It may be that the most important of these long-distance runners is Bob Moses, for he would bring our students many gifts that are sorely needed in our time, beginning with the gift of his story. The story is of his movement from a Depression-time Harlem beginning, to a teaching position at a comfortable private school in New York City, to the profound sense that he must join the great drama unfolding among the 1960s student movement in the South. The story is of Mississippi and its magnificent grassroots Black leaders who risked livelihood and lives to welcome and work with Bob and the small band of nonviolent shock troops who helped open the narrow, blood-bought crevices that eventually became a new beginning for Mississippi and the nation. Let him speak, if he will (for he is not as famous for speaking as he is for acting with such wisdom, courage, and integrity that others are empowered to find their own voice and action).

But for our students and for our contemporary movement, it will be even better if they are able to learn how he literally ran away from the fame and adulation that mounted around him in the South, how he went to Tanzania with his wife and co-worker, Janet, and, while teaching there in a rural school, began to raise a family, began to explore the world of yoga, of meditation, of silence. Perhaps one day we can videotape him as he quietly (always quietly) reflects on the way in which his love and devotion to his four children led him to use his skills as a math teacher on their behalf. Let him tell about how that eventually expanded into his teaching as a volunteer in their schools and finally how that focus opened up an opportunity to develop a new program for teaching math to young people who had been convinced by the schools and the world around them that they could not learn. Someone else will probably need to share the stories of how this organizer, teacher, and yoga practitioner was also a cook, baker, and house-husband in the years of his wife's attendance at medical school. Someone else will probably have to say that he, too, has been a MacArthur Fellow. More important, without anyone saying it, our students will be able to see a life committed to love and service, beginning in his own family and spreading to many other places. The most observant among them will surely see the connection between the commitment to help people break into the arena of full citizenship participation and the commitment to nurturing young people into a mastery of one of the major skills and languages of the modern world. All grounded in love, courage, and a willingness to serve others. A signpost toward life.

Of course, Bob Moses and the others we have named can only begin to touch the surface of the biographical resources available to us. Still, we know that their great value is not in numbers, but in the questions they allow us to raise with ourselves and our students, questions that may open us toward sign-posts. For somewhere along the line, as students consider such lives, they do try to make sense of them. They do ask what such lives mean, especially as they span decades of commitment to a difficult and often unpopular cause. For instance, not long ago a high school senior in Denver reflected on what she had learned about long-distance runners like the Boggses, Farmer, Rustin, Moses, Nash, C. T. Vivian, June Johnson, and others. Her imme-diate comment, in a very reflective mode, was this: "You cer-tainly can't make too much money doing things like that, can you?"

Obviously, she was raising a most important issue of values, and in that classroom it led to serious conversation about life-styles, wants, and necessities, and the sacrifice involved in being a signpost. In the same way, another question naturally arises out of our reflection on such lives: What is it that keeps people going for so long a time? In almost every case those women and men who have essentially given their lives to the long work of humane social change answer that question by speaking of some gradual inner development, often unexpected. They tell of the slow nurturing of deep spiritual resources within them, usually connected to regularly practiced disciplines of meditation, prayer, silence, community with others, at times moving outside the conventional paths of America's organized mainstream relig-ions. They speak, like Bob Moses, of constantly discovering how crucial is the work of "internal organizing" for anyone who seeks to work at serious reorganization of the world around us. Clearly these are questions and responses we might ordinarily try to avoid, but when students are in search of signposts, they have a right to expect us at least to explore with them the ways in which other persons have nurtured the resources to keep their lives going.

Moving with our students into such uncertain arenas is the least we can do once they have been awakened to the issues, once they have ventured into the path of self-discovery. For a profound engagement with the lives of authentically human women and men reminds us that such seriously crafted signposts point not only to a way out of the darkness of self-destructive lifestyles and socially constructed traps, but they do more. Such beacon lives and the questions they raise also urge us all toward deep and often untapped levels of our own inner universe, opening issues we might otherwise wish to escape.

So the signs may be for us as well, driving us back to an insistent set of questions: What is the purpose of our teaching? Where are our assumptions, our actions, and our content pointing our students? To take such queries seriously is to be directed back toward Dorchester, where we began. Poised on those grounds, some of our students may finally feel freed enough by signpost lives to ask real questions about the purpose of their own learning and their own lives. Some of them—regardless of their color—may begin to ask what they should do with the inspiring model of the young men and women of Dorchester who have taken their degrees and their gifts into the service of a community in need. Is that a sign?

To open the way for exploration of such fundamental questions may be one of the greatest privileges of our teaching. To join our students in personally coming to grips with the magnificent signpost lives of our times may be one of the rare privileges of our existence. For it is possible that among the most uniquely humanizing forces we can know and share is the experience of informed gratitude. In that spirit we are able to return to such a sign as was provided by a young Black sit-in heroine in Tallahassee, Florida, thirty years ago. There, Patricia Stephens sat in jail, serving a two-month sentence for her participation in the struggle for democracy, and wrote to a friend: "We are all so very happy that we were (and are) able to do this to help our city, state, and nation. This is something that has to be done over and over again, and we are willing to do it as often as necessary."[5]

With words and lives like Patricia's, the signs and their direction become visible, leaving students and teachers the great privilege of choice, opening a thousand Dorchesters to our view, providing constantly new meaning to Bob Moses' invitation to the organizing of our souls, to the transformation of our nation, "over and over again."

2

Advanced Ideas about Democracy

Rediscovering Humanity's Great Lessons at Home

In the spring of 1989, at a time of the year when renewal and transformation seem natural to the life of many parts of the planet, hundreds of millions of people all over the world were watching Tiananmen Square in Beijing. With the aid of an encircling electronic network, we were all witnesses to a great struggle for democratic renewal as it was being waged in the heart of one of humankind's oldest and most tradition-oriented civilizations. For the most part, even into the last, terrifying stages, it was a creatively nonviolent movement, focused with greatest intensity in the lives of some three thousand students who were fasting for democracy, offering their lives as a sacrifice. But they were surrounded and cared for by tens of thousands more young people who occupied the square for weeks, and all were increasingly enveloped and undergirded by hundreds of thousands more Chinese citizens of all ages and conditions, expressing a profound need for new beginnings in their nation, offering a moving and eventually dangerous sense of solidarity with the students.

Throughout those weeks of hope and anguish the spokespersons for the demonstrators made it clear that while they called for the dismissal of certain political leaders of their country, their deepest desire was for the expansion of democracy and

the diminishing of corruption in their beloved nation. This was
the theme of a poem written by one of the hunger strikers to
his mother. He said,

> No, Mother, I'm not wrong, not a bit.
> You might have been told: "Your son rioted!"
>   "Your son disrupted law and order!"
>   But Mother, do you know:
>   What kind of law and order I am disrupting?
>   What are the things I am fighting for?
>   Is it wrong to fight for democracy and freedom? . . .
> It is precisely because I want to help build up China
>   Into a land where people can enjoy
>   democracy to the fullest extent
>   That I disrupt the so-called law and order![1]

As we listened to such sentiments, as we watched the developing, enlarging scene, it was possible to tie these events to the
original hopes of the people's revolution in the Philippines, to
the struggles that were going on in Poland and the Soviet Union,
to the constantly reviving, decades-long freedom movement in
South Africa. For it appeared that these were no isolated events
and yearnings. We were witnessing the rise of a global passion
for democracy. (But few of us dared dream in the spring that
this magnificent historical thrust would soon transform the European continent, threaten the cohesion of the Soviet Union, and
upset all the conventional wisdom of the Cold War world.)

Then, as we watched the events of Tiananmen Square in
Beijing, we saw two great symbols of the democratic quest begin
to appear, affirming and testifying to the profound meaning of
the student-led uprising. One was the goddess of liberty (which
was duplicated in other cities), seen by many people in the
United States as nothing less than a replica of the Statue of
Liberty. The other symbol that caught our attention was a set
of powerful and very familiar words: "We Shall Overcome." On
banners above the crowd, on shirts worn by the students, on
leaflets distributed everywhere, the words appeared; the statement was unmistakable and the implications were stunning.
These students of the world's most populous communist-led

society were at once offering their loyalty to their nation and their party's right to leadership, and at the same moment claiming the best of our own country's democratic traditions — not only claiming them, but risking their lives to proclaim and make them real in their land, in their way.

For our purposes, especially in the context of these reflections on the Black-led freedom movement in the United States, the appearance of "We Shall Overcome" in Beijing held great significance. The Chinese students seemed to be saying that they recognized and were inspired by the power of our African-American struggle. Their signs were new evidence and confirmation for us, if we needed it, that this American freedom movement of the post–World War II period was no relatively narrow contest for the "civil rights" of Black people alone, important and endangered though those rights were and still are. The life-risking students in Tiananmen Square were claiming our movement for what it really was: an epic, life-affirming, nonviolent struggle for the expansion of democracy, a great contribution to the twentieth century's movements for human renewal and social transformation. For them, this African-American movement was one of America's most important offerings to humanity's continuing evolution toward its best possibilities. (And in their choice of organized Gandhian fasting they may have offered us a challenge, to consider what may be some of the best expressions for the next possible stages of the American pro-democracy movement.)

This is the context in which we may understand and communicate to others the meaning of the experiences of one of the American university students who appeared on television here shortly after he returned home from the rising dangers of the student-occupied square. Almost incredulously, Daniel Silver of Brandeis University reported that American students were greatly valued by the Chinese young people who were leaders in the movement there. Actually, he said that the Beijing students expected their American friends to be their "mentors" in the ways of the democratic process. We were the experts. Wasn't that the meaning of our statue? Wasn't that the essence of our slogan and our song? Believing such things, respecting our assumed experience in democratic struggle, our Chinese sisters and brothers prepared to face the tanks. And the poet-demonstrator completed the message to his mother:

> At present we are all fainting, we may fall any
>   moment,
> But soon trees of enlightenment will grow up where
>   we fall.
> Cry not for me, mother. Shed no tears.
> But slacken not to water the trees with your loving
>   care.
> Surely god will bless the growth of enlightenment
>   in China
> That soon will shelter all its people.

Eventually, of course, we learned that neither trees of hope nor the democratic yearnings that gave them life could be confined to any one place, even so vast a place as China. So while the students were temporarily crushed in Tiananmen Square, their dreams and aspirations continued to live and soon found new manifestations in Eastern Europe. For the grounding, the rootage, the deepest concerns were very similar, though many of the expressions of the pro-democracy movement on that continent were different. Still, in Leipzig and in Prague we heard the anthem again—just as we had continued to hear it in South Africa—and we realized anew how deeply intertwined are all human quests for hope. We shall overcome.

From this perspective, the Black freedom movement, symbolized by its marching song, becomes essential to an understanding of America's most important possibility for the world. And our students surely need to know that what the marching, singing, organizing, dying men and women around the globe want in the most humane recesses of their hearts is not our glut of material and militaristic goods, with their accompaniment of homeless citizens, drug-addicted young people, uneducated children, uncared for elders, and poisoned environments. Rather, what they see in us is the possibility of a large, multiracial, democratic and just society, a nation of nations, true to its own best aspirations. This is still only a possibility, but people all over the world have not only grasped our living essence but have understood the centrality of the African-American pro-democracy struggle to the realization of our most basic dreams. This is part of the inspiration that sends them into the streets, that contributes to the empowerment of all those people who once thought they had no power.

In the presence of such hope, courage, and totally unpredictable ventures toward democracy, it may seem painfully ironic to realize that so many teachers in America have seen our students and our nation in a very different light from that of the pro-democracy Chinese martyrs and their European and South African sisters and brothers. Indeed, it has not been unusual over the last decades to hear serious questions raised among us about the future of democracy in the United States. On the most superficial level our concerns have been aroused by the statistics that continue to tell us that only 50 percent of the nation's eligible voters expressed their right and responsibility to participate in the most recent presidential election, that we have not reached 60 percent any time in the 1980s. However, while the record of voter participation is an important indicator, those of us who spend many hours in the formal and informal classrooms of our nation are often pressed toward other, deeper levels of concern.

For we have seen rising levels of cynicism among all age groups in the face of the manipulative attacks on democracy and its institutional safeguards that have repeatedly emanated from the highest levels of our government.[2] We have also learned how limited is our students' knowledge concerning the roots, the costs, and the responsibilities involved in the continuing development of so fragile a system of government, a way of life. Undoubtedly part of what we are witnessing is also the sense of alienation experienced by everyone who realizes that a political order, whatever its name, has not recognized them as worthy, authentic participants in its constant re-creation. (The excited response of many people, young and old, to the promise of Jesse Jackson's campaigns is a sign of what enthusiastic participation can be elicited from those who seem to have been permanently disconnected.) Of course, another explanation for the lack of engagement in the democratic process is the general tendency in our society to encourage passivity and spectator status, to value consumers and audiences more than actively engaged citizens.

When we allow ourselves to absorb the implications of this nonparticipation in action and knowledge, for whatever reasons, it is clear that we are faced with a dangerous phenomenon. Nearly half the citizens of the nation seem regularly detached from the democratic process (which at its best involves much more than voting), and distant from crucial democratic assumptions. Central to these assumptions, of course, is the critical importance of their own active, informed, and persistent participation to the best functioning and development of a people-powered American government. As a result, we also undermine one of the great assumptions of humankind, and that is that we know something about the care and nurturing of the trees of democracy. Meanwhile, as struggles for human transformation and profound institutional reconstruction continue to roil the waters of the world, we may find ourselves unable to comprehend the depth and meaning of the quests, may interpret them as simply attempts to mirror our "free market" materialism, may miss our most vital connections.

In the light of the magnificently perplexing realities of our world and our nation, those of us who teach cannot avoid the disturbing reality that faces us every day: We know more about the nurturing of capitalism, athletics, pop culture, and high technology than we do about the care and development of democracy. But at the same moment, students like those in Tiananmen Square call on us and look to us. Strikers in South Africa depend on us. Marching citizens who cause divisive walls to tumble while singing African-American religious songs affirm the connections. And here at home, if this nation is not to fall victim to its own materialist, technological Frankenstein of a world view, we certainly need new, compassionate workers for building democracy.

So we are challenged to explore every possible pedagogical resource for awakening ourselves and our students to the fact that our best identity in this society, in this world, is not as mindless consumers, status-driven accumulators, or even occasional voters, but as thoughtful, active, responsible citizens who care (like the best of our Native American sisters and brothers) about the well-being of the seventh generation to come. Our nation sorely needs such benevolent engagement. Our world expects it from us. And as for us as teachers, the work of Paulo Freire, the Brazilian liberation-oriented educator, and others has reminded us over the years that we can often contribute to the larger spirit of passivity or of active engagement as a result of the very methods we use in the classroom, including our choice of materials.

Considering such methodological wisdom, and remembering our need to create a greater sense of democratic citizenship responsibility, let us consider a possibility. What better *Primer for Democracy* (how's that for a text title?) could we find than the African-American freedom movement, the post–World War II, Black-led struggle for the expansion of American democracy? Through a variety of print and audiovisual resources, through living Black and white veterans of the movement, through creative uses of role-play, dramatization, and student research, much can be done. Indeed, using these resources and more, we will be able to offer our students a fascinating opportunity to reflect on what widespread, inspired democratic participation in the re-creation of America can look and feel like, in all of its unpredictable, surging, and often costly manifestations.

I have seen students of every kind literally moved to tears and to new questions, opened to excitement and new personal resolves, when they have been creatively exposed to this dramatic story of human beings risking all to renew and transform their lives and their communities. Thus the exciting struggle for democracy has come alive for them. They have been able to imagine what it was like not long ago when American citizens, often led by young people, took their rights and responsibilities so seriously that they, like the white Founders of 1776, were prepared to risk their lives, their fortunes, and their sacred honor to create a more just, a more democratic, nation. These were the new founders of the emerging multiracial American nation for the twenty-first century, and they may help our students understand the meaning of the continuing creation of American democracy, watering the trees of enlightenment.

At the same time, as we open the development and meaning of American democracy to students, we also need to introduce many of them to critical uses of documentary evidence, oral interviewing, concrete examples of the democratic process at work—and at fault—as well as confront them with powerful ideas, institutions, and people. Engaging in this process via the freedom movement history, comparing it to pro-democracy movements in other countries, it would be helpful for us all to remember a Chinese student in Shanghai who was interviewed for American television just before the valiant occupation of Tiananmen Square in 1989. In an exchange with the American broadcaster, she said that the only thing the Chinese students and intellectuals wanted from the United States was its "advanced technology." Then she was asked if they weren't interested in any American ideas—such as ideas of democracy. Her response was immediate and powerful. Yes, she said, "but only if they are *advanced ideas* about democracy."

Keeping that comment and challenge in mind, we can explore specific events and developments in the story of the Afro-American freedom movement that provide solid material for our *Primer for Democracy*. Of course, remembering the Shanghai student—and continuing to stand close to Tiananmen Square— we may want to move as quickly as possible with our students beyond the primer level. Or, in a more pedagogically flexible way, it may be good to realize that the examples we choose can be geared to primary or advanced levels, depending on the context and the students. This is something that might be done as a freestanding set of sessions, or as part of our teaching of history, political science, American studies, religion, race relations, or a dozen other courses.

The concrete historical examples we can choose from the post–World War II freedom movement are endless, but a number of them, outlined below, will suffice to suggest the richness of the resources available for our exploratory workshop in democracy:

1. *Brown* v. *Board of Education of Topeka*. Students sometimes have a vague idea of what this landmark Supreme Court decision was about. Perhaps they understand that the *Brown* case overturned the once accepted American legal concept of "separate-but-equal" schools (segregating the races in the South and elsewhere). But the story is so much richer that the possibilities for teaching are extensive. For example, using a resource like

Richard Kluger's *Simple Justice*,[3] we have a chance to introduce our students to the original plaintiffs in the cases that became *Brown*, allowing them to consider the human price that was paid by ordinary citizens just to get such cases into the Supreme Court. The pro-democracy role of justice-oriented national organizations (such as the NAACP) and local citizens' groups becomes another element in our understanding of the deepest democratic meanings of the case. Of course, using *Brown* as our base, we are also able to think together about the strengths and limitations of the courts in the process of establishing democratic goals—and our students will certainly want to know why another *Brown* case, with Linda Brown (one of the original plaintiffs in the 1954 decision), now a parent petitioner, is still in the courts in the 1990s.

Now, in the light of the current ideological makeup of the Supreme Court, this topic provides an excellent opportunity to re-vision the amount of dependence that can be placed on the nation's highest court as a source of democratic expansion. It will therefore also be important to discuss creative alternatives to the Court in the democratizing process. (When we realize that it was only in the second half of this century that Afro-Americans felt they could depend on the Supreme Court as an ally in the quest for democracy, the current conservative moment becomes somewhat less portentous.)

2. *The Montgomery Bus Boycott*. Although the boycott is best known as the setting for the public emergence of Martin Luther King, Jr., it is also a source of much material on the role of grassroots citizen initiatives (such as the Montgomery Improvement Association—what a fascinating name!) in gaining the enforcement of just laws. The Montgomery experience also provides a significant point of entry into the vast and largely uncharted history of Black women's organizations in the struggle for democracy. There, the Women's Political Council, led by Jo Ann Robinson, was crucial. In other words, both the MIA and its older church and women's base constituencies press us to consider seriously the transformative possibilities inherent in groups who appear to have no conventionally defined power, but who are propelled by a deep conviction that empowers them

in ways that break through the limits of all traditional definitions.

As a matter of fact, looking at the Montgomery experience itself, classes might be encouraged to study the history, purpose, and modes of operation of legal segregation in the United States. Only against that backdrop can most students of the 1990s have any sense of the awesome challenge that was faced and accepted by these "powerless" people of the 1940s and 1950s. The *Brown* plaintiffs, the Black people of Montgomery, later the sit-in and freedom ride participants and the hundreds of thousands of South-wide participants in direct action, won "impossible" victories for democracy against the powerful and violent system of de jure segregation. What does that mean for our contemporary approach to all those democratic struggles for justice and peace that are now called impossible to win? (The Eastern European revolutions of 1989–90 certainly provide much thought-provoking material on the role of the impossible in human affairs.)

Of course, in this desegregation struggle setting we are also able to introduce to our classes the idea that all things legal are not necessarily just or right. As we know, it is this basic democratic insight which leads to the experience of civil disobedience on behalf of justice and truth — or, as King and others called it, "the higher truth." (Imagine the possibility of our sparking related discussions on the purpose of law in society, on the purpose of social institutions in the development of human life — on the purpose of life itself!)

Finally, Montgomery and its nurturing of Martin King give us an excellent opportunity to examine the dialectical movement between an inspired and inspiring people and an inspired and inspiring pro-democratic leader. For we remember that it was the courageous initiative of a determined Black community which first called King to his larger leadership and helped him to begin to see the deeper purposes of his life. As he moved into that role and explored these purposes, he opened a never-ending dialogue with his people, lifting them and being lifted by them to heights that neither had previously dreamed possible, with him finally being opened to the strange privilege of martyrdom.

3. *The Little Rock School Struggle.* Again—and we cannot have too much of it—we are presented with a chance to focus on the role of ordinary citizens, with little or no conventional political, economic, or military power, as they invest real life into the democratic decisions of a Supreme Court. (Suggesting, perhaps, that in the struggle for democracy courts are never supreme?) We see, too, the significant human costs of such democratic commitment, and we recognize in Little Rock a major example of the special contribution of children and young people to this recent, Black-led opening of American democracy. On the other end of the spectrum, the Little Rock drama is also a setting for the study of the role of presidential leadership (or its abdication) in the growth of democratic social change in our still developing nation. (By the way, I have found it essential to keep reminding myself and my students of the fact that our nation is still very young as nations go, and that our serious commitment to experiment with a democratic, multiracial society has hardly begun. Therefore, in the things that really matter for the future of the human experience, we are really a developing nation, needing all the creativity, courage, patience, and hope we can muster.) Finally, Little Rock allows us to explore the relationships between state and federal governments in the struggle for democratic change.

4. *The Sit-ins and Freedom Rides.* Reflection on these signal events of the early 1960s can only deepen our continuing sense of wonder at and appreciation for the powerful role played by young people in the mounting of awesome challenges to southern anti-democratic practices, in the calling of the entire nation to its best self. What strikes us no less sharply is the fact that the distance from the sit-ins and freedom rides to Tiananmen Square is far shorter than we may imagine. For in both situations we are drawn by the great courage and moral authority of costly, nonviolent civil disobedience led by young people who are willing to die for the advancement of democracy in their society.

Facing these audacious actions, focusing on the sit-ins and freedom rides, it is impossible to escape certain central, continuing themes and questions crucial to the study and practice of expanding democracy: the role of youth, the power of sacrificial, often joyful, nonviolent direct action, the inevitability of frequently violent resistance from those who seek to maintain the status quo. And, of course, there was always the important question: How shall nonviolent democratic activists respond to violent acts of repression? (During much of the sit-in and freedom ride action, there was a conscious decision to respond to violence by regrouping and advancing even more deeply into the contested territory, refusing to allow the momentum to pass into the hands of the attackers.[4]) Finally, one of the most important issues brought to the fore by the study of the sit-ins and freedom rides was the capacity of such movements—largely by virtue of their audacity and sense of moral authority—to attract participating allies from the white majority and thereby offer them a new purpose in life.

5. *Mississippi Summer and the Rise of the Mississippi Freedom Democratic Party.* In addition to all there is of history and culture, of symbols and meaning, to share with our students through the Mississippi story, this is also one of the key strategic occasions for them to be introduced to the world of democratic community organizing. Nowhere in the freedom movement's history is there more material accumulated on the specific experiences of the dangerous, creative, and costly organizing that went on day after day, night after night, in homes, in churches, in prisons, in groves of trees lost in the darkness. This unromantic organizing action is still the largely untold, unknown center, the heart from which so many lives were empowered to challenge an unjust, undemocratic, and terroristic system. While the world saw marches, heard singing, and mourned martyrs, while our attention was focused on daring confrontations and open political challenges, the essential source of so much of this was hidden. Mississippi Summer of 1964 is a marvelous starting place from which to go back in history and forward in time, to revision the breaking of the iceberg.[5] Indeed, it is crucial that our students and all citizens catch at least some glimpse of the costly, step-by-step processes that extended over years. This is what was necessary in order to organize with a people, to develop their best contribution to the growth of democracy, to expand their own great hidden gifts. In a time of quick fixes, this story of years of work brings an essential message.

Unfortunately, the most popular reference to the organizing

story, the film *Mississippi Burning*, is totally, abysmally blind to the heroic, Black-led organizing that eventually began to remake the state. Even the best visual description that we have, in the first part of the *Eyes on the Prize* series, only begins to catch the genius, the frustration, and the power of community organizing under such circumstances. What it meant to take on an "impossible" task and stay with it for the sake of present and future generations is an epic account that must be shared. For these events were at least as central to "the defense of American democracy" as any overseas warfare at any time in our nation's history. And the Mississippi movement ties us in profound and inextricable ways to those who call out now from the creative turmoil of Eastern Europe and the Soviet Union, from the hidden sanctuaries, prison cells, and burial grounds of China, from the struggle lines of South Africa, and from many similar places yet to be revealed.

Of course, we also tell the story of this courageous, democratic organizing because it ties us to all the contemporary American marchers, workers, boycotters, confronters who fight against the drug trade, the crack wars, the jaws of poverty, miseducation, and joblessness, who fight for the lives of an endangered generation of young people. This is a critical struggle, for if we lose the young people, who will continue the fight for the expansion of democracy? And if democracy does not deepen and expand, what are its hopes, our hopes?[6]

6. *King's 1966 Chicago Campaign.* This is an important counterpoint to the Mississippi story, for it provides significant lessons concerning some of the differences, and similarities, between organizing for justice and democracy from southern, rural-based settings, and carrying on such organizing work in the quintessential bastion of northern, urban, de facto segregation. (How Chicago came to be such an archetype of American racism, and at the same time developed some of the nation's most powerful Black urban cultural gifts, is another fascinating and paradoxical story for our students to explore.[7])

The immediate failure of Southern Christian Leadership Conference's (SCLC) relatively whirlwind kind of organizing approach, compared to the years of digging in, planting, nurturing, and harvesting that went on in Mississippi, is most instructive, especially for those of us who seek to work for justice and democratic development in such northern settings. Many important questions are raised here concerning the goals, methodologies, and focal points for pro-democracy work in the deteriorating cities, in the cities where poorer Black folks and their middle-class kindred are living farther and farther apart. (Some of these issues are best seen, of course, from a perspective like the story of the election of Harold Washington as the first Black mayor of Chicago, some seventeen years after King's 1966 campaign.) Here, too, as we consider the power of the forces of Mayor Richard Daley, it is possible to introduce and reflect on the role of urban political machines and their Afro-American constituents. What has been their function as proponents of, or hindrances to, the flowering of serious democratic development? At the same time, the King-Chicago story cannot be approached without our cultivating a sense of the great, explosive urban pressures that were building in the United States by the time King's organization arrived in that city, thus providing a very different and far more volatile setting for community organizing than had been known before. Indeed, one of the most important questions that arises out of the Chicago experience is the part played by the urban uprisings in the expansion of American democracy. How many doors to democratic participation were opened because of the fires on their threshold? What happens to such doors and the participatory access when the fires are banked—or when they begin to burn inwardly, out of control, consuming vital parts of many young lives?

7. *The Poor People's Campaign.* For most students of all ages the Poor People's Campaign is at best a source of vague memories. However, as we explore the story of the struggle for the expansion of democracy in America, it is important to grasp the original vision of the campaign. It raises with us crucial issues, especially concerning the relationship between political and economic democracy. Do the limits set by our society on economic opportunities for all really limit the possibilities and narrow the range of democratic political participation as well? Another obvious issue has to do with methodology and strategy in the struggle for democracy. We may wish to ask, for instance, how much of the kind of organizing that led to breakthroughs in

political democracy might be utilized in working for greater economic opportunities for all Americans. As an example, toward the end of his life King was explicitly moving to test the possibilities of using nonviolent direct action, particularly "massive civil disobedience" in the nation's capital, as a means of confronting our political leadership (and the nation at large, through the media) with the serious and profoundly systemic problems faced by the poor.

The use of nonviolent direct action on behalf of a more just (and therefore more democratic) economic order is still a relatively unexplored area among us. But as the interracial gap between rich and poor, between relatively comfortable and very uncomfortable, continues to widen (and as thousands of young people and others attempt to fill the gap from the bloodied cornucopia of drug-based cash), King's vision of audacious, nonviolent revolutionary challenges to the status quo is more than a quaint religious oddity. How shall we deal with it?

Finally, one of the hallmarks of King's Poor People's Campaign plan was not only its radical nonviolence but its bold attempt to mobilize poor people and their allies across racial lines, especially targeting poor whites, Hispanics, and Native Americans to combine with his African-American base community. Can the struggle for economic justice in America be envisioned without such a coalition? Is the Rainbow Coalition a contemporary substitute? If so, how can the Rainbow become more than an emotionally driven piece of election year machinery? In other words, can the poor, especially people of color, again become powerful subjects rather than mere objects of social change? Might our students have any thoughts, any role, here?

8. *The Struggle for Black Studies and Black Education.* Although we do not often place this powerful educational, cultural, and political thrust into the context of the quest for the expansion of democracy, it certainly belongs there. For the partially successful, continuing movement for a Black-orbed revisioning of American education was actually one of the "advanced ideas" of democracy that emerged out of the freedom/justice movement, out of the creative quest for self-determination and Black consciousness. Indeed, it will be important

for our students to realize that this particular educational struggle did not come from the initiatives of formal educational institutions, was not a reflection of a benign liberal enlightenment on the part of our "best" white mainstream colleges and universities. Rather, the initial calls for a more authentic Black educational and cultural vision (a more faithful American vision) came from hundreds of local Black communities, from highly charged forums, conferences, debates, and discussions on the educational implications of Black power and Black consciousness, on the responsibilities of a people to define their own past as well as their present and future. In many ways it was part of an urgent thrust to develop a more democratic understanding of the truth of America itself.[8]

For there was much more here than a demand for additional Black professors, students, or pages in textbooks. All of these were a part of a larger, democratic movement to break an unjust and unenlightened white male cultural, intellectual, and political hegemony. The essential questions being addressed in the late 1960s and early 1970s were: Who shall participate in the crucial process of defining the good, the true, and the beautiful in our society? Who shall determine what (and who) is worthy of being studied, especially by our children? As we have seen, the answers to those questions are filled with explosive psychological, cultural, and political implications. In that context, the struggle for Black studies—which paved the way for an expanding multicultural educational vision of America—was an attempt to open the arena, to say that there is more to American history than white-defined history, more to American literature than white-established canons, more to "the American people" than a collection of blond and blue-eyed Norman Rockwell creations.

Students at every level surely need to reflect on how educational systems and assumptions are formed, to recognize the hidden politics of education, to ask how education itself can contribute to a more democratic society. So it will be helpful for them to recognize in this movement a firm determination by many kinds of Black people (and a significant minority of white allies) that the democratic, Black and white truth of America be acknowledged, be researched, be published and taught at every level of our nation's life. In other words, it was (and still is) the quest for an American education true to the best visions and values, true to the subjective and objective realities of its peoples. More Black books, stories, poems, students, and faculty were only necessary means to the larger goal of a truthful democratic singing and seeing of the nation. So let our students hear Paul Robeson sing, "The House I Live in," beginning with the words, "What is America to me?/ A word, a map, a flag I see/ A certain word, democracy." He may help them, and us, to understand. For his words and his life surely carried "advanced ideas" about democracy, and he paid the price for them. Let us hear him.

It may be, then, that if our students understand these things, they will also see and hear more clearly the meaning of educational/political struggles like the one that the second part of the *Eyes on the Prize* series documents from the Ocean Hill-Brownsville section of Brooklyn. For in this and similar settings across the nation, Black parents sought to take greater democratic responsibility for the education of their children. They did it partly in order to break the hegemony of insensitive, often destructive, white-defined and controlled education in their schools. They did it as well in order to test the possibilities of democracy and the great, untapped potentials of their children. In a sense, they were parenting both their natural offspring and the possibilities of their nation. Because we are still young in our life as an officially democratic, multiracial society, this struggle for a democratic content and organization for the educational process must continue for a long time. We will probably be amazed by the capacities of our students to see the meaning and participate in the continuation of this movement, and it will likely be our task to face with courage all the untidy, disorderly implications of truly democratic educational experimentation. But how else can democracy be nurtured?

9. *The Black Panthers and Community Control.* Although we have not often seen them in this context, the Black Panthers of the northern urban centers were, for a relatively brief explosive moment in history, an example of the search for "advanced ideas" of democracy carried out by young people who were both well equipped and clearly handicapped in the quest. Early on, our students may want to consider this: One of the most obvious

and ancient manifestations of democratic responsibility is the establishment of control and protection for one's own community. At their best, this was one of the central concerns of the Black Panther Party for Self-Defense. (Their original, entire name is important.)

However, the Panthers were not operating in an open, flexible setting, where such matters could easily be explored and experimented with over time. They were organizing in the superheated years of the late 1960s and early 1970s, years when officially sanctioned violent subversion and assassination had become too common, when Black communities were electric with protest, anger, creativity, and rebellion. It was a time when white, status quo establishments and their heavily armed police forces were shouting "law and order" and were often hostile and afraid of any movements that threatened their anti-democratic visions of "order." To control and defend one's community in that setting meant, by definition, to challenge the white power structures and, most directly, the predominantly white police—the "occupying armies" as they were often called in the anti-colonialist consciousness of the time.

In this volatile, disorderly context the young Panthers had bought into much of America's worst romance with the gun, saw revolution as requiring the use of the gun, perceived themselves as a vanguard force who had to demonstrate armed, fearless, macho confrontation with the police. (As they said, they were "policing the police.") This was a setting designed for drama and tragedy. It was a situation in which police, the FBI, and local white communities (and a surprising number of Black people) could feel at least justified in the murder of these young men and women.

But the story must not be taken out of the context of the struggle for democracy. For the Panther experience provides important resources for exploring the harsh but crucial relationships among race (and racism), the quest for local community control, and the search for the expansion of democracy among an economically, politically, and racially constricted people. For many persons at the time—and since then—the Panthers were central to the larger question of how people can break out of the subtle and overt structures of an internal colonialism to find the life-nurturing spaces of democracy. As a result, we must also ask: How shall we best evaluate a movement that encouraged young Black urban males to see themselves not simply as victims but as prime actors in the unfolding drama of the transformation of America and the world?

At the same time, somewhere in our discussion of the Panthers, it would be important, especially for educators, to acknowledge the fact that many of the leaders of this unconventional group did not allow themselves to be intellectually constricted but attempted some important, expansive steps of self-education. For instance, students might be helped to explore for themselves the books that Huey Newton was reading when he founded the Panthers with Bobby Seale, books like Frantz Fanon's classic *The Wretched of the Earth,*[9] Walter Rodney's *How Europe Underdeveloped Africa,*[10] the writings of Chairman Mao — and Plato's *Republic.* Or if some observant, well-read person looks carefully at *Eyes on the Prize II* and examines the bed where Illinois Panther chairman Fred Hampton was murdered by police, she or he will find that *Malcolm X Speaks* was the volume that remained on the martyr's blood-soaked mattress.

10. *COINTELPRO and the Uses of Repression.* That the Panther experience with police and FBI repression was part of a larger, federally based campaign of official subversion, repression, and "dirty tricks" is still hard for many of us to acknowledge. But the story is now well-documented and deserves the most serious consideration from us and our students. (The most recent and relentlessly careful telling of a part of the story is found in Kenneth O'Reilly's *Racial Matters: The FBI's Secret File on Black America, 1960-72.*[11]) How shall we help each other to understand the fact that a program such as COINTELPRO was aimed not only against the Panthers, whose armed and zealous status could provide some inadequate justification, but that it was turned against a full array of nonviolent pro-democracy forces as well? For at the heart of the matter is the need to realize that elements of the federal government, with basic sanctions from the highest levels, responded to the Black-led quest for the expansion of democracy in deceptive, repressive, often violent and destructive ways. For those persons behind COINTELPRO, the search for advanced ideas and expressions of

democracy was dangerous, especially when led by a people they had learned to fear and despise at worst and tolerate "in their place" at best. It is a harsh and often ruthless story, but for anyone who is committed to continue the historic struggle for a more democratic society, it is a necessary, cautionary tale.[12]

Here it would certainly be important to have our students meet people such as C. T. Vivian, Staughton and Alice Lynd, James and Grace Lee Boggs, James Bevel, Bob Moses, Myrlie Evers, Zoharah Simmons, Anne Braden, Bob Zellner, and scores of others who have lived through the repression and who continue their commitment to the re-creation of American democracy. Such powerful witnesses are surely among the best safeguards against cynicism on the one hand and mesmerizing fear on the other. As the old folks used to say, "Freedom ain't free."

11. *Attica*. One of the most difficult and yet one of the most imperative events to approach with our students is the story of the Attica prison uprising of September 1971, especially as it is conveyed to us in *Eyes on the Prize II*. There are, of course, many reasons for the difficulty: We are initially uncomfortable with the inner world of prisons, for we often put men and women there so that we will not have to face them, fear them, think of them any more. In Attica, as in many other places, we are dealing with men who have committed real crimes, sometimes terrible and ferocious crimes, and we are ill at ease in their presence. Besides, the Attica story—when it is vaguely remembered—seems to be one of great, unmitigated tragedy, and we do not see how it fits into our explorations of the expansion of democracy. We certainly wonder how young people, or church folk, or synagogue members—or prisoners—would respond to the often chilling images and the no less chilling thoughts that the *Eyes* film promotes.

Nevertheless, serious teaching about American democracy demands serious attention to America's penal system and all its anti-democratic elements. More specifically, any of us who are exploring the story of the Afro-American freedom movement for its contributions to democratic expansion must confront the fact that there is a vast and wounded army of Black young men (and women as well, but the Attica focus is on the men) wasting their lives in prison, unavailable to any pro-democracy movement. But the Attica uprising—as well as the attention to Malcolm X earlier in the *Eyes II* series—suggests that there are other messages here. There is more to Attica than meets our first glance.

For instance, one of the most powerful themes at work in this story is that of men who are trying to remake their lives and their community under hostile fire, under the glare of television, and so very late in their lives. No matter how late they are, they testify to the continuation, even under the harshest circumstances, of that deep and hidden spark, that human desire to participate in re-creation. On one crucial level, the Attica rebels were attempting to build, physically and spiritually, a new, more democratic society in the courtyard of the old—under the guns of the old. In the *Eyes* film, New York state legislator Arthur O. Eve, one of the observers who went into the besieged prison, remembered the spirit he found there. He said, "It was almost a community within a community. And it was very, very impressive that they had said, 'This is our home and we're now going to make it as livable as possible.' And there was a tremendous amount of discipline there within the yard."

That was true. After the first terrible and confused moments of the rebellion, there was no striking out by the men, no torturing, no beating up of hostages or anyone else. Rather, their major energies were being spent on building and maintaining the integrity of their new community in the prison yard, on testing the possibility of their new lives (isn't that what the home-made dashikis meant?), on challenging the authorities to let them experiment with self-determination and self-reform, either in the United States or in overseas exile.

We ponder this not only because of Attica, but because Black young men currently make up nearly half of the nation's prison population, and if transformation is not possible within those walls, what is our future, as a nation, as a people, as a democracy? These are crucial questions, and the testimony of the observers who went into Attica must be taken seriously. They said they found love, compassion, and a sense of integrity and responsibility among those "rejected stones" of our society. What are the implications of such testimony? Can these men and others like them really be cast aside if democracy is to be expanded and rebuilt in America? Somehow inmate Frank "Big Black" Smith, in all the sheer strength of his awesome story-telling presence, confronts us with these issues. When we guess at who he once was, when we hear his story of the transformative and terrible Attica experience, when we realize that he is now serving others as a worker in a social agency, we are faced with the issue of hope, the question of possibilities, the vision of transformation. How shall the best gifts of wasted men and women be rescued and harnessed for the great work of building a democratic and healing society? In the context of such questions, if we face them, Attica may become a gift, a watering place for the trees of enlightenment in America.

12. *The Gary Convention.* One of the signal characteristics of the African-American freedom movement has been its basic resiliency, its capacity to recover from harsh blows, to persevere against literally murderous pressures. The story of the National Black Political Convention in Gary, Indiana, in 1972 is another example of that vitality. This important gathering of Afro-Americans took place in the midst of the repression and subversion, while the mourners' songs continued to echo in our hearts. And yet Gary was still able to evoke and embody the persistent African-American search for a creative tension between our calling as the prime keepers of the flame of American democracy and our responsibility to create and develop independent visions and institutions that nourish the Black community. If students can understand—indeed, feel and appreciate—that tension, they may learn the difference between racial solidarity and racial separatism.

Perhaps a study of Gary on film and in some of its documents will help us to recognize the vision of a new society that contin-ued to emerge out of all the terrors of the old. For instance, it might be helpful to share with our students portions of a doc-ument that became the basis for many of the convention's state-ments on the necessity of independent Black political organizing. For many people of that time saw such empowering Black organizing as a prerequisite not only for Black life here, but for the advancement of democracy and the transformation

of the American nation as a whole. Here are excerpts from the
Gary Declaration, the call to the convention:

> Let there be no mistake. We come to Gary in a time of
> unrelieved crisis for our people. From every rural com-
> munity in Alabama to the high-rise compounds of Chicago,
> we bring to this Convention the agonies of the masses of
> our people. From the sprawling Black cities of Watts and
> Nairobi in the West to the decay of Harlem and Roxbury
> in the East, the testimony we bear is the same. We are
> witnesses to social disaster.
>
> Our cities are crime-haunted dying grounds. Huge sec-
> tors of our youth—and countless others—face permanent
> unemployment. Those of us who work find our paychecks
> able to purchase less and less. Neither the courts nor the
> prisons contribute to anything resembling justice or ref-
> ormation. The schools are unable—or unwilling—to edu-
> cate our children for the real world of our struggles.
> Meanwhile, the officially approved epidemic of drugs
> threatens to wipe out the minds and strength of our best
> young warriors.
>
> . . . So, let it be clear to us now: The desperation of our
> people, the agonies of our cities, the desolation of our
> countryside, the pollution of the air and the water—these
> things will not be significantly affected by new faces in the
> old places in Washington, D.C. This is the truth we must
> face here in Gary if we are to join our people everywhere
> in the movement forward toward liberation.
>
> A Black political convention, indeed all truly Black pol-
> itics, must begin from this truth: *The American system does
> not work for the masses of our people, and it cannot be made
> to work without radical, fundamental change.* (Indeed, this
> system does not really work in favor of the humanity of
> anyone in America.)
>
> . . . So we come to Gary confronted with a choice. But
> it is not the old convention question of which candidate
> shall we support, the pointless question of who is to preside
> over a decaying and unsalvageable system. No, if we come
> to Gary out of the realities of the Black communities of

this land, then the only real choice for us is whether or not we will live by the truth we know, whether we will move to organize independently, move to struggle for fundamental transformation, for the creation of new directions, towards a concern for the life and the meaning of Man. Social transformation or social destruction, those are our only real choices.

... The challenge is thrown to us here in Gary. *It is the challenge to consolidate and organize our own Black role as the vanguard in the struggle for a new society.* To accept that challenge is to move to independent Black politics. There can be no equivocation on that issue. History leaves us no other choice. White politics has not and cannot bring the changes we need.

... So, brothers and sisters of our developing Black nation, we now stand at Gary as a people whose time has come. From every corner of Black America, from all liberation movements of the Third World, from the graves of our fathers and the coming world of our children, we are faced with a challenge and a call: Though the moment is perilous we must not despair. We must seize the time, for the time is ours.

We begin here and now in Gary. We begin with an independent Black political movement, an independent Black political Agenda, an independent Black spirit. Nothing less will do. We must build for our people. We must build for our world. We stand on the edge of history. We cannot turn back.[13]

If we can help our students grasp the vision and the passion represented in these words, then they may see the great tension that continues to mark the African-American struggle for democracy and integrity. In the context of our own present moment, it will probably be illuminating to help students obtain documents of the 1989 National Black Political Convention, held in New Orleans this time. What will comparisons reveal? What would our students write today if they were asked to compose a similar document faithful to our time and their vision?

Perhaps at some point in this discussion we will find the courage and the right spirit to ask another version of a necessary but very painful question: In the light of the central, exemplary role played by African-Americans in the historic struggle for the expansion of democracy in this land, what do the depredations of joblessness, poverty, drugs, class gaps and the weakening of older institutions of support mean for the future of Black people, for the future of democracy in America? Are we still, with the Gary convention, "at the edge of history," still fervent seekers of the "advanced ideas"? And when we set ourselves in the context of the 1990s, are African-Americans the only people who need to face and address such questions?

13. *Electing the Mayors, Envisioning the President: The Strengths and Limits of Electoral Politics.* In the post–World War II freedom movement some of the most exciting events in the expansion of American democracy have come in connection with the election of Black mayors—usually the first of some kind. Somehow, at least for a moment, the intense organizing and the joyful grasping of the reins of the office have symbolized for us a certain coming of age, a claiming of responsibility for ourselves and others. If nothing else, it has felt like a long-overdue recognition of our significant gifts and talents as democratic grassroots leaders.

In *Eyes on the Prize II* we see three Black "firsts" elected to office: Carl Stokes of Cleveland, first Black mayor of a major American city; Maynard Jackson, first Black mayor of a southern metropolis (Atlanta); and Harold Washington, first Black mayor of Chicago, the city that is still called the most deeply segregated urban center in America.

The films make it possible for us to catch some of the almost religious fervor involved in the campaigns, suggest the transformative power inherent in such actions. Especially in the Harold Washington segment, there is much for us to ponder as we consider the laments in our own time about citizen nonparticipation, and then are able to see a young Black woman obviously experiencing a new level of release and engagement as she reflects on the meaning of her involvement in the victorious Washington campaign. Rosie Mars's face testified to her sense of jubilation as she announced that "I felt like I was a part of something— making history. I was the small person in the corner that wouldn't get the big headlines, but I made it happen. I was part of it." Clearly the Washington campaign was a pathway, at least a temporary one, to marvelous self-liberation for her. Of course, it also became something like a new day for the vast majority of Black people in Chicago, as well as for their white and Hispanic allies. They were making history, re-making Chicago.

Recognizing all the limits of electoral politics, it is crucial to reflect on the great potentials of such a sense of engaged empowerment. Can it be taken to even deeper levels, over longer periods of time, in the continuing quest for a more democratic society? Can such a spirit join up again with groups like the pro-Washington Hispanics? Was the death of Washington and the return to internecine warfare among Chicago's Black political leaders at the end of the 1980s a temporary experience or testimony to a more permanent loss of vision?[14]

All these kinds of experiences and questions were expanded almost exponentially in Jesse Jackson's two campaigns to win the Democratic nomination for the presidency. Here, it is possible to focus our reflections on what happens when mainstream American politics is directly confronted by the legacy of the Black-led freedom movement in its multiracial, pro-democracy manifestations. As a result, it may be helpful to see the Jackson experience as more than "the first Black presidential campaigns," which they were not, and more than the study of one charismatic individual's remarkable development.

For our teaching purposes it will be much more helpful to provide a historical context for the campaigns. For instance, we may wish to ask how the Mississippi Freedom Democratic Party's challenge to the Democratic National Convention of 1964 was connected to the Jackson campaigns and the conventions of 1984 and 1988 — how the death of the martyrs and the organizing of the living helped to water the trees of democratic (and Democratic) enlightenment in our land. It will be crucial to remember the capacity of the earlier freedom movement to engage white commitment and participation, and then to note the important and growing percentage of white primary votes cast for Jackson, especially in 1988. Was this yet another stage in the continuing and costly education of our nation to "advanced ideas" of democracy, a process long nurtured by the Afro-American freedom movement?

We can, of course, move from such questions to the memory of King's last campaign and its attempt to build a populist-based multiracial coalition. When we place the Rainbow Coalition in the context of the earlier Poor People's Campaign it is more clearly anchored. In the same way, when we remember the appeal that the Black movement has always had overseas, Jackson's immense capacity to capture the hopes and imaginations of Third World peoples and others becomes part of the same great historical energy.

Finally, it will be important to explore with our students the speeches and position papers of the Jackson campaigns, helping them to sense where this offspring and representative of our American pro-democracy movement was seeking to take the country in its domestic and international development. Perhaps that will not only inform them, but supply sources of inspiration and suggestions for their own movement toward the twenty-first century.

It was clear that both Jackson and Harold Washington had tapped human resources that had not been galvanized by electoral politics before. To some degree we observed the same phenomena in the campaigns of Doug Wilder and David Dinkins. At least temporarily, these campaigns opened possibilities of democratic participation and leadership to women and men who had long experienced themselves outside the structures of political engagement. How far that casting of the net, that gathering of the rejected stones, can go within the parameters of the American electoral system is unknown. And its limits can only be ascertained as new forces beyond the mainstream test it at every point along the way. Will our students be part of those new forces?

In the end, even the most cursory glance at cities like Chicago, Cleveland, Detroit, and Atlanta today will clearly repeat to us the truth of the Gary Declaration—no one victory, by no one person (no matter how charismatic and rainbow-based) is enough to deal with the crises of our society, especially the harsh realities faced by the majority of Black and poor people in our nation. As a result, we are challenged to ask older questions:

Where do we go from here? What are our advanced ideas about
the development of political, economic, and cultural democracy
in the United States of America?

Such questions remind us that whether we choose these thirteen examples of the struggle for democracy, or dozens of other
equally accessible points of reference from the Afro-American
freedom movement, certain themes emerge consistently. Certain
experiences underlie all events, constantly challenging us and
our students to consider our relationship to the quest for a truly
democratic and participatory citizenship.

By now it is obvious that the Black freedom struggle has been
at its heart a challenge to the entire nation, a call for the deep-
ening and development of the best possibilities of democracy—
a quest for the healing and advancement of us all. So no American can study these matters solely from the outside, acting as
if these were the struggles of other people. But when we move
in we see both the beauty and the costs. Advancing democracy,
healing the nation, developing humane institutions—whatever
we call it—is a grand and costly vocation. Some have paid the
cost with their lives, on behalf of us all, but the cost continues.
For what is also obvious by now is that the fulfillment of democracy is a continuing task, one that each generation must actively
take up, coming to grips with the harsh enemies of apathy and
ignorance, cynicism and immobilizing fear. Of course, we must
also come to grips with all the cooler, more respectable opponents of expanding democracy, such as the eminent scholars who
say they believe that "the effective operation of a democratic
political system usually requires some measure of apathy and
noninvolvement on the part of some individuals and groups."
Thus they search for "desirable limits to the indefinite extension
of political democracy"[15]—throwing themselves into that search,
strangely enough, just when peoples of color are rising to new
levels of participation, just when the political map of Europe is
being redrawn.

In the late 1980s, when the *Eyes on the Prize* team was interviewing Black and white Chicagoans for their memories of
SCLC's campaign in that city, a sympathetic suburban white
woman who lived in one of the segregated neighborhoods where
the movement was marching offered more wisdom than she may

have known. She contrasted herself and most of her friends to what she considered a minority of "Nazi-types," to use her disapproving words. She noted that the latter group harassed and attacked the freedom movement's open housing demonstrations. On the other hand, the woman identified her group of friends as middle class, and said that they had neither joined King's demonstrations, nor had they stood with the attacking white forces. Rather, she said, "Middle-class people just want to be left alone."

That section of the interview eventually became part of the mountain of materials that the filmmakers had to edit out, but by then its image had etched itself on my consciousness. For I became convinced that in an oblique but powerful way this Chicagoan may have presented a serious and compelling challenge to those of us who are the teachers of the nation. Her own struggles prod us to ask if we are satisfied to be crucial participants in the creation, or justification, of an orderly, respectable middle class (of many colors and backgrounds now) whose major activities will be the acquisition and protection of all the things we are urged to accumulate. Will the hidden message of our teaching be a call to students and teachers alike to work hard to avoid involvement in any costly, unsettling movements toward our best humanity? Or have we discovered that none of us can be left alone within the familiar conventional boundaries when a great democracy and its advanced ideas are still in need of nurturing?

As we allow ourselves to be confronted by such questions, we realize what the statement from the Shanghai student really means: Neither advanced technology nor advanced democracy is developed without great commitment, sacrifice, and creative experimentation. Ultimately her ideas connect with the words of Martin Luther King, Jr., in *Stride Toward Freedom*, challenging our desire "to be left alone." Back in the 1950s, King wrote:

A solution of the present crisis will not take place unless men and women work for it. Human progress is neither automatic nor inevitable. Even a superficial look at history reveals that no social advance rolls in on the wheels of inevitability. Every step toward the goal of justice requires sacrifice, suffering, and struggle; the tireless exertions and passionate concern of dedicated individuals. Without persistent effort, time itself becomes an ally of the insurgent and primitive forces of irrational emotionalism and social destruction. This is no time for apathy or complacency. This is a time for vigorous and positive action.[16]

Now, more than three decades later, there can be no escape from the direct significance of King's words to our own situation in America. Now, from the vantage point of all the pro-democratic struggles that are shaking the old post–World War II order, we may approach the heart of the matter with King. For now we realize that "to be left alone" is precisely what the words say, to be isolated from the great challenges, the harrowing risks, and the magnificent joy of building a just and compassionate community. And the other message opens up: to explore advanced ideas of democracy, to create primers or progressive texts with our lives is all the same, is watering trees, is immersion into the great river of humanity's most authentic life. Who really wants to miss that?

3

More Power Than We Know

Recollecting the Young Warriors

Only the passage of time, the cultivation of creative reflection, and much persistent, democratic experimentation of our own will help us to understand the remarkable gifts and messages that have been made available to the citizens of our nation through the surging pro-democratic struggles that shook the globe and closed the decade of the 1980s. When the images began to pile up and to crowd our minds, entering, expanding, from Soweto to Tiananmen Square, to Leipzig and Prague, they were not always easy to manage. But one thing was clear: Young people were everywhere. And in every setting where they challenged the possessors of conventional power their faces and voices seemed filled with a combination of innocence, wisdom, great courage, and heart-piercing vulnerability.

Even as we watched, some of them were killed for their commitment to democracy. Others were beaten down into the streets or hauled away to meet their torturers. In other streets, at other borders, young men and women, often inspired by the Chinese martyrs, continued marching, standing, contending, leading the lines of democracy's nonviolent armies. We saw them climbing the Berlin Wall, organizing a national general strike in Czechoslovakia in nine days, providing the impetus and inspiration for so much of the rising tides of change in South Africa. Young people, high school and college age, sometimes younger or older.

And very near to us, closer than we often dare to feel, just such youth have also borne the brunt of the less televised but very active battles for democracy in Central America.

Partly because our historical attention span tends to be rather short, it was often difficult for us to come to terms with these images of young citizens playing such leading roles in the serious, joyful, uncharted struggles for the future of their nations. For in the United States, young people are more often seen as necessary evils, as targeted consumers, as hedonistic creators of major social problems, or at best as unprepared and reluctant apprentices being trained to compete to fill whatever job slots the operation of "the free market" makes available. In other words, it is not easy for many people to conceive of the American young people we know as our own pro-democracy leaders, as major participants in the humanizing transformation of our society.

Too often our young people have appeared to accept their elders' narrow judgments concerning their best possibilities, and they have tended to act accordingly. Fortunately, there is much reason to believe that this apparent acceptance of irresponsibility is nothing more than a patina, a gloss which fends off hard questions and issues about their real capacities and responsibilities as citizens of a democratic community. My own experience has been that whenever they have been taken seriously, both in their brokenness and their strengths, whenever a level place for engagement has been cleared, American young people of every variety are prepared at least to explore the questions of their great power and potential for assuming more responsibility in the building of democracy in our land. Again, what they often seem to lack are "signposts," models of responsible action.

As we might expect, young American women and men have been most fully encouraged to recognize their own best possibilities when they find signs and models who are other young people, even from another generation. Indeed, I have discovered that when we have ventured together into the American past to witness other marching, organizing, sacrificing, challenging groups of students emerging from our own nation, coming from relatively familiar cities, towns, and rural areas, sometimes from their own families, the shock of recognition has been salutary and enlightening.

Access to such empowering United States history is not difficult. For instance, we may wish to remind our young students (and their older fellow citizens) about the conventional wisdom that dominated the early 1950s, when social scientists were convinced that the young people of that time were a selfish, apolitical, pleasure-seeking group who were not likely to engage in any serious citizen causes. Even as contemporary youth ponder the familiar ring of that description they can be helped to discover the fact that the surveys on which these conclusions were based in the 1950s had totally ignored the presence of African-American young people, and had not really touched the deepest longings of the white informants they interviewed and observed. Against that background, we are able to understand the great surprise so many Americans experienced when the youth of the African-American movement boldly began to present living evidence that contradicted and uprooted the conventional wisdom. Pressing forward with great insistence, creativity, and dignity, a generation of Black young people entered the post–World War II movement for the re-creation of American democracy. Before long they stood at the center of the struggle.

As we accompany the young students of the present generation on their explorations of the earlier movement—which brought such powerful democratic changes to America—we have many reasons and resources for introducing them to their valiant counterparts from the recent past. Indeed, it is impossible to miss that vital force. For wherever we look in the films, the book illustrations, the old posters and photos, whenever we hear the records or audiotapes, we are confronted with the faces and the voices of children and young people, those whom Lillian Smith once called the "Tender Warriors." In their lives they bear testimony to the amazing potentials of young, positive change-agents. Like their global counterparts today, they deserve close attention from students, parents, and teachers of every generation.

When we focus on them we realize that these junior warriors were sometimes as young as six and seven, bravely walking the gauntlets of hate and fear to pry open schools once closed to the democratic participation of all the children. They were in New Orleans, they were teenagers in Little Rock, Arkansas, entering the school under the protection of the National Guard—but with no protection at all in the classrooms, locker rooms, and lavatories, where they faced ostracism, threats, and violence on their own.

By 1960 they sat-in at lunch counters, knelt-in at churches, waded-in at beaches, slept-in at motels, and courageously took the punishment such a struggle required in hundreds of cities and smaller towns across the South. College students. High school students. Children. They were challenging the nation to become a far better place for everyone than it had ever been. They were part of the vanguard of American democracy. Young people were the heart of the movement. Let today's young people discover them.

On the freedom rides in 1961, they rode the buses, and their vulnerable lives demanded that the federal government enforce its own laws. In the course of their pro-democracy action as responsible, creative citizens they were brutally beaten, sometimes hospitalized, but they refused to turn back in the face of violence, and they refused to add their own reactive link to the terrible chain of destructive force. Instead, strengthened by faith and by one another, convinced that they were working for the truth of a people, a nation, and their own individual integrity, they continued moving forward, until many of them ended up in harsh, threatening prisons, from Virginia to Texas. Still, they would not stop, and in jail these children, these teenagers, these young women and men sang and prayed and refused to desert one another. Eventually, their courage and determination—and blood—forced their government to defend democracy, made it possible for everyone in America to have the freedom to ride, to sit, to eat, to go to the rest room, just about wherever they wanted to (and could afford to), and with whomever they wished. Suddenly it strikes us: It was a phalanx of children, teenagers, and young adults who did so much to break the back of the deadly, generations-old system of legal segregation in America. It was an inspired group of young people who sowed so many of the seeds for the rising forces of democracy, for us and for the world.

We cannot, must not, avoid these pioneers of the post–World War II movement, partly because we owe them so much in the contemporary, continuing struggle to rescue this nation from its worst self. And even though we are often tempted to feel that nothing has really changed, anyone who lived with American racism and legal segregation in the 1940s and 1950s, especially in the South, surely knows that much has been changed, even as so much remains to be done. So if we are serious about continuing, multiplying, expanding the democratic realities of this nation, we need to ponder these young people and the costs they paid. Indeed, we simply cannot pass them by in any humanizing educational process, for they present models, signposts, for us all, but especially for our current generation of young people. They did not carry on their battles in China, Eastern Europe, or South Africa. They were here (connected to everywhere). They were us. We cannot, must not, escape them. For they are children, high schoolers, college students most often supported in faith and hope (and bail money!) by parents and church congregations and their relatives in the North, creating cross-generational bonds.

To see them clearly is to be strengthened in the possibilities of our own humanity. And we do see them when we enter seriously into a study of this nation's struggle for democracy. We see them marching in Birmingham—children, young people, facing dogs, refusing to let go of each other when the brutal pressure of fire hoses sends cannonades of water crashing against their tender bodies. It is important that our students see them— young, afraid, but refusing to turn back, even when the antidemocratic, anti-human powers in Mississippi, Alabama, Georgia, and elsewhere vow to chase them out or destroy them.

Indeed, it is essential that each generation of young people experience this introduction to their forebears who refused to be chased or destroyed, while absorbing significant losses. They need to meet these recent ancestors who opened many doors they now take for granted—or do not take at all. Someone needs to remind us all that Frederick Douglass was right when he declared that human progress, human struggle, and sacrificial human commitment are indissolubly linked. As a matter of fact, some of us already know that there are powerful epiphanies of hope in store when our students finally hear and see this story of the post-1955 period, realize that these were Black young people and their white allies, their own ages, successfully taking on some of the most destructively powerful political leaders and systems in the country, and doing it without guns. There are deeply moving moments waiting for us when we accompany our students to meet these southern-based community organizers in their teens and twenties, facing guns and flames and threats of death, but determined to make democracy more real than it ever was in this land. I have seen students of all ages and races (but particularly the young) deeply moved and challenged by these stories, especially when they see them on film.

When we direct our attention to the northern, urban manifestations of the Black-led struggle for democracy in America it is not always easy to see young people in the same light, but they are very present, often very heroic, and our teaching is surely able to illuminate some of these realities. Indeed, at times it may be even more important that we lift up the significant role of young people here, toward the end of the 1960s, as the epicenter of the freedom movement passed out of the South to the North. For they are sometimes lost or unappreciated in the telling of the more explosive, episodic northern story. So, it is good to remember that even before the movement's focus shifted, the same Black young people who carried on powerful community organizing on behalf of freedom and democracy in the South were the ones who were most prominently involved in raising the provocative and necessary call for Black Power, a cry that finally joined the southern and northern struggles in a new set of connections. We need, too, to recollect that it was Black high school youth—often inspired by older veterans of the movement such as the Harlem-based historian-activist John Henrik Clarke—who first voiced the demand for Black history in their schools, carrying it to the level of a major challenge to America's cultural gatekeepers as well as to its educational bureaucracies. And it was Black youth, moving to popular songs like "Keep on Pushing," displaying great amounts of creativity and courage (not to mention hair), who appeared at the forefront of the Black consciousness manifestations of the movement, demanding a central place for Africa-connectedness in the development of a more democratic American society. So too, in many settings it was Black young people who insisted on keeping the galvanizing memory of Malcolm X alive.

Of course, there is no way to avoid the powerful Black youth presence in the northern urban rebellions, but we need to realize that these were the children of both King and Malcolm. Often inspired by their counterparts in the South, but finding themselves in a different inner and external space, they responded in a different way. They literally became the carriers of fire, often seeking to call attention to all the fires burning within them, all the desires for a more just, more humane society in which they could live and grow. It is crucial to see them not simply as the proponents of "Burn, Baby, Burn," but as young people who were attempting to act out in some very public way their powerful concerns about their life in America, about the "American Way of Life" itself. Now, when the fires of destruction seem to be burning only in the inner lives and hearts of young people, now that the urban explosions have often become self-destructive personal and collective implosions, it is easy for us to forget that even with the fire in their hands these young people were actively taking a role in their society. They were moving in the public squares, calling attention to injustice, exploitation, anger, and fear, refusing to adapt to the status quo, refusing to lie down in darkness. Strange though it may sound, they cared enough to burn. They believed enough in the possibility of change to try to rebel.

For anyone who doubts the meaning of this youthful participation in, often leadership of, the urban uprisings of the 1960s, it may help to see other images of the same young people. For many of them were very much drawn to Dr. King, and we need to watch them in Chicago and Newark and Detroit as he sought them out, spoke to them, and especially as he invited some of the gang members to participate in the Poor People's Campaign of 1968, to become unarmed marshals for what would eventually be Resurrection City. Many of the gang members listened to King closely, for they realized that this was more than a public figure speaking from a platform. Like their beloved Malcolm, this was a Black man who cared about them, who cared so much about them and others like them that he was constantly putting his life on the line for them. (Perhaps they realized that their own best lives were also at stake.) Now, in our time, it is important to recollect that many of these young people actually accepted King's invitation, volunteered to go with him to Washington to challenge the nation's leadership to deal with the needs of the poor. It is, indeed, crucial to recollect that these young people temporarily agreed to put down their guns, to work on their underdeveloped weapons of courage, hope, creativity, and social commitment, and were prepared to join King in a struggle for the continuing democratic transformation of America. So when we caught a glimpse of many of these same young men and women in the light of the flames that tore through the Black communities of America after King's assassination, it may well be that they were carrying the fires of mourning, as well as of rage, that they were earnestly in search of their own most valiant futures by the light of the funeral pyres of their two great fallen heroes.

These young people deserve our closest attention, for when some of them appear again in the story as organizers and leaders of the Black Panther Party for Self-Defense they bring another powerful message for us and our students. (For many Americans, even those who lived consciously through the time of the Panthers, the organization had faded, or been pushed, to the background until the murder of Huey Newton in the summer of 1989 revived our memories.) Here, again, re-membering is crucial, putting the story and its meaning together for ourselves and our students. Perhaps the Panthers are most important for us here as a youth-conceived and youth-led organization whose initial purposes were actually filled with great hope and commitment on behalf of their community.

At their best (and how else shall any of us wish to be judged?) this defiant organization of young people opened new possibilities for Black people, especially for Black young men. Recently, one of the Panther leaders of the late 1960s and 1970s, Elaine Brown, told the *Eyes on the Prize II* interviewers that the Panthers offered urban Black young men "the opportunity to make their lives meaningful."[1] Clearly this was a central contribution of these young, audacious, often misguided young Americans: They challenged their sisters and brothers, their neighbors and friends in some of the most difficult urban communities of this country. They challenged them to refuse simply to be objects of social service, passive recipients of the benefits of someone else's social planning, or mere victims of police brutality. Rather they called them into a new status, as subjects, as makers of their own history, as protectors of their own community, as participants in the worldwide process of revolution. And it is essential that we recollect the response they evoked. At their height, it was tremendous. Whatever we think of the Panthers' style, their immaturity, their arsenal of offensive language, and their guns, it is important to remember that thousands of Black young people across the country (and perhaps too many white hero-worshippers at times) answered the call, said by their actions that they wanted to become active participants in the struggle to change their own lives and the life of their community. It is important to recollect the dazzling mixture of emotions that caught many of us adults as well.

That was slightly more than two decades ago. As a result, we and our students need to share with one another some obvious questions and concerns. There are powerful discussions to be raised, for instance, about whether such potential for organizing urban young people to transform themselves and their communities still exists. (There are provocative questions to ask concerning whether we prefer serious Panthers, with all their problems, or serious drug dealers and addicts. Or serious Black clones of white mainstream America. Are those our only choices?) Meanwhile, if we remember anything about the Panthers, it may be best to recall some things the cameras of the media did not seem to catch—like the hundreds of Panther members who were up at five o'clock every morning to do calisthenics and to serve in the breakfast programs. Or we may wish to recall the scenes of Panthers escorting older members of the community to the banks and currency exchanges to make sure they were safe when cashing their social security and pension checks. In the light of those memories we may understand more fully why one of the segments in *Eyes on the Prize II* shows us some of the thousands of older people who lined up in Chicago's harsh winter weather to examine the apartment where

Panther leaders Fred Hampton and Mark Clark were murdered by the police.

Ultimately, both we and our students may need to come to grips with the significance of the Panthers for today, particularly for the separate racial and economic camps in which we live. Huey Newton may help that process, not only as we study his life and death, but as we read his words in *Revolutionary Suicide*:

> Gradually the Black Panthers came to be accepted in the Bay area community. We had provided a needed example of strength and dignity by showing people how to defend themselves. More important, we lived among them. They could see every day that with us the people came first.[2]

Seven years after the founding of the Panthers, Huey reminded us here that the guns we associate with them were not their most important legacy. Rather it was their willingness to live with and work among the ordinary people of their community.

Now, after "many dangers, toils and snares," Huey Newton has gone on his way. What do our students think of him as they search for the essentials of the Panthers and their meaning for today? Early in Huey's development, he was an avid student of the great post–World War II scholar-revolutionary Frantz Fanon. It may be that the Panthers and other youth of the northern movement cannot be comprehended without at least some exploration of Fanon, especially his classic, *The Wretched of the Earth*. Indeed, it is likely that Huey's often broken, but very real, attempt to live faithful to "the people" can only be understood when we introduce our students to the words that Fanon wrote very near the close of his powerful life. In December 1961, a few days before his death, Fanon wrote to a friend, "Death is always close by. And what's important is not to know if you can avoid it, but to know that you have done the most possible to realize your ideas." Then the thirty-six-year-old Martiniquan wrote words that may have later been read by Huey of Oakland: "We are nothing on earth if we are not first of all slaves of a cause. The cause of the people. The cause of justice. The cause of liberty."[3] Such were the ideas and the examples that youth leaders of the 1960s and 1970s struggled to master as they grasped at "the opportunity to make their lives meaningful." Such were the messages from Soweto to Prague.

Although such words and examples often bring discomfort to those of us who have settled for a tenuous safety and security in our quietly desperate lives, perhaps they can also stimulate us to reconsideration. For the ideas of Fanon and Newton, the models of Bob Moses, James Forman, Diane Nash, and others, remind us that at their best, both in the South and in the North, this phalanx of young freedom workers may well have come close to a universal truth—that there is no real meaning in life that does not involve sacrificial, joyful service to others. Was this the ultimate source of their power, more power than they knew—more power than they were ready to receive?

No one can provide today's students with answers to such questions, but creative teachers can certainly open pathways to similar searching inquiries. We can, for instance, encourage contemporary youth to do their own research in the history of the earlier youth movement, making use of the copious oral histories and primary documents, discovering such moving works as Howard Zinn's[4] and Clay Carson's[5] histories of SNCC and several of the powerfully told stories of the Mississippi movement, along with important studies of the Panthers and a number of autobiographical reflections. Let them discover for themselves the faces and the words in the films and tapes. Through role playing and the creation of their own docudramas let them *become* the Panthers, the first Black Student Union members, the SNCC organizers, the children of Selma, the courageous pioneers of Little Rock—and much more.

As the power-filled lives of the earlier times begin to make connections with their own existence, perhaps two natural developments might be encouraged among our own youth. First would be an experience of gratitude. For both the profound humanity and the sense of power and potential in our students will best be nurtured as they gain a deeper sense of appreciation for the many young forerunners. Their lives will be empowered as they are helped to see their own connections to the sacrifices, the contributions, the gifts that have been offered to us all by those who struggled for the expansion of American democracy before us, who refused to let their youth become an escape from responsibility. Indeed, it may be that it is only in the cultivation of gratitude for the work of our forebears that we are freed to consider our own accountability to the unborn, our own responsibility for the trees of enlightenment. Perhaps it is only in our reconnection with the past and the future that we discover the deepest power of our humanity, more power than we know. Clearly youth itself is no hindrance to such serious reflections, to such responsible action.

The second development flows directly from a sense of gratitude and connection. For when our young people are faced with the powerful potentials of their youth, a power that is far greater than consumerism or private rebelliousness (or strictly personal religiosity), when they begin to see themselves as transformers of American life, as participants in an ongoing global movement for democracy, they are opened to even richer reflections on their youthful ancestors.[6] Now we can encourage them to move more deeply into the kinds of questions and careful considerations evoked by this history of the pro-democracy movement in the United States, especially as it was led by African-American young people. So they might be engaged, for instance, by the thoughts of Dr. King, reflections he offered from the heart of the movement shortly before his death. Considering the role of Black youth, especially, King wrote,

> It is difficult to exaggerate the creative contribution of young Negroes. They took nonviolent resistance . . . and developed original forms of application — sit-ins, freedom rides, and wade-ins. To accomplish these, they first transformed themselves.

Then King went on to offer examples of the self-transformation accomplished by his youthful co-workers in the struggle for democracy:

> Young Negroes had traditionally imitated whites in dress, conduct, and thought in a rigid, middle-class pattern. . . . Now they ceased imitating and began initiating. Leadership passed into the hands of Negroes, and their white

allies began learning from them. This was a revolutionary
and wholesome development for both.[7]

Here was power, flowing from deep inner resources, in the
lives of high school and college students. It was creative power
to take ancient, spiritually grounded weapons and reinvent them
for the purposes of the American movement. It was power to
transform themselves, to affirm that they were more than the
invisible men and women of the social science researchers, that
they were responsible, committed young people with a vision
and a purpose. As a result, they developed a great attracting
power, eventually drawing into their ranks thousands of young
white people who found a deeper sense of themselves in this
magnificent struggle for the transformation of their country, who
found their separated sisters and brothers as well. And King,
with his typical insight, recognized that this shifting of Black
young people into a leadership role in relation to their white
counterparts was indeed one of the most profound revolutionary
developments of the century.

But King did not stop there. He was too much of a pastor,
teacher, and preacher to miss the opportunity to make a point.
So he continued to reflect on the meaning of the power that had
been developed in the lives of Black youth and their white allies:

It is ironic that today so many educators and sociologists
are seeking methods to instill middle-class values in Negro
youth as the ideal in social development. It was precisely
when young Negroes threw off their middle-class values
that they made an historic social contribution. They abandoned those values when they put careers and wealth in a
secondary role. When they cheerfully became jailbirds and
troublemakers, when they took off their Brooks Brothers
attire and put on overalls to work in the isolated rural
south, they challenged and inspired white youth to emulate
them.[8]

Obviously, King's words — and example — are a continuing, powerful challenge to "educators and sociologists," to pastors and
political leaders, to parents and friends of this current genera-

tion of young people. Is it really possible that certain kinds of power come to us only as we let go of things rather than accumulate them? And what of those youth who feel they have never had anything to let go of? What is their path to the power that can transform both individuals and nations? What fascinating exchanges might evolve out of a panel of young people and adults grappling seriously with the meaning of King's words—and example—for today, especially if our youth recognized some willingness among us to move eventually beyond words to powerful deeds, to continue in the heritage of those who were transforming America and inspiring the world?

As we encourage this generation of young people to claim its transformative ancestors in the freedom movement, they will be introduced to many more questions and reflections like King's. For the history of the earlier youth movement is very suggestive, and our role may be primarily to encourage their serious struggle with the issues, questions, and meanings in the materials. Central here is the matter of power, the creative power of young people, the potential of the young to change themselves and change their world. Exploring the history, it becomes evident that the earlier generation found that when they committed themselves to work for change, to serve the cause of justice, to help excluded citizens develop traditional avenues of power—such as the right to vote—then they discovered many other forms of power that were available to them.

They learned the power of patient, persistent organizing. They discovered the power of commitment to each other and to the service of "the people." They found that they had power to cross generational lines and rediscover the unity of human life. That is surely what we see in the classic photo taken during the Meredith march through Mississippi where a group of young SNCC organizers hold up on their shoulders the exultant 106-year-old El Fondren as they celebrate together his first time of registering to vote. (And which students will be assigned to research the meaning of *that* name in Greenwood, Mississippi?) It is also the power we catch in a ninety-year-old Alabama woman who said of the students, "They helped me to be a brave woman." And what we certainly know is that the help was mutual, a source of great power for the movement, a power that could also be felt in Oakland when the young brothers in berets and shiny black jackets and boots carefully escorted the old folks to cash their checks. More power than we know.

Of course, that earlier generation learned much more as well, left much to be shared with our students. They learned the power of tough and courageous loving, the power of unyielding commitment to truth in the face of violent denials of our oneness and our needs. They learned that they could be disciplined, nonviolent warriors in the midst of the most frightening provocations. Others eventually learned that it was not their guns that were the ultimate source of their power, but their undying commitment to the people—who needed (and still need) their courageous and compassionate presence much more than their provocative guns.

Everywhere, in every setting, these young freedom workers learned the power that grows out of a willingness to work and sacrifice for the creation of a new society. Consistently, all the history and testimonies regarding the period make it clear: Here were young people, South and North, who discovered the power that comes to those who see themselves as challenging the old order, opposing the keepers of the conventional power of the status quo, on behalf of new, more human possibilities for children not yet born. Even when they were wounded we could see it in their eyes: They found a power that is reserved for those who risk their lives on behalf of what they really believe is the compassionate order of the universe, the will of God, the creation of a divinely ordained sisterhood and brotherhood of all humanity. In that power the southern forces were able not only to call white young people to follow their lead but also to challenge white labor leaders, white church and synagogue members, calling each, calling all to be faithful to their own best commitment and hope. And in the midst of the common grounds, both the young callers and their allies discovered and rediscovered the great, suffusing power of the Black churches, especially when that beautiful force is linked to the struggle for a new and loving society on earth ("Thy will be done on earth as it is in heaven"). And, of course, if they had not done so before, they learned the power in music, in their own specially created songs such as, "We'll never turn back/Until we've all been freed. . . ."

That is a powerful heritage, one filled with questions for reflection, discussion, and action. It is a heritage each new generation needs to know, perhaps to claim as a source of power, as a path toward the discovery of its own largest possibilities. Whenever I meet contemporary young people I sense they are more ready than we realize to engage their ancestors, and we usually try to discuss certain key issues of that engagement. One is the question of what, if any, are the differences and similarities between today's generation and those young people who blazed a path for the expansion of American democracy in the decades following World War II? The question offers much opportunity for self-reflection, but I have usually tried to help students avoid the temptation to offer excuses for copping out of their role in the ongoing struggle for democracy. (The excuses can be both numerous and creative, whether they emerge out of life in the housing projects, the affluent suburbs, or the broad spaces in between.)

Ultimately, the direction in which we move in our conversations is to explore the meaning and relevance of the empowered forebears for today's generation. Do we possess such power? If so, how can it be discovered, tapped, developed, and made available in the constant movement toward the re-creation of America? Of course, there is always space for them to express their feelings about whether they really want to find that power, to share it, to be transformed by it. (Interestingly enough, as a result of our study of the earlier youth movement there is never any extensive debate among Black or white students about the choice between self-help and governmental assistance. For the history of the freedom struggle tells us from the outset that this has never been an either/or question for African-Americans. Certainly the young movement stalwarts of the post-Montgomery pro-democracy struggle were always involved in a three-pronged action: they worked to change themselves; they challenged others to participate in the struggle for the transformation of self, community, and nation; and they continued to challenge the United States government to take up its proper responsibilities in the enhancement and expansion of a democratic society. For they knew that one of the original purposes of American government was "to form a more perfect union.")

When they are asked about some of the important issues and challenges we face today in the struggle for a more just, compassionate, and peacefully democratic society, the current teenagers and young adults are not slow to identify them, if somewhat vaguely at times. They speak of the scourge of drugs, and we wonder together what we can learn from the earlier youth-led organizing experiences of South and North that might be applied to this great challenge. We often explore dreams that bring together combinations of committed, Panther-like (but unarmed) patrols, and local community organizers to build courageous challenges to the dealers and their sources. We envision volunteer mentors, counselors, and substitute grandparents to reach directly into the lives of the endangered youth. Together we can catch a glimpse of new institutions—such as risk-taking churches—establishing themselves in the heart of some of the most needy situations, following the example of the Freedom Houses in places like Mississippi and Alabama in the 1960s. Like King and Malcolm, they are deeply concerned about the need for humanizing values.

The conversations and creativity are always encouraging, continuing some of the same uses of history and hope when we discuss the need for much better schools, for committed teachers, for decent housing, for all-encompassing health care, and for good paying jobs for everyone who wants to work. They speak, too, of the need to rid the world of the threat of nuclear war, eventually moving to look at all war, especially as they consider what we lose when we spend so much of our time, energy, talents, and money on preparations for war. Often there is great sensitivity among them to issues of world poverty and to economic injustice at home. Ecological concerns are usually present as well. Naturally enough, the continuing issues of race and racism arise. We recollect the powerful experiences of the earlier period when Black and white young people not only worked together for justice and peace but were willing to live and die for one another in the cause of building a more democratic society. So we wonder aloud about whether there can be any new building of racial unity among us without common, challenging tasks that draw us together for the good of our nation, for the good of our world. In that context, they tend to be very happy about what they understand concerning the most recent breaking of the grasp of the Cold War on us all.

In the midst of such discussions with young people about the contemporary challenges, and about the historical models, we usually begin to talk even more directly about what all this means for them in their own lives. Most often I find that many youth want to be invited to expand their horizons, although they are not always sure how to move from the path they have already begun to walk. In the light of all the things they identify as needing to be done, I ask them to consider their own calling, their own sense of vocation, their own role in working for a more humane American democracy. This often brings us to careers, to discussions of what life is for, to reflections on ways in which they can possibly enter the long historical stream of men and women who have worked for justice, peace, and human unity.

We consider the possibility that some careers might bring them closer than others to the sources of inner power that seemed so important to the generation that spent years on the firing lines. We often talk about varieties of conventional power, discuss the importance of working for economic, political, and administrative power. But we also recognize what so often happens to persons who devote themselves to the achievement of such conventional power without any reserves of the hidden creative inner forces: They forget their original purpose and direction; often they are lost to the struggle for democracy.

When we think of the lists of challenges our students can compile, it seems clear that one of the most crucial careers today is that of teaching, at all levels. Because that is not currently a very popular direction, it is fascinating to see students struggle with the logic of the importance of the profession, with its need for many more compassionate, creative, and power-filled teachers, with its relatively low pay scales. So, too, with all the professions that bring us in most direct contact with people who need human encouragement, modeling, and guidance: social workers, community organizers, pastors, youth workers, law enforcement officials. None of these is usually high on the agenda of today's students. But that is what teachers are for. That is what teachers brought to me: stimulation, reasons to consider vocations I had not thought of, encouragement to take my verbal concerns and move them toward the center of my life, encouragement to go into a traditional profession and help reshape it for the good of us all.

In the temporary absence of a high-profile, challenging, pro-democracy movement in America, it will take wise and creative guides to help our students find ways in which their lives can join with those of Bob Moses, Prathia Wynn Hall, Annelle Ponder, Charles Sherrod, Bob Zellner, and the thousands of others who discovered that they had more power than they knew. But many of the students are open, especially after immersing themselves in the story of the freedom movement. They are open to becoming new kinds of lawyers, more committed to justice than to status. They are open to becoming engineers and architects who will build and design with the needs of human beings and ecological balance foremost in their minds. They are open to helping to create new definitions of religious leadership, political leadership, film-making, social analysis. They are prepared to explore how business skills might actually be used to empower others, not from a trickle-down perspective, but far more directly. Indeed, one of our most compelling callings may now be to help students who are moved by their forebears to discover new professions, to reshape the more traditional ones, to create transformative vocations for the coming century.

But at the center of it all is our own vocation: to help draw forth from them their best selves, their best strength, their most powerful visions of a more democratic society, of a more just and peaceable world. At *our* best it is we who remind them of their connections to the past and to the future, of the powerful inner resources at the center of their lives, resources that tie them to the lives of young carriers of hope across the globe. It is we who point them toward Fannie Lou Hamer's statement, made shortly before her death in 1977: "Because of these young people, I think for the first time we have the chance to make democracy a reality in the United States."[9]

The rest is in their hands, and in their hearts, places of great power.

4

Fighting for Freedom
with Church Fans

To Know What Religion Means

My devotion to truth has drawn me into politics; and I can say without the slightest hesitation . . . that those who say that religion has nothing to do with politics do not know what religion means.
—*Mohandas K. Gandhi*[1]

After decades of shunning classroom discussion of religion, fearing that it was too divisive a subject or that church-state separation might be breached, many American public schools are now moving to incorporate it into their curriculums.

The change results largely from a sentiment that schools have too long ignored religion as a force in American and world culture, and signs of it are far-flung.
—New York Times, *March 19, 1989*[2]

For those of us who seek to anchor our teaching in the daily realities of the modern world, certain harsh encounters are difficult (and undesirable) to avoid. When we call the attention of our students to the possible presence of profound truths just beneath the surface of mundane events, none of us can escape the many times when great light, sometimes terrible beauty, is revealed to us through unspeakable tragedy. That was certainly my response to the murder of the six Jesuit priests and their friends in El Salvador in 1989. Those martyr deaths evoked both memories and anguished hope. For I saw not only Ignacio, Joaquin, Julia, and their companions but I remembered the Maryknoll women workers, and others who had been killed in service—as well as the assassinated Salvadoran archbishop. As a matter of fact, my memories went even deeper, longer, extending to other bearers of truth, embodiments of compassionate religion in the midst of life-affirming social movements. My memories embraced Martin and Malcolm. I heard Gandhi's dying chant of affirmation. I visited Steven Biko's grave, among so many other mounds of hope. I stumbled on the body of David Walker in nineteenth-century Boston. And these were only the tokens, representatives of the hosts.

It was in the midst of this great company of witnesses that I grasped again the meaning of Gandhi's words: "My devotion to truth has drawn me into the field of politics." For that is precisely what had happened to each member of the community of memories—their work for truth, for peace, for justice, for human solidarity had emerged naturally out of their deepest religious convictions. And these convictions, that work, had led them to identify with the expendable people, the exploited ones, the rejected stones. For each of them there came a time of discovery when, as King put it, "silence is betrayal," when they were faced with the impossibility of neutrality as a religious calling.

It is important to keep such persons close to us when we learn that there is a movement among America's school constituencies to find ways in which we can explore more fully the role of religion in our national past and present. We who are based in the classrooms are now being asked to consider and teach such subject matter in a richly pluralist—but often religiously biased—society. And although some of the proponents of this interest in religion may be more restrictive in their vision than we would like, the stirrings are important and need to be experienced and encouraged. They are signals of the return to a vaguely familiar, necessary, and wider-ranging search. For it is clear that ever since the time of the earliest, agonizing prayers on the African-laden slave ships, and the religiously founded civil compacts of the European settler-disrupters, the ubiquitous double-edged power of the search for the holy has been a source of both division and healing among us in our strangely native land.

Now, at this supposedly "secular" moment of our modernity, there is much evidence that we have begun to learn, again, that we cannot properly understand ourselves or others without some sense of the world of the numinous, that world which drives, defines, and shapes us, which frightens or repels us, and which feeds our deepest needs. Somehow we have come to see that the crossing places between religious faith and public action, between spiritual convictions and social commitments, need to be explored if our classrooms—whether in public and private schools, community centers, or religious institutions—are to catch any real reflection of the vibrant, mysterious center of human life and struggle.

Indeed, what better way is there to teach and learn about religion than to explore the ways in which this sense of engagement with the ultimate has invaded and grasped human beings so fully that their lives have been transformed? And what happens when we are able to track the movement of those who live such lives, carefully watching as they move beyond their once accepted limits to become more fully realized persons and more compassionate participants in our common pilgrimage of responsibility? Might such explorations open our students to a richer, deeper sense of the meaning of religion than that which comes from the most famous of our religious television stars, or from mild and toothless Sunday school versions, or from soul-scarring introductions to deities of vengeance and fear? Is it possible that some serious exposure to the ways in which religious commitment can draw women and men into the task of creating a more just and humane society may be one of the best means for introducing children and adults in a pluralistic society to the amazing hope that so many persons find in the power and meaning of religion? In other words, rather than teaching only doctrines and comparative styles of worship, we may all learn more by also exploring compassionate lives on fire with faith and hope, human beings with beating hearts in search of a more just and loving society.

As we have already realized, there are witnesses from El Salvador to Romania and South Africa who can assist us in this approach to the places where religious faith and liberating social responsibility converge. But we are all served well at home. For by virtue of a sublime and tortured history lived out on the stage of our nation and the world, the Black struggle for freedom, at its best, provides just such openings into the power and mystery of a life-affirming religion at work. Carefully explored with our students, the freedom struggle—most obviously in its southern manifestations—not only provides us all an entry point to the world of Black religion in the United States (an important and deeply moving subject in itself), but also demonstrates some of the ways in which the humanizing force of any religion can draw to its side valuable companions from other religious traditions. We can also watch as these seekers are able both to embrace each other and to continue their search to find the best meanings and hopes in their own religious faith, to re-vision and re-experience their own essential ground of being. (Surely this was what Gandhi sought when he rejected the sometimes arrogant Christian calls to cross-religious conversions and urged instead that we stand in communion with one another, working sacrificially for the coming of a more just and loving social order, thereby developing the best possibilities and potentials of life in our own religious traditions. He said, "Our utmost prayer should be that a Hindu should be a better Hindu, a Muslim a better Muslim and a Christian a better Christian."[3])

As we reflect on the post–World War II African-American freedom movement, nothing illustrates this powerful gathering and affirming tendency more fully than the vibrant interfaith mass meetings that were held at the height of the southern movement. Scenes from such explicitly religious (but not sectarian) meetings in Albany, Georgia, Birmingham, Alabama, Greenwood, Mississippi, and other similar settings are captured with great power in the *Eyes on the Prize* series and elsewhere. But many of our students of every chronological age will need us to help interpret the unfamiliar images, to call their attention to both the seen and unseen elements of the often ecstatic meetings. (Religious ecstasy in the midst of a dangerous socio-political freedom movement? What does that mean? Is it possible? Perhaps the deeper question is this: Can there be any real movement to freedom without deep ecstasy?) For they *were* meetings, deep engagements with things visible and invisible, with other human beings, both friends and oppressors, with fears and exultations. Sometimes they seemed to be great wrestling meetings between our lesser and better selves, shout-pierced, wing-spread engagements between humble men and women of the earth and the exalted spirits of the universe.

Usually the meetings were most powerfully experienced in the midst of times of crisis, when a local Black community had committed itself to struggle against the unjust system of segregation and white domination, and while public demonstrations were going on—often at great personal cost—in the area. In many cases the people who spoke and sang and prayed in those mass meetings had already begun to experience jailings, beatings, loss of jobs, and other forms of economic, physical, and psychological attempts at intimidation. Tensions and fears might be high. Dangers were real. That's why they *had* to sing, "Ain't Gonna Let Nobody Turn Me 'Round." That's why they had to sing songs taken from the deep reservoirs of their forebears' religious genius and then respond with their own revised versions of majestic hope. That's why they had to sing everything they could sing.

Dangers were real, but so were the great resources of their religious heritage. (Perhaps we should let our students hear those songs. Even better, let them try to break loose from inhibitions and fashionable disengagement—or lame adult excuses—to take on the songs, to take in the songs, to let out the songs themselves. Then perhaps there can be real conversations about the relation of singing and shouting and chanting to a variety of religious and liberating experiences. Perhaps it might even lead to an exploration of the holy vocal organs and cavities of our body and the tremendous power of breath which fills them with sounds that sometimes become more than we understand ourselves, sounds which some religious faiths believe are tying us to the breath of life, the breath of God. Maybe that's why they had to sing—in mass meetings, in jail, at funerals, on picket lines, in lonely times of prayer. Perhaps that's why Bull Connor heard the songs of life bursting out of crowded, rhythmically rocking police wagons in Birmingham and had to say, "If that's religion. I don't want no part of it." But perhaps it was too late. Perhaps some seven-year-old child on the way to "freedom jail" had already breathed on him.)

In the midst of such situations the local movement leaders sometimes called in larger, more experienced organizations, like SCLC, SNCC, the NAACP, and CORE. (What stacks of reports and papers and poems and songs, to be created by our students, lay hidden in those acronyms!) They in turn often called upon their Black and white allies in other parts of the country, and such persons soon flooded the relatively unsegregated airports and arrived on the scene. Almost always the movement leaders and others chose to organize mass meetings, sometimes every night, at least two or three times a week, depending on the intensity of the local struggle. On one level, the meetings were held to build cohesion, to convey necessary organizing information, to carry out planning—but there was always much more to them.

At the heart of the mass meetings was the experience of Black religion. The sessions were held in the Black churches, often changing location from night to night—partly for ecumenical purposes, partly for security. The powerful, roiling sessions brought together Baptists of all varieties, AMEs, CMEs (the pregnant acronyms again!), Pentecostals and Black Lutherans, Roman Catholics, Methodists and Episcopalians. The mass meetings were, in other words, a great African-American ecumenical revival-type gathering, where denominational rigidities and rivalries were temporarily cast aside. (Had they discovered "post-denominationalism" before the theologians and historians?) And beyond Black ecumenism there was more. Few things were more striking in these sessions than the sight and sound of Jewish rabbis, white priests and nuns, and visiting white Protestant ministers and laypeople of many northern varieties, all singing, swaying, and shouting "Amens" in ways that probably surprised no one more than themselves. They had been drawn to a wondrous meeting place.

Here it was: The religious common ground so often sought

at conferences, symposia, ecumenical services, and countless teas, was here on this ancient southern ground. Breaking—at least temporarily—against bloodied barriers of human construction, women and men of many faith persuasions had been brought to a sacred space of struggle, sacrifice, and hope. In small, simple church buildings, lined up on streets facing dogs and guns and fire hoses, sharing Mason jars of tepid water in sweltering prison cells, the human temple of the divine Creator had been drawn together, perhaps by the breath of hope. And the mass meetings expressed it all, reminded people of the central promises that appear in so many manifestations of the divine, promises that said we human seekers would be met most urgently by the great spirits not in the magnificent and fabled temples of religion but at those beleaguered places of most urgent human need, where struggling, hoping, committed women and men were willing to risk their safety for the sake of a compassionate quest for justice, reconciliation, and peace.

Perhaps we can help our students to sense the constantly surprising, often jarring, role of religion, and encourage them to recognize the power of its call, especially when that summons emerges out of the lives of men and women who have committed themselves to the creation of a more humane society. To introduce them to these mass meetings, this freedom religion, this divinely obsessed search for our separated kindred, this spirit-filled movement toward a righteous community, has nothing to do with proselytizing, but it has even less to do with "neutrality" in our teaching. Rather, it takes a stand with all those who have sought a compassionate way toward the release of the best, most humane, and life-affirming qualities in us. And it certainly at least calls attention to those tendencies or institutions (even within a freedom movement) that stifle the grace of creativity, self-reliance, and mutual responsibility in any of us. So we discover anew that it is impossible to study "religion" without serious examination of our own values and visions, without facing King's question: What are we prepared to die for?

In that spirit we take our students again to the mass meetings as a central paradigm for the meeting of religion and social responsibility (a better term for "politics"). We remind them of the ways in which the movement context was always presenting the nightly participants with an opportunity "to live the life I sing about," to "walk your talk," as the old folks admonished. This, of course, is central to the teachings of heart-deep religion everywhere—faith and work, beliefs and action, walking our talk. So at the mass meetings there was praying and singing; there were women, men, and children testifying to divine assistance when they were in jail, or facing the billy clubs or the hoses; there were songs and more songs. There were solos, quartets, and choirs leading the singing. But when they had sung "Go Tell It on the Mountain," or "Leaning on the Everlasting Arms," or "We Shall Overcome," then they had to go out into that dangerous night or prepare for the next morning when they would test the faith and courage they had proclaimed, offering themselves as living, public witnesses to the power of the religion which so moved them inside the churches.

Eyes on the Prize caught one of the most vivid and revealing testimonies to the power and meaning of such religion as it told the story of the Albany, Georgia, freedom movement. There the cameras caught the face of a Black woman in a mass meeting as she sang and fanned herself with one of the ubiquitous cardboard church fans. Soon after, in another scene, probably the next day, she was present again, now kneeling with others in prayer, visibly moved by the spirit, right in front of Albany's combination jail and City Hall. As she rose to be arrested and escorted into jail this woman of faith and action was still waving the church fan, testifying in that simple motion to the fact that the religion which moved her life was one and the same in the church building and in the public square—and it would remain the same in the city jail. (Meanwhile, she and other such nonviolent freedom fighters would find some of the priests and rabbis and white Protestant allies also in prison, joining in the singing about "Paul and Silas bound in jail. . . ." Certainly it would be good to encourage our students to ask what were the elements in those other religious traditions which might prepare their practitioners for voluntary entry into jail, for serious response to the call of the Black freedom movement. Perhaps we should also entice them into the longer history of the movement, encourage them to investigate the African and earlier African-American sources for its stirring combination of religion and political struggle, to understand why they felt the authority to call others and expect a positive response.)

There is a good chance that such scenes from the struggle would help our students to understand the significant statement by Gayraud Wilmore, one of our most perceptive historians of Black religion in America, when he wrote, "Between 1955 and 1960 the South experienced a revival of black religion – a revival that did not break out with sawdust trails and mourners' benches, but with picket lines, boycotts and marches through the downtown sections of scores of southern towns and cities." For Wilmore, the hundreds of Black preachers involved in the struggle, "most of them unknown and unsung, were there only as the instruments – sometimes the reluctant instruments – from which the theme of freedom rose like a great crescendo from the depths of the people."[4]

It might be helpful to take Wilmore's statement into our varied classrooms and build on it, opening for exploration some of the many meanings of religious revivalism. What has that experience meant in American history, going back as far as the eighteenth century? What does revivalism mean as we see it in other-than-Christian religions in the world today? Such questions are important, for even as the African-American, Christian-led "revival" was taking place in the Deep South, for instance, we might ask how it was related to the parallel "revival" of the Black American version of Islam, most widely known as the Black Muslims. Opening the world of Islam through the Black Muslim experience offers many important pathways, including an opportunity to understand why people change their names, like Kareem Abdul-Jabbar and Muhammad Ali – or like many Roman Catholic sisters and monks. What is the spiritual significance of new names? All of which might bring us back to revival, for some of our students may want to know what actually happens in the lives of people who are "revived" or renamed.

Against the background of such crucial questions, one of the discoveries we may make with our students as we move into the religious core of the Black freedom movement is that religion, when taken with heartfelt seriousness, presents a great challenge. At its best it is a challenge to its practitioners, to their immediate communities and to the world around them. So we can begin to understand why the Black religious expressions of the freedom movement participants were often so threatening to their sisters and brothers in the southern white churches, parishes, and synagogues. Perhaps we can also help each other to understand some of the reasons why there should have been such turmoil in the northern-based religious institutions when Brother Martin Luther King, Jr., moved into their precincts to challenge urban poverty, American militarism, some of the northern varieties of white racism—and the acquiescence of religious people in all these betrayals of human community.

In the same way, it would be fascinating for students to discover James Forman, the former SNCC executive secretary who led what was called the Black Manifesto Movement of the late 1960s and early 1970s. Forman's movement was an audacious and often powerful (and slightly revolutionary) attempt to face the northern churches of the United States with their responsibility for white American racism. It was also a demand on them to make concrete financial amends in the form of reparations for the wrongs and exploitation suffered by Black people over many generations. But perhaps the most difficult part for the churches and other institutions to deal with was the Manifesto's call for the interracial redistribution of power in white-dominated religious institutions and the encouragement of Black self-determination everywhere. Comparing the responses to the call for money to the call for shared power, comparing the responses of the northern white churches and those in the South to the challenge of Black demands for justice—all this would be a marvelous lesson in the ways of religion, as well as other important American institutions. Of course, it also provides an excellent opportunity for our students to investigate the explosive rise of Black theology in the United States, not as an arcane academic or ecclesiastical set of formulations, but as a vibrant, controversial expression of judgment and hope, surging forth from the daily experiences of the African-American communities, annealed by fire. Once they see this American development, then the global rise of liberation theologies in the quest for democratic transformation becomes easier to comprehend.

The sources for such larger explorations are legion. For instance, the story of the Black freedom movement can take us into fascinating realms of history, sociology, and gender studies when we explore the long tradition of men and women in the African-American experience who combine the role of political and spiritual leader. Beginning with Africa before the slave ships, then remembering the ministries of survival and hope that were shared beneath the decks of those floating nightmares, we are eventually brought face to face with persons like Frederick Douglass, Sojourner Truth, Nat Turner, Harriet Tubman, Bishop Henry McNeill Turner, the Honorable Elijah Muhammad, Malcolm X, Adam Clayton Powell, Jr., Reverend Herbert Dougherty, and Martin Luther King, Jr. In this generation the tradition flourishes even more formally with pastors who are members of Congress, such as William Gray of Philadelphia, Floyd Flake of New York, and Walter Fauntroy of the District of Columbia (who was a youth leader with King and SCLC at the outset of his career). Can our students eventually meet one or more of them, and people like them, in local political and religious leadership?

From another, related perspective, the rise of Black caucuses in predominantly white churches (and everywhere else) in the period of great rage and hope at the end of the 1960s and beginning of the 1970s presents one more fascinating subject for study. When the members of these ubiquitous caucuses were charged with "separatism" by a majority of their white Christian sisters and brothers, why did so many of the African-American leaders remind the white (and Black) churches that Jesus of Nazareth had taught people to love their neighbors *as* they love themselves? Is healthy self-love really a religious imperative? If so, how does a society, a school, a religious institution encourage self-love among those who have been told for so long that their racial ancestry automatically makes them inferior to whites (or is it their overly long exposure to "the culture of poverty" that disqualifies them?)? Is this powerful quest for self-affirmation and self-determination really more than a matter of social issues or court cases?

In a society increasingly populated by peoples of color, by those who have known the disdain and domination of the Euro-American world, it would be fascinating to ponder self-love as a religious calling. How are people, beginning in their earliest years, nurtured to act with self-respect and self-responsibility? How are they/we encouraged to move through the world with a spirit which un-self-righteously challenges everything that threatens to crush the human spirit, the human ability to love ourselves and others? Can we explore such fundamental questions with our students, wondering aloud with them about the fascinating possible spiritual connections between the capacity to love ourselves and the willingness to love and serve others? As we approach the end of the twentieth century in the United States, how can we afford not to engage such essential human issues with our best resources, with our greatest and most imaginative energies?

These quests for the human truths opened up by the religion of the Black freedom movement could help us to understand why Malcolm X, with his insistent call for self-affirmation and self-determination, became the "Black shining prince" to so many of those he left behind. They might explain the scene in *Eyes on the Prize II* when a Black Roman Catholic priest in Chicago bursts with joy as he recounts the experience of hearing a room full of young African-American children affirm their special sense of identity with Fred Hampton, recently martyred Black Panther leader.

The study of religion, like religion itself, is surely filled with surprises, and they come from every direction. For instance, as we linger over the image of the African robes of the Black priest, as we see Carl Stokes of Cleveland and Harold Washington of Chicago campaigning—and receiving blessings—in the familiar precincts of the African-American churches, we may be tempted to miss a powerful fact of the northern-based freedom struggle: From many outward appearances, the Black churches of the North seemed less central to the movement there than had been the case in the South. Now, that is not an undebated issue, and exposure to the debate would surely be helpful to our students. However, if it is true, then what does it mean, not just about the Black churches of North and South, but about our understanding of the basic similarities and differences between the northern and southern Black experiences? For now we must look back and ask, How much did the evocative, central power of the Black churches, their beliefs and their rituals, their life rhythms and their leaders, have to do with the character of the southern freedom movement? How did the shifting, perhaps less central, role of those churches in the northern Black communities help account for the more episodic, relatively unfocused and physically explosive movement that developed in the North? In other words, when it comes time to carry on a struggle for fundamental social change, is it better to start from a setting in which you have known your "place" for a long time, where you have had ample opportunity to nurture networks of both resistance and accommodation? Is it also important to ask what kind of religious manifestations are developed within experiences of uncertainty and uprootedness, in the crisis of migration and the search for place? Or are the differences we see as the movement moves north more a function of Black people's entering more deeply over time into all the antic unknowing of the twentieth century, paying the century's hard price for our passage into the ambiguous world of modernity?

Of course, none of these questions must be allowed to drive our students, or ourselves, away from our wrestling with one of the most important elements of all explorations of religion. In our search for the Black churches, it *is* certainly crucial that we remember that religion at its deepest levels has never been confined to churches, synagogues, mosques, or any places made with human hands. Indeed, it may be that some of our most fascinating and searching discussions will grow out of an attempt to discover how much of the deepest religious undercurrents of the northern freedom movement are to be found among its ever-expanding non-church-going (sometimes church-bashing) participants, women and men with no apparent current connections to any religious institutions at all.

This path may lead us to sentiments like that expressed by Langston Hughes in his poem "Personal":

> In an envelope marked:
>   *Personal*
> God addressed me a letter.
> In an envelope marked:
>   *Personal*
> I have given my answer.[5]

Even more importantly, and publicly, we may all begin to understand religion as being every truly compassionate expression of the great human longing for participation in the wholeness of the universe. Thus we may absorb more fully Gandhi's equation of the religious quest with the search for truth. We can explore with our classes the religion of the Hebrew prophets, hear the powerful announcement that true religion consists of love for God and humanity, that true love leads to service, especially to the poor, the weak, the oppressed. They may look through the window of the Black freedom movement and discover a religion beyond buildings and institutions that is a profound personal and collective recognition of the oneness of humankind. They may see that religion is that commitment to give our best self to the work of nurturing and defending the great connectedness, through personal disciplines, collective work, and public witness. If students apprehend the ways in which the human quest for meaning most often begins in the depths of our own truth-seeking lives and emerges into a sense of connection with the cosmos, then they may see fascinating things, beyond the churches, beyond all institutions (and also within them), at the heart of the northern-based freedom movement.

For instance, from such a point of view we may recognize the emphasis on Black self-love that rose out of the late 1960s and moved into the next decade as a necessary preparation for the love of neighbor and of God. They may grasp the possibility that the affirmation of God's blackness (so puzzling and offensive to some), of Jesus as a man of color, may have been crucial openings to an authentic sense of African-American oneness with the Divine (as well as an important recognition of the color realities of the Middle East). As they explore the renascence-like movement that grew out of the post-assassinations decade, students may find religion in strange places: the magnificent, creative out-pouring, exploding out of saxophones and trumpets, resounding from drums, singing from guitars, lifted up by poets and playwrights, unfurled in living colors on Black community "walls of respect," focused on canvas squares by artists of many talents and visions, the sculpturing of every conceivable material into throbbing statements of the heart. Perhaps all this rediscovery and reshaping of the African-American creative forces of that period can be recognized as a re-encounter with the image of the divine Creator within us, a reclaiming of our best selves, a statement of our ultimate hope.

When religion is seen with new eyes we may re-vision all the Panthers (and others like them) who really believed their lives were meant to be lived for "the people," especially the poor and intimidated among the people. Then our students may recognize these apparently strange, often cursing, angry, and defiant young women and men in the light of the story that appears in the twenty-fifth chapter of the Gospel according to Matthew. For it may well be that some day, somewhere, some of the young Panther folks who often seemed so frightening to so many people in their time will be surprised and sustained by the joy of the timeless, simple words, "I was hungry and you gave me breakfast. . . . Come."

Who knows? Perhaps religion really is about the fact that all of us, by the very reality of our humanity, are called to serve the poor, to open doors for prisoners, to work on behalf of the exploited, to seek for a new order of sharing, forgiveness, and compassion in this world. If that is the case, then Gandhi is teacher to us all, and religion really cannot be separated from responsible public participation in the shaping of our community — politics at its best. Exploring such insights, our students will have every right to ask about where love-possessed "doers of the word" might be today. They might ask who has been called in our own time (and what does *calling* mean, does it have anything to do with making as much money as possible?) to release and serve, to heal and bring good news? And which of our students will wonder aloud about what *is* "good news" in the last decade of the twentieth century? Does it have anything to do with the tumbling of walls, with the opening of borders, with the freeing of prisoners of conscience? Or is it the invasion of a small, helpless nation? What can we say?

Somewhere in the exploration of the various expressions of the African-American freedom movement, somewhere in our attempt to understand the convergence of religion and politics in that singular experience, such reflections and questions may well arise. The least we can do is prepare ourselves and our students for surprises, from within and without. Religion has a way of doing that, especially when we track its movement among people who have nothing to lose but their pain. Finally—or is it initially?—if we are open and caring, our students may well ask about our own religion, our own hope, our own commitments. Are we ready?

5

"God's Appeal to This Age"

The Search for Alternatives to Violence

He was only five years old, so the morning news report did not reveal his name. We were told only that the child lived in the Bronx and that there was now a security guard assigned to his elementary school, because he had brought a loaded handgun to the school. That was more than enough for me.

Perhaps the brief report struck with such force because I remembered my own kindergarten days in Harlem, my high school years in the Bronx. But I was certainly not alone in claiming this little boy. Many of us knew his name. It was written on the consciousness of concerned parents, teachers, neighbors, and ministers of religion everywhere. We recognized his face, in all its manifestations, in all its pain, innocent confusion, warped pride, and fear. Whether five or fifteen, or caught in any of the dangerous manchild ages between and beyond, he was recognizable to us. There, standing naked to the world, robbed of his childhood, recruited into the force-ripened armies of drug runners, gang members, macho men, in danger of early corruption by some of this country's worst values and by its terrible romance with the gun, he was our child, reminding us of so much, warning us.

Everywhere in America there is a deep, often unarticulated fear that the violence of our culture is out of hand and that our children may be among its most vulnerable victims. How do

teachers address this great threat to our humanity, participate
in the rescue of our most valuable endangered human
resources? Obviously, there are no quick fixes here. The dislo-
cation of our values, the destruction of our play-filled childhood,
the acceptance of women and children as punching bags and
outlets for male anger, the fixation on lethal weapons as stan-
dard equipment for the American family—all these run deep.
But the resources that lead us out to alternative, healing paths
are perhaps deeper; at least that option must not be closed
down. So we search, inviting our students on the pilgrimage.

Again, it may be that one of the major resources in the struggle for the humanity of our children—and ourselves—can be
found in a careful exploration of the still-unappreciated experiments with creative nonviolent social action that were developed in the course of the post–World War II African-American
freedom movement. Indeed, even more important than the specific experiments with nonviolent responses to injustice were the
larger human questions the movement was raising about the
spirit of violence within us, about the violence of the powers
that be, about the creativity and courage that are necessary if
we are to develop alternative ways of challenging a destructive
status quo.

As a matter of fact, it was not long after I had heard the
news of my five-year-old brother-son from the Bronx that my
wife and I were given new reasons to suspect that embedded in
the story of the freedom movement there might be unexpected
hope and help for the child and the rest of us. We had been
invited to West Germany by a group of American peace workers
to meet with some of the thousands of U.S. military personnel
stationed there, especially army and air force people. In classrooms, chapels, and living rooms, our March 1989 meetings
focused on the meanings that King and the nonviolent freedom
movement might possibly have for people who were involved in
an institution that legitimized and justified the uses of massive
violence. (At every point of encounter it was clear that many of
the men and women we met had not made the choice to enter
the service because they were militarists, but because civilian
life offered them so little in the way of remunerative employ-
ment, a sense of dignity and security, or a relatively desegregated

opportunity for advancements in nonprofessional work—to say nothing of safety. Indeed, more than one Black male reflected on the dangerous community from which he had come and said, "I came to the military to save my life.")[1]

Our visit occurred shortly before the magnificent upheavals in Eastern Europe, but even then, without exception, the conversations we had were candid, stimulating, and often moving. Most important for our Bronx child, though, was the openness of the men and women we met, their willingness to explore, raise questions, examine beliefs, and especially to re-collect old truths and powerful hopes that had sometimes been long repressed beneath the camouflage of their uniforms and their lives.

Perhaps the most vivid example of these encounters took place in a company chapel one afternoon where more than a hundred enlisted persons and officers gathered for a presentation I was making on Dr. King. As I faced the group in the chapel it was obvious that the power of the freedom movement had already been at work, for that earlier struggle in the United States had made it possible for us to have a meeting in Germany in which so many of the military participants were people of color, were women, and were in positions of responsibility. Considering such fascinating paradoxes, I raised with them one of King's central concerns through the use of a story and a set of questions.

We were talking about the Birmingham, Alabama, campaign of 1963, where the attention of the world had been drawn to the cannonades of water smashing against determined, young bodies, and police dogs snapping at the limbs of courageous, nonviolent demonstrators. Two of the Black young women in the chapel had grown up in Birmingham during those years, and they helped recreate the feeling of the situation, reminding us of the city's well-earned nickname, "Bombingham," because of its record of violent attempts at intimidation, especially against any Black initiatives for justice. Recollecting that danger, I asked, "When King and SCLC were invited by Reverend [Fred] Shuttlesworth to come to this violently segregated city to challenge its unjust ways, how many guns did they take with them?" I could feel the sudden pause in the movement of the conversation. I watched the questioning eyes, almost heard them saying within, "What are you talking about? Are you crazy, mister?" Aloud, several persons declared at once, "No guns, they didn't carry any guns."

It was an exciting moment for a teacher whose students (and fellow-seekers) were all wearing U.S. Army uniforms. Pressing them into the logic of their own announcement, I said, "What do you mean, they had no guns? How could they go into that violent city without guns? Aren't we taught here that you meet violence with violence, that you have to talk the language that people understand?" I continued the questions. "Aren't we taught here that you have to fight fire with fire?" For a moment no one spoke. Then, out of the eloquent silence, a young, Black enlisted woman sitting up front spoke slowly, thoughtfully, emphatically: "You don't fight fire with fire," she said, "you fight fire with water." As I had seen in so many other classrooms, when the essential wisdom came not from a "teacher" standing up front, but from one of the fellow-seekers in the group, her profoundly simple statement released remarkable energies. Other significant, moving comments came forth, exploring, probing not only the meaning of "water" in Birmingham and across the American South of the 1960s, but what the "water" might mean now in their lives, in their works as the keepers of the great, consuming fires, hidden in the forests of Germany.

Somehow I felt that the Black, white, and Hispanic soldiers who were searching there with Rosemarie and me had been given permission by the Birmingham story (and others like it), had felt freed at least to make some tender, tentative moves into crevices of their own selves, touching places that they had not often entered (just as I had to explore those parts of my own being where I held captive the knowledge of my taxpaying participation in the purchasing of their/our weapons of destruction). Reflecting on the experience later on, remembering the leading role in the discussion that some of the Black soldiers — male and female — had taken, recalling the seriousness of their very personal probing for "water" as they stood around for nearly an hour after the meeting, it seemed exactly what King and his fellow nonviolent warriors would have hoped for.

Of course King and the movement belonged in that setting.

I could almost see his playful, serious eyes dancing in the midst of the situation. For we were dealing with themes that formed so much of the early teaching of the southern freedom movement — and it was a self-consciously teaching movement. Indeed, in his first mass meeting sermon/speech in Montgomery in 1955 King called for the Black people who were rising up to a new level of struggle to see themselves as the once-rejected servants who were now destined to infuse "a new meaning into the veins of history and civilization." At the heart of this messianic — and therefore dangerous — calling, according to King, was the combination of courageous, self-disciplined contestation for a new and just America and the uses of well-organized, militant nonviolent action to bring it about. So in his first book he dared to declare, "This is a great hour for the Negro," dared to recognize that Black people might become "the instruments of a great idea," dared to hope that "it may . . . be possible for the Negro, through adherence to nonviolence, so to challenge the nations of the world that they will seriously seek an alternative to war and destruction." King understood and tried to convey to others his conviction that "today the choice is no longer between violence and nonviolence. It is either nonviolence or nonexistence." So he placed the descendants of America's slaves into a healing, cosmic context, proposing that "the Negro may be God's appeal to this age — an age drifting rapidly to its doom."[2]

Clearly his was a vision that pressed on far beyond civil rights and legalities. It was the same vision put forward in more earthly ways by the early members of the Student Nonviolent Coordinating Committee in their founding statement of purpose. They said, "We affirm the philosophical or religious ideal of nonviolence as the foundation of our purpose, the presupposition of our faith, and the manner of our action. Nonviolence as it grows from Judaic-Christian traditions seeks a social order of justice permeated by love."[3]

In the light of the degradation of the word *love* in our contemporary culture, it will be important for our students, whether in prisons, synagogues, churches, or schools, to rediscover what these earlier nonviolent warriors meant by the word. Exploring the writings, speeches, and actions of King, James Lawson, their teacher Gandhi, and thousands of movement participants, we are soon enlightened. We recognize a deep, soul-level force, a will to seek out the best possibilities of oneself and the opponents, a refusal to ignore or desecrate the divine image in any of us. We sense this love as a powerful commitment to the forces of good, an opening toward the creative powers of the universe. In the minds of many members of the church-based southern Black community, such love was a natural, modern manifestation of Jesus' call to live out our divine kinship by loving our enemies. So, from this perspective, we are able to understand the love of the nonviolent warriors not as a soft, sentimental kind of flimsy emotion but as a great, rock-ribbed, empowering force that makes it possible for women, men, and children to stand fast in the face of death, and thereby explore new paths to life, to the redeemed and compassionate community.

The nonviolent action that flowed out of such commitment made it possible for the early SNCC organizers in Mississippi to take harsh physical beatings and still confront the forces of destructive segregation without losing their basic sense of direction and purpose, without surrendering their humanity. As a result, they inspired thousands of other persons there to recollect their best selves, to stand and move forward, to break through their ancient fears. (Of course, the young workers constantly testified to the many ways in which they were also sustained by the wisdom and strength of the people they came to encourage.) This was the nonviolence that filled the Nashville student group with the determination to keep the freedom rides going, refusing to retaliate or to back down, opening doors no one can finally count or close. Watching carefully, you can catch glimpses of this alternative way of being deep in the eyes of Charles Sherrod, the dauntless SNCC leader in Albany, Georgia, as he remembers on film what it was really like to rally the grassroots forces of freedom in that dangerous city. We hear it in the voice of Annelle Ponder, one of SCLC's most resourceful staff members, when she stumbles out of the Winona, Mississippi, jail, badly beaten for her commitment to justice but calling out through her swollen lips, "Freedom!"

These and thousands more were the embodiment of the movement's greatest vision—the rising of new soldiers of freedom and democracy, armed with love, courage, and fierce determination, empowered by a relentless commitment to an emerging, but unrealized, democratic America. Turning away from the weapons of violence, manifesting the disciplined, healing energies of a profound soul force, for a time they seemed to be precisely what King had foreseen, "God's appeal to this age." And when their stirring images were carried across the globe by the news media, men and women everywhere responded to the message of their lives at levels that only the passing of decades could begin to reveal. Now the freedom songs echo back. Now we see King's words on signs above swirling throngs in distant squares. Now we realize how deep his example and his comrades' hope penetrated into Czechoslovakian lives, how they engaged South African hearts, reinforcing the model of Chief Albert Luthuli, reaffirming the people's own deepest longings for a democratic, nonracial society, for a nation at peace with itself.

Who dares raise such hopes in the United States today? In the face of many forms of personal and structural violence at home, listening to the misguided applause for bullying and immature military intrusions abroad, considering the thousands of families for whom the military offers the only possibility for a decent income in our unjust economy, who dares to remember and to dream of nonviolent alternatives? Obviously, we must dare. We who seek to inform our teaching with some real vision for the advancement of democracy in our country and the world—we are the witnesses. It is we who realize that our telling of the story of the Afro-American freedom movement can be authentic only as we reveal these original, magnificent dreams of nonviolent transformation, recollect the quest for creative alternatives, and suggest these connections to the world's best dreams of new democracy. For this is a unique and compelling story. Never before in our nation's history had the participants in a major social movement grounded themselves in so magnificent a hope, dared to dream a possible human transformation so deep—and then proved willing to put their lives on the line in courageous acts of faith. For those who stood on the front lines of battle against the terroristic system of American segregation were indeed displaying great faith, in themselves and their mission, in the power of courageous love, in the capacity of their enemies to change, and sometimes in a divine reality whose central identity is compassion. Perhaps this is part of what made our experience so attractive to those hidden crevices around the world where the seeds of democracy were germinating.

In such a context, for the sake of the five-year-old gun wielders who wrench our hearts, for the sake of hundreds of millions of men and women everywhere who are in search of new hearts, those who teach the freedom movement are presented with a marvelous opportunity to open vistas. For many persons the new approaches will at first be only dimly seen and superficially understood. Still they must be shared. For the movement's bold strand of nonviolence (and we will surely teach that there were other, sometimes competing, strands) provides a chance and a challenge that cannot be left unmet. It allows us to go with our students as deeply as we choose toward the sources of that lifestyle, delving, for instance, into the experience and experiments of Gandhi and his movement, into the paths of the Buddha, working our way toward Jesus of Nazareth and his justice-obsessed brother and sister prophets of Israel, moving quietly, firmly into the river-deep meditations of Howard Thurman — perhaps even reading more of King than the worthy and well-worn 1963 March on Washington "I Have a Dream" speech.

We must work our way into the depths of spirit which supplied the movement with so much of its early power. For someone needs to help our Bronx-American child, and so many adults and children like him, to understand and to care why great teachers and spiritual guides of every age and tradition have come to affirm the same nonviolent vision of life. Who knows, perhaps with insight, courage, and serious study we could introduce ourselves and our students of all ages to some of the basic tenets of this nonviolent way, exploring such convictions as:

1. The fundamental unity of all creation, including our essential oneness with those we call "enemy."

2. The deep and often hidden capacities in human beings to become much more than we realize; to approach much more closely the essential oneness of life; to create many more social, political, and economic manifestations of our unity than we dream.

3. The purpose of true civilization is not to focus on higher and higher technology or greater material wealth; it is to help us live more deeply and grow more fully in the humanizing work of mutual responsibility and respect.

4. The necessity of challenging anything—or anyone—in society (or in ourselves) that appears to destroy the God-ordained oneness, or which seeks to damage our great capacities for an ever-expanding development of our humanity.

5. The greatest necessity of all is to seek out and hold firmly to the truths of our oneness, our hope, our mutual responsibility, our capacity to create, our refusal to destroy. Included here, of course, is a willingness to die, if necessary, for such truths. but not to injure or kill others.

6. The constant, disciplined quest for personal and collective communion with the One, the divine and ultimate source of all our unity.

It is amazing, isn't it, where a bus boycott can take us if we allow ourselves to be gathered into the center of the movement? In this way we understand anew the power, courage, and creativity of those who were willing to absorb hatred and violence for the sake of a transformed society in which hatred and violence would continuously be diminished through audacious nonviolent struggle. From this perspective we can understand and convey the essential strength and courage of the citizens of Lowndes County, Alabama, who faced one day the shotgun-carrying sheriff's demand to turn around and give up their persistent quest for the right to vote. In the light of that county's history of white sheriffs, their guns, and what they had done to Black people, we may be able to understand and communicate the grandeur of the simple story told by a SNCC worker accompanying the citizens. When the sheriff ordered them to go home, one of those attempting to register to vote said to the SNCC organizer, "We ain't going nowhere today. If we back up now, we'll be backing up for the next hundred years." And soon all the people who had come to register started saying, "We ain't going nowhere today. You're going to have to kill us right here." Armed only with their courage, refusing for many reasons to pick up the weapons of their oppressors, the man and his companions stood their ground and were eventually able to move forward in ways that surprised even them. With the help of SNCC, they created a county-wide independent political party and chose as its emblem the defiant black panther that would shortly thereafter inspire Huey Newton and Bobby Seale to name their new organization the Black Panther Party.

Of course, as we have already discovered, this quest for non-violent alternatives in the movement is not a one-strand story. For instance, anyone who uses a resource like *Eyes on the Prize II* to follow the story of the Lowndes County movement, or the rise and fall of the northern-based Panthers, or the fiery explosions of the urban rebellions, will be presented with a marvelous opportunity to teach. For we, like King and the other nonviolent warriors, must struggle with ourselves and our students to absorb the pain, the fierce determination, and the broken hopes that finally led to urban fire, to popular calls to "pick up the gun," to demands for defensive and occasionally revolutionary violence.

Let that intense and powerful debate on the value of violence and nonviolence be picked up from the past and carried on in the classrooms, as we encourage close listening to the developing arguments. Let us be sure to recognize how clear King was by the late 1960s that nonviolent protest had to evolve beyond its southern-based experience into even more dangerous and militant nonviolent revolution, eventually challenging the federal government and all the anti-democratic status quo values and structures of the entire nation. Let them read his last book, *The Trumpet of Conscience*, and hear him say in the midst of the explosions of the cities and the anguish of poverty and war:

> Nonviolent protest must now mature to a new level to correspond to heightened black impatience and stiffened white resistance. This higher level is mass civil disobedience. There must be more than a statement to a larger society. There must be a force that interrupts its functioning at some key point.[4]

Go with our students, through film and print sources, to the "key point" for nonviolent confrontation that King was choosing at the very end of his life, the federal establishment in Washington, D.C. Help them envision what he might have had in mind for his multiracial Poor People's Campaign in the nation's capital, his campaign of "mass civil disobedience on behalf of economic justice and democracy." Then students and teachers alike may understand the larger context of his assassination. Then we will be walking on far more controversial ground, accompanying a much less safe and smoothed off national hero. Can we be faithful to our students, to the movement, to our five-year-old brother, without such a walk? Can we understand those who died in China, who shake South Africa, or those who now transform Eastern Europe without a sense of this part of our own powerful history?

Whatever our answers to these questions, it will be crucial to ponder with our students why it was that a clear majority of the people who were most deeply committed to the way of nonviolent struggle for justice and humane social transformation in the movement are still at work on that path. (Perhaps we could share examples like that of C. T. Vivian and his current work against racism, Bob Moses and his creative experiments with empowering children to master mathematics, Diane Nash and her determination to create a nonviolent army, Bernard Lafayette going into prisons and police departments to teach nonviolent alternatives to guards and officers, Reverend James Lawson lifting up issues of justice, peace, and nonviolent action from his Los Angeles pulpit and in his pastoral work every week—as well as many others.)

On the other hand, most of those freedom workers who once announced most loudly the need for "the gun" are no longer making such calls, publicly or privately. Among other reasons, many of them have surely seen too much of what the gun has done in the Black and white communities of America. They, too, know our brother-child in the Bronx kindergarten, and they realize that his deepest needs cannot be met by guns, neither the ones children bring to school nor the ones our country stockpiles in the name of "security." For all these guns have left our child naked to the enemies of fear, ignorance, self-doubt, and insecurity, have abandoned most schools and communities of the poor (and many in the middle class) to a shameful state of deep educational and spiritual unprotection. And all these guns are obviously being challenged by the unrelenting forces of nonviolent revolution now at work in the world.

Our students know such things. They recognize such children, too. And at hungering levels of the soul they are longing for alternatives to violence for other lives as well as for their own. In the course of our teaching, then, it would be fitting and helpful to be sure that they are introduced in person or on tape to Martin and Coretta's youngest daughter, Bernice "Bunny" King, born in 1963. For she is a beacon and a sign. Continuing a great tradition in Black America, she has studied to be both pastor and lawyer, deeply concerned about young people caught in the "justice system" of our land. Moving across the country, she is calling for the development of a nonviolent army whose backbone will be young people, whose work is to continue the struggle for the creation of a just and humane American nation, whose very existence will be a testimony to the possibility of a creative alternative to all the ways of nonviolence, all the ways that deny our oneness and our great reservoirs of goodness. It is startling to realize that Bernice is just about the age her father was when he began his public leadership in the struggle for a transformed people and a revolutionized nation. Is there any place for her vision, for our vision to join hers, for all of us and our students to discover our best possibilities, and begin to build on them?

In the light of the self-destructive violence that stalks our land, that now seems endemic among Black young men, in the light of the curse of drugs and the drug economy that is partly a result of our refusal to create an economy of compassionate sharing for our society, is it too late? Is it too much to hope that some of the young people and adults in our classes, from every racial background, will find alternatives for the many forms of violence they are experiencing in their lives? Is it too much to hope that some of those who have broken through to high school and college and jobs and "security" will recognize the fragility of any security built on the wasting of our children in the Bronx? Is it possible that some of them (us) will move in compassionate firmness and skill toward that gun-carrying child, holding him, challenging all the conditions that have helped to create him?

Is it even possible that some of my early-retirement friends who leave the "security" of the U.S. military will become recruiters for a new army, a gathering of nonviolent rainbow warriors? And do we dare dream that one of those peace-force sisters or brothers will eventually find our child from the Bronx, help him to grasp the beauty and creative power within him, and move forward with that manchild into the next stage of our nation's never-ending struggle for its own best truths? Will that self-respecting child eventually be accepted into one of a score of American peace academies that we must create, or find his way to a U.N.-sponsored peace brigade, serving skillfully, nonviolently, in the midst of some setting of armed tension and fear? Somehow I choose to imagine him bringing his audacious creativity to participate in the expanding international explorations of civilian-based, nonviolent national defense forces. I hear his voice among the rising chorus of those younger persons who will soon challenge much of our old thinking about national security, military strength, and the power of disciplined soul force. I see him becoming all that he can be on behalf of human life and creativity.

Such dreams and visions concerning the life of our young brother and son return us to the large and fundamental questions for us all, prompt us to wonder if it is too much to hope that some of us may be drawn into King's great dream of an alternative to the ways of destructive violence. Is it possible that we might all become part of what he called "God's appeal to this age"? Is that one meaning of the amazing democratic developments around the world—a divine appeal, arising as much from within us as from any outer ranges of the universe? What a marvelous possibility: The ferment across the globe, the life-affirming hope that our own movement helped to engender, may be a sign that there is still time for us all to rediscover our creative calling, time to nurture our best responses to the divine summons away from violence and destructive fear, moving toward sanity, toward humanity, toward home—a new home, a new beginning for our Bronx manchild, for all God's children.

Is that too much to dream? And if dreams die, what is left? At its best, teaching is dreaming, isn't it, believing in possibilities that no one else sees, and being willing to work sacrificially toward the realization of those potentials? In essence, this is the deeper story of the freedom movement: By our dreaming, in the crucible of active hope, we begin to create new realities. Who can teach without dreams? Who dares to dream without acting?

6

Gifts of the Black Movement

Toward "A New Birth of Freedom"

We the People of the United States, in Order to form a more perfect Union, establish Justice, insure domestic Tranquility, provide for the common defence, promote the general Welfare, and secure the Blessings of Liberty to ourselves and our Posterity, do ordain and establish this Constitution for the United States of America.
—Preamble, United States Constitution, 1787

From these honored dead we take increased devotion to that cause for which they gave the last full measure of devotion—that we here highly resolve that these dead shall not have died in vain—that this nation, under God, shall have a new birth of freedom—and that government of the people, by the people, for the people, shall not perish from the earth.
—Abraham Lincoln, Gettysburg Address, 1863

The black revolution is much more than a struggle for the rights of Negroes. It is forcing America to face all its interrelated flaws—racism, poverty, militarism and materialism. It is exposing the evils that are rooted deeply in the whole structure of our society. It reveals systemic rather than superficial

105

flaws and suggests that radical reconstruction of society itself
is the real issue to be faced.
                                                    —*Martin Luther King, Jr., 1968*[1]

During the course of the Civil War one of America's most
perceptive social critics made this observation: "Among nations,
no one has more need of full knowledge of itself than the United
States, and no one has hitherto had less." When we reflect on
what we have all probably learned in our own lives about the
costs of a lack of individual self-knowledge, there is surely something troubling about the existence of such a state of ignorance
in the life of a nation. And now, more than 125 years after
Orestes Brownson's astute commentary on the shortcomings of
American self-understanding, we are faced with the fact that it
is still too accurate, and that it has a painful and special relevance for many of us who teach. At times Brownson's words
seem pointed particularly to the women and men who labor
valiantly to make American history come alive, but we know that
the afflicted population is really deeper and broader than that.
Indeed, the issue is far more than academic and the consequences are of great importance to the future possibilities of
our nation. For it may be that we will find no creative grounds
for the common life of this wonderfully diverse people until we
are able to establish some solid and knowledgeable foothold in
both the hopes and the terrors of our national past.

At least that is what I think I see as I continue to encounter
a generation of white young people (and too many of their parents) who have been taught that the great freedom struggle of
post–World War II America was really about nothing more than
"rights" for Black people. In response, they often pass it off as
something old, finished, and essentially irrelevant; and they
object to any continuing attention to a somewhat murky cause
that seems to ignore, or even diminish, their own "rights" as
modern, often wounded and very uncertain, white persons. At
the same time, many younger Black Americans who have
received the same historical message are tempted to think that
nothing remains for them now except to protest the continuing
lack of adequate rights, or to turn toward a defensive individ-
ualism that denies their need for any special attention. Mean-

while, observing the whole process are the other peoples of color, whose grasp of the history of the modern struggle for the expansion of American democracy is usually at least as weak as everyone else's (and who often display a palpable ambivalence about their own relationship to the "dominant" whites and the "subordinate" Blacks). Often their understandable response is to enter into a quest for *their* rights, with the assumption that there are only so many "rights" available, that African-Americans have gotten at least enough, and now they must carry on their own, independent struggle, as Asians, as Hispanics, as Native Americans.[2]

Obviously, such a misunderstanding of the Black freedom movement—and therefore of the history of this country—has dire consequences for everyone, especially for all of us who believe that there is still the possibility of creating "a more perfect Union" in this land. As a result, one of the major challenges available to teachers in every possible institution is to introduce ourselves and our students to an alternative vision of the movement, to see it as a great gift for all Americans, as a central point of grounding for our own pro-democracy movement. To do that, it is necessary to call attention to the deepest commitments of the Black participants and their allies, to allow all of us to experience the urgent concern for the expansion of American democracy and for the healing of a schizophrenic nation that burned at the core of the struggle. In the process, our own teaching may well become part of the therapeutic experience.

In other words, for the sake of "a full knowledge of ourselves," what we must all learn is what so many African-Americans have known from the founding period of the nation, from the early days of their struggle: First, that American democracy could not be realized in any basic integrity unless the fullness of democratic life was shared with its enslaved people, with its newly freed people, with its legally segregated people, with its exploited people. And the second knowledge went even deeper, that the nation could never be whole—released from its "disease" of saying one thing about freedom, justice, and liberty, and doing another—until Black Americans were whole, internally and externally. The terror and the beauty of the dialectic have always been inescapable.

Thus it is that we return to one of the most powerful aspects of our vocation as teachers over this next period: to help the entire nation understand that the freedom struggle of its African-American citizens has always been a gift of life and truth to the whole society. Always.

Even though the focus of our exploration has been on the post–World War II period, it will be important at least to call the attention of our students to the earlier times, to the very beginnings of the nation. For if we look at formative statements such as the Declaration of Independence, or the Preamble to the Constitution, we see not only the best democratic intentions of the founders but also the ways in which the interdependent relationship between the freedom of Black people and the truth of democracy was established from the beginning. Our students must recognize how important were the ceaseless questions, protestations, and courageously rebellious acts that rose out of the Black communities during that early nation-building period. They need to reflect on the fact that without this persistent, costly questioning of the meaning of "all men are created equal," or the identity of "we the people," the white male, slave-holding/trading founders might have found it even easier to live out a tragic falsehood, a betrayal of their own best selves, a denial of the extraordinary possibilities of this new nation.

So, from the very beginning, those Black people and their allies who created difficulties, who raised questions, who deserted the ranks of slavery, who rebelled against the system of bondage, who challenged the wisdom of the conventional definitions of truth and justice, were actually sharing a great gift with the nation. They were offering an opportunity for America to be true to itself, to live out its most democratic pronouncements. Unfortunately, as we all know, it was not until many slave rebellions had been quelled in blood, not until tens of thousands of freedom-bound Black fugitives had exacerbated the rising tensions between North and South, not until white families and churches and territories were split apart and deeply wounded over the issue of slavery, not until Black and white abolitionists daily risked their lives to call the nation and the world to sanity, not until all these contradictions and more had exploded into the most costly war of the century (a war whose coming many

Black people had predicted, if the nation held to its inhuman and anti-democratic institution of human slavery)—it was not until then that increasing numbers of the nation's citizens and their official leaders began to see that the nation could not exist half slave and half free. (Shall we prepare for a contemporary question from our students: "And what about half poor and half affluent?")

In the same way, it will be important for our students to know that during the Civil War, our country's great humanitarian president sincerely longed for "a new birth of freedom," and later saw the closing of the terrible civil conflict as an opportunity "to bind up the nation's wounds" and to build "a just and lasting peace." But once again, through the war and the post-war period, African-Americans challenged Lincoln and the nation in words and deeds to consider how new freedom, new justice, and new health were related to the future of the children of Africa, who had shed so much of their own blood as participants in the struggle for freedom. For these determined Black freedom fighters were certainly in search of a government that would really be "of the people, by the people, for the people." But they knew that no such government could exist in truth for anyone here unless they, the formerly enslaved people, were fully welcomed as crucial, participating elements of "we the people of the United States." Anything less would be dangerous, costly, and undemocratic. Black people knew that, said that, persistently organized in the light of that truth. But the nation constantly tried to bargain for less, was not ready for full Black citizens, was not prepared to pay the price for their protection and empowerment, especially as they lived out their lives in the midst of their former owners and oppressors. Soon the white supremacy of the South joined ranks with the white supremacy of the North and temporarily strangled the vital Black thrust toward their own version of Lincoln's new birth of freedom.

So with the death of Reconstruction those African-Americans who carried the dream of true American democracy within the deep places of their lives dug in for a long and very costly struggle. They were bearers of the gift and they would not give up. In their best hours they understood that their movement was not simply for Black rights, or even for "equality" with a wounded white American populace, but for "a new birth of freedom" in the blood-soaked, fire-singed land. Our students need to know and feel that. They need to realize that all the most profound leaders and spokespersons in the Black-led struggle for a just and non-racist democracy expressed this dialectical set of goals as they fought their way into the twentieth century. Whether Black or white, these men and women of courage and hope understood that African-Americans could not be truly free for our best future until the rest of the nation was delivered from its anti-democratic and white supremacist past. At the same time, they realized that the nation could not achieve its truest human possibilities until African-Americans were fully appreciated participants and leaders in the creation of the new democratic reality.

With our assistance, this running outline of history helps to provide our students with a logical setting for the rise of the post–World War II African-American freedom movement. Placed against the earlier background, set in the context of anti-colonial struggles around the world, the developments of the 1950s and afterward can be seen as a powerful, sometimes explosive continuation of the centuries-long struggle for the truth of America, for the freedom of its Black people. In this context we may help our students understand why, for instance, a Black American marine would receive word of the *Brown* v. *Board of Education* decision in 1954 and say, "I was sure that this was the beginning of a new era of American democracy." (Part of the educational process consists also in understanding how this marine, Robert F. Williams, could end the decade as a fugitive from American justice, the result of his armed fight for democracy in his native North Carolina.) They will also be prepared to catch the meaning of the way in which Martin Luther King and the Southern Christian Leadership Conference constantly defined their task in the 1950s as a movement "to redeem the soul of America." What greater gift could a nation receive? And what struggles lie ahead if the nation does not know its soul?

In order to develop this theme in the modern time of freedom struggle, it might be valuable to explore with our students a number of the manifestations of the "gift" quality of the movement. As we do so it is possible, and necessary, to reflect on the kind of wisdom and maturity that are needed if individuals or collectivities are to recognize the possibility that those who challenge our status quo may be offering us all a gift. The central idea is not hard to grasp, even for younger students: there are times in our experience when we are living lives which contradict and deny the best truths that we claim for ourselves. Therefore we are crippling ourselves, damaging our spirits, but have grown accustomed to the process. At such times, people in our families, or those unfamiliar to us, may offer a magnificent opportunity for us to disturb and re-collect ourselves and return to our most authentic commitments, when they challenge our direction, when they raise questions about what we're doing, when they refuse to cooperate with our self-destructive actions, or our equally damaging acts against them.

That challenging role has been a central characteristic of the Black struggle for freedom in America. The men, women, and children who carried its banners have insisted that the nation and its institutions ask fundamental questions about all the issues and actions that go to the heart of democracy. The movement has opened opportunities for us all to develop new definitions of what it means to be an American, has pressed us toward a continuing rethinking of the meaning of "a more perfect union," of "the general welfare," has insisted that we consider the needs of the weakest and most vulnerable outcasts among us in our concern for "the common defense," in our quest for "equal protection under the law." In that tradition, then, one of the great gifts of the post–World War II freedom movement has been its continuing pressure for the creative opening of the Constitution, the courts, the executive branch, and Congress to deeper explorations of democracy (more "advanced ideas," in the phrase of our Shanghai student) than ever before.

Becoming even more specific, it is likely that most of our students under the age of forty have no real idea of what it meant to live in an America that proclaimed its democracy to the world and yet encompassed large portions of legally segregated existence. That this physically and socially coerced segregation was included in "the American way of life" did not make it any easier to explain to young Black children why they could not play, eat, go to school, or use the restroom where other children were obviously doing so. (And how did white parents explain the great Black absence from public places such as restaurants, hotels, and theaters?)

Only a brief time of reflection may be needed for students to understand that those tireless freedom workers, who determined to overcome the power of the long reign of legal segregation, who relentlessly challenged the official, heartrending denials of democracy, were doing much more than opening formerly closed doors to Black people, were seeing greater visions than "integration." Generations of white Americans had also been prisoners, held bondage to the illusion of white supremacy, denied access to their separated Black sisters and brothers, encouraged to live daily lives in absolute denial of their prayers, speaking with forked tongues to their children. How they needed release! In the 1950s, an entire nation was calling itself "leader of the free world," and yet carrying out on many levels a freedom-denying system of apartheid. Therefore those women and men, and all their children, who challenged the system, who offered their lives in courageous opposition, who fought for democracy on these embattled shores and became models of "a new birth of freedom," were actually presenting a great gift to us all, were *being* a great gift for us all. They were offering the nation a chance to begin the journey out of its woundedness, its schizophrenic illusions, on the pathway to integrity. In fits and starts, with periods of great denial, America has tried to respond, often has tried to do only what is minimal for its healing, but it can never go back to the pre-1950s again where race is concerned. That is a magnificent gift. Perhaps the nation needs some great living monument of gratitude to those who brought them kicking, screaming, longing, yearning, rebelling, regretting, hoping, out of that past. Is celebrating King's birthday enough? Is it understood?

While reflecting on such questions it may be helpful to turn the attention of our students to one of the most important and resonant institutional examples of the gift—that is, the experience of the white American churches. With important exceptions, before the 1950s they had generally accepted and usually blessed "the American way of life" with its segregation and strident anti-communism. It was understandable that out of such institutions there should arise by the end of the 1950s a significant conversation concerning "the death of God." But it turned out that the only God who was dying (who needed to be buried) was the irrelevant, mirror-image deity of the white, segregationist, accommodationist, idolatrous institutions of religion in the United States. For the early, post-1950 Afro-American freedom movement was sending out a different, powerful signal, a life-affirming call from its base in the Black churches of the South, inviting men and women of faith to come and see and feel the movement of divine love in their midst and to commit themselves to work on the frontiers of struggle for justice and love.

Before long, the Black-led movement for the expansion of American democracy had become a powerful source of religious awakening, offering revival to all those people of faith who wanted to be revived. (At the same time it was also offering encouragement to millions overseas—from Nicaragua to Vietnam—who were deeply moved and encouraged by our struggle.) Those spiritually charged gatherings of nuns, rabbis, priests, and Protestant lay and clerical forces, singing, shouting, "We want freedom," refusing to be moved from the movement's struggle lines, were unforgettable experiences. American religion had never before been aroused to such ecumenically broad and persistently active responses to human needs for justice, truth, and democratic hope. (Nor had some of the church and synagogue folk ever sung anything so loud and spirited as they sang "We Shall Overcome.") Even though there was controversy about their involvement in the struggle, the movement that inspired such new life among the churches was recognized by many of the members as an extraordinary blessing. Indeed, it was so powerful a gift that *some* of the religiously based white participants in the freedom movement's far-flung struggles actually went back to their local settings and began to work anew for justice there—and some have never stopped.

Eventually the movement helped create our own American brand of twentieth century liberation theology, beginning, appropriately enough, with themes of Black liberation. In essence, then, the white American churches were being pressed to discover what the Black churches had long been forced to know: At its best, the struggle for the expansion of democracy is a struggle for the sensitizing and enlarging of the human spirit—indeed "a new birth of freedom" that is at the heart of all true religion. Eventually, as we shall see, the opening created by the churches' responses to the call of the Freedom Movement also made possible an unprecedented religious dissent to the expanding war in Vietnam and a powerful church-based resistance to some of our leaders' worst intentions in Nicaragua. (Unfortunately it was no ultimate deterrent to our government's racially integrated, but still racist and colonialist invasions of Grenada and Panama.)

Perhaps it was the profoundly spiritual quality of that democratic quest for human renewal which helps to explain the arrival of the young white southerners who were among the first allies to embrace the gift of the Black freedom movement. It will be good for our current students to know that while we often focus our historical attention on the hundreds of white persons who entered the freedom struggle as Mississippi Summer volunteers in 1964, there were many others who came years before them, including young southerners. These were among the earliest of the student forces who were beaten and jailed in the course of the sit-ins and the freedom rides, who risked their lives with their Black comrades in early voter registration campaigns in terrifyingly dangerous rural counties of Georgia, Alabama, and Mississippi, and elsewhere in the South.

I knew many of these southern white young men and women, and it was very clear that they considered the movement, and the significant supporting role they were allowed to play, as a great gift for their lives. Many of them had been shaped in the fiery cauldron of this nation's southern white religion (which, of course, was partly African at its base), and then had turned away from what seemed to be the racial hypocrisy of their home churches. When the movement opened itself to them it was like being born again. For here was a familiar religious ethos, touching them at deep places of memory and pain. But now it was tied to a just and righteous cause, the cause of freedom and justice, the cause of reconciliation and unity. Their faith was renewed. Their love was set free. They gained a new sense of purpose, direction, and hope. On dangerous country roads, facing hostile white mobs (who were especially angered by the sight of *their* white faces and the sound of *their* southern drawls) they found a cause worth living and dying, but not killing, for. They believed they were working for the cleansing of American life, for the advancement of democratic hope, for a more perfect union—perhaps even for the glory of the coming of the Lord. Even though they often had to bear many forms of abuse from family, friends, and others, even though the necessary rise of Black consciousness and the call for Black Power later put them on the edges of the movement, many of them took the gift and went on to new points of struggle for democracy. Whether in the Southern Student Organizing Committee or in the better-known Students for a Democratic Society, these white young people made it clear that they had been opened to a new vision of their society and their role as agents for democratic change. Our students need to reflect on this gift, especially when we consider that one of the most important manifestations of the continuing white student presence was soon expressed in the rising, organized opposition to the war in Vietnam. It is important to know that there was a direct and compelling line between the Black-led struggles for democracy in the South and the recognition that the war in Vietnam was a great danger to the development of democracy everywhere, but especially in the United States.

This insight and connection came not only through the lives of white movement veterans, but from the earliest anti-war words and deeds on the part of SNCC and such individual African-American freedom fighters as Bob Moses, Stokely Carmichael, Diane Nash, and Jim Bevel.[3] Of course, the best-known Black opponent to the war was Dr. King, and he made it very clear that there was an indissoluble link between his struggle for the soul of America at home and his call for the nation to cease denying and destroying others—and its own children—abroad. Again, it takes significant maturity for persons and nations to welcome rather than subvert or kill their prophets, but we can certainly see from this distance that King and his Black and white movement-shaped comrades were bearing a gift, offering us a release from a self-destructive path. In his most famous public statement against the war, the speech he delivered at New York's Riverside Church on April 4, 1967, King said that those who chose "the path of protest and dissent" were actually "working for the health of our land." (This is, of course, an important opportunity to explore again the role of principled dissent and noncooperation in the building of a democratic society, a chance to reflect with our students on the dangerous and healthy pro-democracy dictum of Walt Whitman: "Obey less and resist more.")

The crusade against the war in Vietnam was not the only social movement that was fed directly by the African-American freedom struggle. For instance, many of the nation's religious institutions found continuing inspiration from their participation in the movement. Not only did the revival of social concern lead the churches and synagogues to unprecedented wartime dissent during the Vietnam years, but the spirit persisted, and often showed itself in the process of internal struggle and renewal of the institutions. For instance, it is fascinating to study the pictures of the southern marches of the early 1960s and to note the first appearances of Roman Catholic nuns in their traditional full habits. Then, over time, we see them persistently on the freedom lines in a number of movements, but we also see a change of external appearance, and we may even be able to catch the new sense of internal empowerment that their participation seemed to bring with it. Of course, none of this came without significant cost, and the price is still being calculated within the lives of the women and the structures of the churches.

Not only the nuns, but many other faith-based veterans of the freedom movement became part of the costly heart of pro-democracy struggles here. So Black movement history, methods, music, and leadership continued to inspire a powerful church- and synagogue-based participation in the struggle against nuclear weapons, in the work for noninvasive solutions in Nicaragua and in the development of the Sanctuary movement on behalf of Central American political refugees. Indeed, the Sanctuary network went back as far as the days of Harriet Tubman and the antebellum Underground Railroad in its claim on African-American freedom movement inspiration. And the fact is that wherever the predominantly white churches and other religious institutions engaged in struggles for justice and peace and for the expansion of democracy in the United States from the 1960s onward, their testimony was the same. From Witness for Peace in Nicaragua, to Jubilee Partners in Philadelphia, to Ground Zero in Washington state, to the Sojourners Community in Washington, D.C., and the Jubilee Community in Georgia, they have all expressed a sense of profound indebtedness to the formative and continuing gifts of the Black freedom movement—its spirit, its songs, its vision, and its heroes. In many cases they have also paid the price.

Even though the gifts and connections are manifested in different ways with different movements, once they are opened to the linkages it will not be hard for students to trace the path of the Black-led struggle for democracy through the life of other American struggles. For instance, the revival of the women's liberation movement in the 1960s and 1970s was often accompanied by freedom movement songs, methodologies, and concerns about the destructive dominance of white patriarchy in their lives. (At one point, some women in search of an authentic women's identity cast aside their male-identified last names and temporarily called themselves Mary X and Jane X, on the pathway to new identities.) In an even more obvious testimony, the Gray Panthers used their name to demonstrate the debt they owed to the Black movement.

The issue of personal and collective identity, which has been so central to the African-American quest for individual integrity and authentic democracy, soon found powerful resonances among other peoples of color in the United States, and elsewhere. Indeed, as we shall indicate more fully below, it was the Black search for self-definition and self-determination that did so much to inspire Hispanic Americans, Asian Americans, Native Americans and other groups to organize in search of their own new levels of internal and external freedom. For a time (especially after the January 1977 showing of the television adaptation of Alex Haley's novel *Roots*, seen by more than 130 million viewers), everyone seemed interested in ethnic and cultural roots, including people of Polish, Italian, and other previously less-valued European backgrounds. Again, a Black quest had become a national gift—perhaps, in an increasingly pluralistic society, more of a gift than we know.

As we delve beyond the civil-rights-for-Black-folk level of understanding this powerful movement, it becomes increasingly clear that we are really inviting our students to an experience that involves more than the acquisition of new information. Rather, as they consider the contributions of the freedom movement to the development of our nation's other pro-democracy forces, they move beyond information toward insight: insight about the "object" of their study, hopefully even deeper insight about themselves. As always, they invite their teachers on the journey.

This process, so crucial to all humanizing education, is fascinating to observe as we see it lighting fires in faces, eyes, spoken words, or written papers. For instance, as students ponder the gifts of the Black movement those who are not African-American (and some who are) admit that they find it difficult to understand why and how the quest for positive Black identity, Black pride, and Black solidarity, could be defined as gifts for the rest of our society. Now, this is where a sense of compassionate social cohesion becomes important, and our teaching needs to assume that such a feeling for "the general welfare," for the oneness of "the body politic" is within the realm of possibility for most, if not all, of our students. Working from such assumptions, we may need to remind them of the psychological tests of African-American children involving Black and white dolls. First conducted by Black psychologists Kenneth and Mamie Phipps Clark in 1939 and 1940, these tests have been repeated as late as the 1980s. In every setting, too many of the children displayed great difficulty, even pain, in identifying with dolls modeled upon themselves, rejecting them, claiming they were "dirty," saying they were "not the right color," suggesting that the Black dolls represented children no one would want to play with.

When we contrast this understandable (but heartbreaking) sense of woundedness and self-rejection with the powerful attempts at affirmation that were rising in the Black community in the late 1960s and early 1970s we see another picture. We hear young Juanita Bryant in Brooklyn declaring:

BLACK PEOPLE

Who are they?
To me they are the most wonderful
thing that could have happened
to this shrinking world of today
They are people who are not
ashamed of their color
or have fear of the new tomorrow
They are the people who have
tried for hundreds of years
to find their freedom.[4]

Sensitively received, this voice of "the new tomorrow" and the choruses from which it springs are sources of strength and hope for the entire society. For they testify to the possibilities of an abused and rejected people developing a deep sense of self-love and self-confidence. Then each of our students who has arrived at a sense of maturity can be reminded of the difference there is on a personal level when we are relating to persons who love and respect themselves, who bring a sense of self-reliance into the relationship, as compared to a connection with self-doubting, unsure, and insecure partners, who want only to mimic and "please" us. Such reflections take us again to the insight that calls humans to love others *as* we love ourselves. Following such a line of thought it is possible for us to realize that a society, like a personal relationship, is richer, fuller, freer when it is built on a base of persons who love and respect themselves (and their ancestry) and who are therefore prepared to respect, challenge, and care for others. So movements for compassionate self-affirmation within any community become gifts for us all.

Of course, given additional time and space these thoughts often lead to serious questions about the real inner condition of those men and women who seem compelled to deride, diminish, and dominate the "different" others among us. (Howard Thurman, the remarkable Black mystic and teacher, often told of his meeting with a leader of one of the Indian nations of Canada. This man told Thurman, "When I come into town and walk the streets and stop at the door of a white man, I come as one who knows his center and am in touch with that center. When the white man opens the door, I can immediately tell whether or not he knows *his* center. If he does, it is good. Our two centers can meet one another, engage one another, know one another. But if he does not know his center, then we cannot meet. And I leave. For I know that great unhappiness can come from those who do not know their center."[5])

In other words, the struggle for Black affirmation becomes, at its best, part of the necessary preparation for a more healthy and multiracial United States, a nation constantly being challenged to give up all vestiges of its centuries-old white supremacist ideologies and assumptions. For those undemocratic ideas and practices throw us all off center. They become impedimenta to the creation of a more perfect Union, especially in a nation where peoples of color—so-called "minorities"—are steadily moving toward a "majority" status. (I use quotation marks here because I am convinced that a new, truly pluralist nation must find some new language to define its peoples, its great, gift-like variety of humanity. *Majority* and *minorities* are words that carry terrifying, pejorative, historical baggage, and not only are they totally inappropriate for describing the parts of a *community* of humankind, but they lead us to very inaccurate perceptions of the actual human statistics of the planet.)

This is why the rise of African-American educational movements and their continuing siege against narrow Euro-American intellectual hegemony provides another gift, another opportunity to open ourselves to a rich self-knowledge. In that context it is easy to see why the emergence of Black studies was soon followed by struggles for women's studies, Asian studies, Native American studies, and Chicano (or Hispanic, Latino, or Puerto Rican) studies. Sharing the gift of Blackness, all these thrusts are really individual and collective experiments, probes on the way to a new American history, a new American studies. (Of course, the term *American* must either be expanded to include this American hemisphere in its totality, or condensed to the size of the setting we really intend, these United States of America.) But our efforts are relatively new, and that discovery cannot be rushed. Meanwhile, we recognize that it was a good and necessary thing for the wedge of Blackness to open us beyond the tragic coagulation of our old and insufficient formulations. We have not yet discovered the full meaning of "American" studies, partly because the new birth is yet in process; we are still creating these United States of America. Nevertheless, we can surely help our students identify, receive, and appreciate the gifts that forced us out of our unenlightened path. For if the self-knowledge Brownson sought in the 1860s continues to be necessary for us, then it must surely be rooted in our national educational process at every level and in every sort of teaching situation. Eventually we must ask, how can a multicultural nation begin to know itself without a multicultural base for the fundamental story that it tells?[6]

From every angle of approach to the freedom movement it becomes clear that when we focus our attention not on civil rights but on the hope of a constantly evolving nation, nurturing and nurtured by a continuous new birth of freedom, it is easier to see the gifts of the Magi—in this case the Black American Magi. For instance, taking off from the Mississippi Freedom Democratic Party's challenge to the 1964 Democratic National Convention, we are able to draw a direct line to the presidential campaigns of Jesse Jackson in 1984 and 1988. Was Jesse a gift? Beyond his obvious, almost mythic significance for Black people, this direct heir of the freedom movement's glory days became a special opportunity for millions of other Americans as well. For many of them it was the first time they were offered a serious opportunity to break out of the political prison of whiteness, actually freed to choose to vote for a Black person as a presidential candidate. As they received the gift, sometimes with great enthusiasm, Jesse became the political equivalent of what King had been for many searching white Americans—their leader, opening their minds, hearts, and loyalties in ways that would have been called impossible a few decades earlier. (Especially in the light of the Black experience and the stories of the worldwide struggles for democracy, let our students regularly consider the meaning of the marvelous imperative scrawled all over the walls of Paris during the student uprisings of 1968: "Be

Realistic—Demand the Impossible." In many cases it has taken only a few months for "the impossible" to become the morning news.)

Here, again, the very process of gaining a purchase on the significance of these developments may contribute to the maturing of those persons we teach, whatever their age. They may begin to see, to sense the ways by which a nation matures—or chooses not to. For through the singular experience of the Jackson candidacy white Americans were being invited into moral and political development, given a chance to do what African-Americans had been doing all along, choosing a qualified person of another race as their supreme political leader. For individuals and the nation, here was a golden (ebony?) opportunity to break loose from the terrible racial traps of the past, to open ourselves toward "the new tomorrow." Indeed, at his most profound levels, when connected to the hopeful promises of the Rainbow Coalition, Jackson inspired us to recollect Martin King's courageous challenge, the call to face "racism, poverty, militarism and materialism" as the great scourges of American life, the deep threats to our democracy. At his best, he, like King, may have been suggesting that the new birth of freedom for this generation must involve "radical reconstruction of society itself." Anyone who helps us begin to see such things has become a gift, even though it may be very difficult for both our students and ourselves to admit or discern the possibility of a truth like this.

The difficulty is, of course, not hard to understand. It reminds us of the observation made by the radical white abolitionist Wendell Phillips toward the end of the Civil War. Considering the overwhelming changes already wrought by and through the war, Phillips wrote, "The youngest of us are never again to see the republic in which we were born."[7] This certainly resembles our own situation, especially as viewed by many of us who have lived through the passing of the 1950s. One America seems to have slipped away, and its replacement appears so uncertain, so filled with pain. So, too, with the rest of the world: "The old order changeth, yielding place to new," and we are experiencing the traditional human problems associated with profound and rapid social change, change that not only challenges the older realities, but often suggests that much of the earlier life has been built on illusion. Old images of ourselves and others, old scapegoats, old solidities are no longer available in the same easy, almost effortless way. For many people in this country the temptation to engage in escapist nostalgia becomes powerfully, dangerously seductive, and they are lured into the work of creating idols out of the worst elements, the "traditional values," of our life-constricting American past. And often their words, actions, attitudes, and silences cripple their children for the long and necessary journey into a new American nation. But those of us who teach cannot acquiesce in such acts of retrogression and denial. Wisely, courageously, we face such flights from maturity and offer (and accept) the challenge to grow beyond our fears. Here, specifically, we call upon ourselves and others to see the unsettling, unfamiliar, and difficult forces of the freedom movement — and its related democratic explosions — as gifts, as pathways toward the rainbow-hued future many of us might never have sought on our own.

Nor should anyone think that the movement toward the realization of our nation is hard for white Americans alone. We must recognize the fact that African-Americans face a related, but different, challenge. For the Black freedom movement, when taken at its deepest levels, frees us African-Americans to become our best selves, launches us out beyond a position of narrow protest against those who are "in charge," to a responsibility for taking charge, sharing charge, fully manifesting our hidden roles as co-creators of all the new births of freedom yet to come. The struggle for maturity is ours as well. And if the luxury of mere protest ever existed, it is now ended. Either we are "the people," with all the redemptive, responsible meanings of that identity, or we are unfaithful to everything that has been purchased with the blood of our forebears — everything, especially the awesome responsibility of helping to provide leadership for the re-creation of this nation. Can our students grasp the profound meaning of this emergence? I think so.

Of course, having said all that, we are certainly pressed to realize that one of the most fascinating elements of the developing American "people" is yet to be addressed. I refer to that constantly enlarging body of citizens who are neither African-

Americans nor Euro-Americans and who must still decide if the great social struggle of the freedom movement is their gift as well, or if they are simply observers, sometime latecomers to this process. Although many, perhaps most, of such people of color are still wrestling with that question, I have met impressive men, women, and young people who have accepted the gifts of Black struggle and adopted the meaning for their own situation. (For instance, one native of India said to me, "I can't imagine what this country would have been like for us and our children if you Black Americans had not persisted in your freedom struggle. It was really for all of us.") In the process, they have entered fully the continuing quest for a new self-knowledge, the search for an expanded modern response to the old question, "What is an American?" Now, especially since the plunging of the Black wedge into the old order, there can be no integral response to the question of our national identity that is not shaped by memories of Vietnam and Korea, dreams of India and the Caribbean, the realities of Central America and the Philippines. When added to all the ancient recollections of Africa, Europe, and the Native spirits of this land, such a gathering of histories becomes a complex gift to our students and ourselves, and we begin to dream the nation again.

Eventually, these reflections on the varieties of our American peoples and on their responses to the gifts of the Black freedom movement bring us to the final, perhaps the ultimate, gift. For the Afro-American freedom movement has not only helped to prepare us for a new, multicultural nation, it has also opened our society to the realities of the modern world, provided an opportunity for the United States of America to be more than a dangerous, dissenting anachronism in a world so largely populated by peoples of color. Moreover, it is important to remember that many of these people of the planet are still struggling against Euro-American hegemonies, seeking to claim their rightful role in the world, attempting to establish new, more just economic, political, cultural, and spiritual relationships, seeking to exorcise the terrors of the relatively brief but very destructive colonial night. Meanwhile, Europeans and Russians experiment with living their own democratic dreams, and the Chinese wait for the next time.

These, of course, are precisely the issues, concerns, and experiences that have been watered in this country by the African-American struggle. So through all the anguish, terror, and joy of our experience, the movement has actually offered our nation a singular opportunity to develop itself for compassionate participation in the central questions and hopes of the modern world. Again, it is maturity and self-realization we are being encouraged to explore, on both personal and national levels. If we persist in this search, and if one of the greatest gifts of the Black freedom movement is taken seriously, then this nation could turn away from its Grenada and Panama actions to become a leader in the search for a way to make our planet a peaceful, nonviolent, democratic, and demilitarized common ground. As a result, we might recognize in China, Eastern Europe, Central America, the Philippines—and in Russia!—the echo and companion of our own Black-inspired call for a place where all the earth's children may find their own opportunity, in their own ways, for a new birth of freedom.

Marching down a hundred streets at the close of the 1980s the world's peoples shouted, "We need freedom!" "Democracy!" They proudly declared their relentless struggles were "completely without violence." And they sang, again and again, "We Shall Overcome."

To see such gifts is to see our past and our future more clearly than ever before. To call students to such insight is to renew our pledge that the "honored dead" who gave their lives, their utmost gifts, for the cause of liberty in our own time, on our own ground, "shall not have died in vain." Thank you, Martin. Thank you, Malcolm. Thank you, Viola. Thank you, Medgar. Thank you, Ruby Doris and Fannie Lou. Thank you, Mickey and James and Andy. Thank you all, known and unknown soldiers, hosts of witnesses. Thank you for another chance, another hope, a new birth. And with each breath of gratitude we water the seeds of our humanity. We begin to know ourselves. We, the people.

7

Poets, Musicians, and Magicians

Prophetic Black Artists of the New Creation

I say that democracy can never prove itself beyond cavil, until it founds and luxuriantly grows its own forms of art, poems, schools, theology, displacing all that exists, or that has been created everywhere in the past, under opposite influences.
—Walt Whitman, 1871

When the history books are written in the future, somebody will have to say, "There lived a race of people, black people, fleecy locks and black complexion, people who had the moral courage to stand up for their rights. And thereby they injected a new meaning into the veins of history and of civilization." And we're gonna do that. God grant that we will do it before it's too late.
—Martin Luther King, Jr., 1955

When I was in supper clubs and nightclubs, I simply played the things that were applicable to those particular places. . . . But now that my people have decided that we're going to take over the world, I'm going to have to do my part.
—Nina Simone, 1968

Because we have so often chosen to reduce the extraordinary democratic explosion of the post–World War II Black freedom

126

movement into a manageable category called civil rights, it has been difficult, usually impossible, to know what to do in our classrooms with the powerful release of creative energy that was so central to that era of transformation. As a result, we have frequently missed an opportunity to share with our students the rich outpouring of African-American music, literature, dance, cinema, and graphic arts that marked those movement years. In addition, they may not have had a chance to consider the fascinating connections between a liberating art and liberation politics, to reflect on the role of the artist as democratic teacher, or to explore the inner relationships that tend to exist among such significant elements as these: the revival of popular participation in the political process, the opening of new, creative vistas in the arts, and the inevitable emergence of unheralded creator-warriors who arrive from unrespectable places ("Can any good thing come out of Nazareth?" — or Newark?) and mount astonishing, often frightening assaults on the traditional definitions of reality. In other words, a narrow "civil rights" approach may have led many persons of every age group to miss the possibility that the study of artists and their work can be enjoyable, exciting, *and* fundamental to the creation of a more just and democratic society.

Fortunately, it is not too late for us to change the conventional, more legalistic approaches to the freedom movement in order to take up this other remarkable and very necessary task. Nor is it too difficult an endeavor. For any of our students who are alive to the popular culture of our own time (whether consciously or otherwise) have certainly been affected by the continuing fall-out from the phenomenal post-1940s Black explosion; as a result, there is a sensitive and receptive field awaiting our cultivation. Indeed, it will likely prove possible, with help from the current youthful generation, to take contributions such as Rap, Graffiti, Public Enemy, Tracy Chapman, Wynton Marsalis, and Michael Jackson — as well as the political rhymes of Jesse Jackson, *and* the Black music behind countless TV commercials — and allow them all to become a bridge to the past. By this means we may all return to a time when hundreds of concerned and compassionate artists really believed, like Nina Simone, that they were doing their part in a great Black-led movement "to take over the world," to create a new, more democratic reality for our children and ourselves, for all children everywhere — especially those who had been the victims of an ersatz democracy known as white supremacy.

On the bridge we soon discover that we are engaged in a powerful and rewarding exploration, this cohabitation with poets, artists, and musicians, this adventure with the Black magicians of a very recent time. Taken seriously, the experience transports us into astonishing expanses of inner and outer space, moves us by way of Sonia Sanchez and Haki Madhubuti, attuned to Charles Mingus and John Coltrane, by way of Aretha Franklin and Mari Evans, finally opening us to a fascinating and provocative re-encounter with Margaret Walker, Walt Whitman, and Langston Hughes. For the movement of our students, and ourselves, to meet Amiri Baraka and Gwen Brooks, to face the blazing "walls of respect," to enter into the shouts of Mahalia and the screaming explorations of Sun Ra and Archie Shepp actually becomes a new way of understanding Whitman's challenge to American democracy quoted above: "I say that democracy can never prove itself beyond cavil, until it founds and luxuriantly grows its own forms of art, poems, schools, theology, displacing all that exists, or that has been created everywhere in the past, under opposite influences."[1] Surely that was Langston's central message as well: "We, the people, must redeem/Our land ... /And make America again."[2]

Of course, neither Whitman nor the lawyer-artist-merchants of the nation's first revolution could imagine who "we the people" would become, or enter Langston's early dream-visions concerning the fullness of the democratic luxuriance that would begin to flourish on these shores. But in this generation we who teach and learn have been allowed to see, hear, and feel — if we will. We have been gifted with a powerful set of Black witnesses to the magnificent and disturbing possibilities of a democratic art that rises out of the forgotten quarries of despised and rejected stones and attempts to recast the world in images of things yet unseen and unheard. So if we can accompany our students into this largely unfamiliar place, if we can open our own eyes and hearts (to say nothing of our minds) to the fullness of the African-American freedom movement and its persistent democratic themes of resurrection and re-creation, then the evocative messages of the Black poets may begin to rush in on us like some great healing flood. And we will be able to hear Rolland Snellings (who soon became Askia Muhammad Touré, in search of his own healing and new life) crying out of that powerful time of the late 1960s:

> SING of our Race! SING out our Destiny
> to your sons, to your warrior sons—in the ghettos,
>   on the tenant farms,
> in the swelling cities by the Western Sea.
> SING with your soul! SING of the Sun!—SUNRISE
> swelling in our hearts, surging in our blood—as the
>   mighty Mississippi
> rushes to the sea.
> WE are the New! WE are the Rivers of the Spring
>   breaking through
> the cold, white ice of Dying Winter.
> WE—with the Sky, with the Soil, with the roaring
>   of the Sea—
>   are the New!
> SUNRISE: Voices of the Song of the Race.
> SUNRISE: Voices of the Sting of the Lash.
> WE are the New! We will resurrect the earth and
>   flood every heart of Man with our Light![3]

(Was *this* what you had in mind, dear loving brother Walt?)

For many people, especially those in white America, such sunrises were not easy to welcome, especially when the morning sun appeared to explode out of the annealing fires of long-stored-up Black rage. So for many people it was especially difficult in those days of roaring waters and raging urban flames to deal with one of the most notorious of all the stunning poems and the most gifted of all the poets, LeRoi Jones/ Amiri Baraka, whose "Black Art" announced with bold and withering defiance,

We want "poems that kill."
Assassin poems, Poems that shoot
guns. Poems that wrestle cops into alleys
and take their weapons leaving them dead.

It will be now, as it was then, a great challenge to take students
into the world of such explosive poetry, to reproduce the setting
for its vast, often purifying storehouses of anger, to understand
why a Black poet could continue the call with a demand for
poems which would "scream poison gas on beasts in green
berets," and at the same moment seek other poems to "clean
out the world for virtue and love." It will take great patience
and skill (and new visions of Whitman?) to guide our searching
readers into the last measures of "Black Art," helping them to
hear Baraka announcing, pleading,

Let there be no love poems written
until love can exist freely and
cleanly. Let Black People understand
that they are the lovers and the sons
of lovers and warriors and sons
of warriors Are poems & poets &
all the loveliness here in the world

helping them to listen with the ears of their spirits to the very
last words:

We want a black poem. And a
Black World.
Let the world be a Black Poem
And Let All Black People Speak This Poem
Silently

or LOUD[4]

Venturing courageously with our students into the demanding
richness of this Black renaissance (and it was nothing less than
that, much more densely layered and politically explosive than
the Harlem Renaissance of the 1920s), we will discover that the

male-dominated images of a Snellings/Touré or a Baraka (or many others) could not hide one fundamental reality of the time: At the heart of the magnificent ferment there was a powerful, vitalizing presence of Black women poets, erupting everywhere on the landscape, sending down elaborately weighted plumb lines into the depths of our existence.

Some of them—like Sonia Sanchez, Mari Evans, June Jordan, Nikki Giovanni, Julia Fields, Johari Amini, Lucille Clifton and Carolyn Rodgers—were relatively new to the audiences of the 1960s. But others of their sisters had been on the scene, developing their art for a longer, harder time, and the bursting power of the new moment was really their power, and at the same time it filled them with new energies, brought them into previously unexplored settings. So a generation of Black college students, movement activists, and community people were discovering and re-discovering the poetry of Gwendolyn Brooks, Margaret Burroughs, Margaret Walker, and Margaret Danner (who dares speculate about the shared magic of that first name?). Now every conference, workshop, and rally seemed to include and revive Margaret Walker's earlier wrought battle cry:

Let a new earth rise. Let another world be born. Let a bloody peace be written in the sky. Let a second generation full of courage issue forth; let a people loving freedom come to growth. Let a beauty full of healing and a strength of final clenching be the pulsing in our spirits and our blood. Let the martial songs be written, let the dirges disappear. Let a race of men now rise and take control.[5]

Meanwhile, below the level of martial calls, from places where poets have continually found their deepest resources, Mari Evans struck a resonant chord in her simple but resplendent announcement,

I
am a black woman
tall as a cypress
strong
beyond all definition still

defying place
and time
and circumstance
   assailed
      impervious
         indestructible
Look
   on me and be
renewed[6]

At the same time Black women like Sonia Sanchez carried on
another long human tradition, publicly mourned their warrior
princes, like Malcolm, sang songs, chanted dirges of sorrow and
anger that still remain for this generation to absorb into the
marrow of their spirits. Sonia cried out,

Do not speak to me of martyrdom
of men who die to be remembered
on some parish day.
I don't believe in dying
though I too shall die
and violets like castanets
will echo me.

Yet this man
this dreamer,
thick-lipped with words
will never speak again
and in each winter
when the cold air cracks
with frost, I'll breathe
his breath and mourn
my gun-filled nights.

      . . .
what might have been
is not for him/or me
but what could have been
floods the womb until I drown.[7]

Throughout the late 1960s and the 1970s Sonia Sanchez's voice could be heard across the land, singing, shouting, wailing, compressing anger, sorrow, and promise into the cadences of her poetry, providing extraordinary public readings as she sought to stretch the forms (forms Whitman reminds us had been "created everywhere in the past under opposite influences") of the poet's statement. Constantly joining the personal and the political, the search for individual and collective resurrection, she called:

> you you black man
> stretching scraping
> the mold from your body,
> here is my hand.
> i am not afraid
> of the night.[8]

Together, these women and others of that time held out their hands, reached out with their lives, refused to let the night of their wounds prevent them from making connections, taking poetry from the people to the people, constantly performing the serious task outlined by Mari Evans:

> Speak the truth to the people
> Talk sense to the people
> Free them with reason
> Free them with honesty
> Free the people with Love and Courage and Care
>   for their Being[9]

Beyond gender or generation, this was part of the amazing power (amazing grace?) of the Black poets in these years of challenge and re-creation. They were inextricably bound to the struggles of the Black community for the expansion of democracy, for the renewal of their own lives. Always familiar with the traditional language and concerns of poets, they never allowed the personal to become hermetically private. So it was not surprising that in the midst of the rushing Black movement toward the redemption of the democratic dream, the poets were often in a foremost, sometimes vanguard, position. That was one of the great marvels of the time. Poets were in demand! Not only by university audiences and polite literati (wherever they may have been hiding among the explosions of the Black communities), but in community centers, in church conventions, and in Black Power meetings. Read to us, read for us, read *us*, and we shall be whole, the people cried.

So wherever men and women gathered to discuss and fervently to debate issues, to forge the new forms of democratic possibilities, to explore the untested manifestations of hope, they expected Baraka and Sonia, Mari and Haki, Nikki and Margaret, and many others, to be there with them, sharing their gifts, allowing the flooding songs of their stanzas to rise like incense, to provide blessings, to sanction emotions, to open wisdom. They expected the great-souled Michael Harper to take them into the depths of our history, to use the gifts of his well-honed art to bring Harriet and Sojourner and a thousand unnamed mothers and fathers of the tribe back to life again. So poets became community leaders, organizers, publishers, mobilizers, political forces, as well as healers. Almost all became leaders of writing workshops, extending the skills and gifts of their craft to others who were willing to receive, announcing thereby the fundamentally democratic nature of their art. Baraka was the best-known manifestation of the organizer-priest-shaman-teacher tradition, but it was carried on in powerful ways by others as well, like Sanchez, Evans, Madhubuti, Burroughs, Kalamu Ya Salaam, and Brooks in their own distinctive ways. Indeed, the name Baraka itself, a Moslem word describing "the combination of energy, warmth and spiritual charm that makes a holy [person] or healer," could have been applied to all of these poets of the new vision, the luxuriant democracy, the collective resurrection.

(There was, of course, another harsher side to this phenomenon of the poets as active participants in the transformative life of the people. Henry Dumas, one of the most promising—and most mystical—of the new group was murdered in 1968 by New York police in a case of "mistaken identity." Baraka, the most provocative of the poetic community, was beaten and jailed by police. Others, such as Sonia Sanchez and Mari Evans, were aware of constant surveillance. None was allowed to forget the costs of democracy.)

By now it may be clear that in the best of all worlds our students should actually hear these poets, *at least* hear them, to gain some rich sense of the gifts that were shared.[10] And as they listen it will now be less surprising for them when the music begins to break through. For both in their wrestling with the printed words on the pages and in the greater freedom of their charismatic readings, poets like Sanchez, Baraka, Madhubuti, and Touré became singers, cantors of a people's agony, vision, and hope, chanters of tomorrow. Repeatedly, their words, like those of the generations of Black poet-preachers who came before them, broke loose from all constraints of prose and book and began to be songs, calls, cries, began to whoop, became what Rilke called "the language where languages end."[11] And most often — as in the churches that so many of the artists knew and thought they had put aside — the people who heard them also joined them, shouting, applauding, rising to their feet, attempting to soar with the poets, following, sometimes preceding their songs to the magnificent aeries which are approached only by those who have decided "to take over the world."

Writing in the midst of such ascending lives and voices, hearing the music burst forth from every corner of Afro-America, Snellings/Touré reminded us that the experience "of the Black musician and poet as priest-philosopher goes back to the indigenous African civilizations, where the artist-priest had a functional role as the keeper or guardian of the spirit of the nation."[12] Handled with respect and insight, set in the context of poets becoming musicians, democratic seers, and spiritual healers, Snellings's insight creates a tri-level pathway of discovery for our students. On the one hand, it provides them an opportunity to reflect on the religious/spiritual grounding of all truly human art (beginning, perhaps, with such African groundings as those lifted up by Robert F. Thompson in *Flash of the Spirit*[13]). And it reminds us of how crucial it is to engage such creativity in the building of any compassionate and democratic society — especially when the continuous building must overcome ancient rivers of blood and persist through terrible nights of fear. In other words, the Black democratic-artistic renaissance reminds us that reading, 'riting and 'rithmetic are not the only essentials of a humane and democratic education. Rather, we learn that the "three R's" become no more than technical training without the healing gifts, the mold-scraping touch of the artist-priests and high priestesses.

Regaining the metaphor of the pathway, Snellings' statement and the poetic witnesses also move us again toward the democratic vistas of Whitman, provide another way to hear his urgent call to the nation:

> Our fundamental want today in the United States . . . is of a class . . . of native authors . . . far different, far higher in grade than any yet known, sacerdotal, modern, fit to cope with our occasions . . . permeating the whole mass of American mentality . . . breathing into it a new breath of life . . . affecting politics far more than the popular superficial suffrage . . . accomplishing (what neither the schools nor the churches and their clergy have hitherto accomplished, and without which this nation will no more stand, permanently, soundly, than a house will stand without a substratum) a religious and moral character beneath the political and productive and intellectual bases of the States.[14]

Whitman's earnest call for healing, saving artists to rise up on behalf of the nation itself is ultimately an invitation to the third level of the path—the final bonding connections between the poets and the musicians who were redefining the world from the ground of their blackness (from the underground where they had been driven). Let our students watch them, watch with them, as the artists respond to Whitman's call (though most would deny they ever heard it). For what we may all see as we peer over the barricades of our hearts is the astonishing possibility that songs resurrect, that poetry makes alive, that dancing revives the dead, that Gabriel blows a tenor sax, that people who had been physically buried in the American earth were once again shaken into revival by all the freedom songs, all the heroes marching, all the martyrs' blood rising from the South.

Bring the students close enough to hear, to feel, to tremble, and to smell, and they may understand one of the great messages of those years of struggle: A people who had been declared invisible and interred were daring to rise, were announcing their new (old?) identity, were becoming Whitman's "sacerdotal" substratum, holy grounding for the nation at large. Let them listen carefully to poet/priest Lance Jeffers speaking for millions as he says, "My blackness is the beauty of this land." Bring them close and they will hear and feel what Whitman desired: fire breathing, anger breathing, trumpet breathing, drum breathing, "breathing . . . a new breath of life" into themselves, conspiring to redeem the land. Bring the students of every age and color close enough to feel and not fear Haki's audacious announcement. Joining words and motion, perhaps they can create a dance, a movement to accompany his hope:

> blackpeople
> are moving, moving to return
>   this earth into the hands of
> human beings.[15]

(And if some of our students should ask, "Where is that hope now?" or if one spirit-genius should wonder aloud in class, "Are we being slowly, painfully crucified for daring such dreams, for believing such things might be?" do not stop the flow. For they feel the public death all around them. They have tasted the despair. And it may be that they must walk and talk and scream their way, our way, through that valley, experience and confess that fear. For it is likely that there can be no resurrections by proxy. Each person and each generation may be called to stand anew—but not alone—at the river.)

Ultimately, what I am saying is this: In the moving, in the breathing, in the rediscovery of the hidden sources of the beauty of the land, the musicians may well have been the highest priests, the most eloquent companions through all the shadowed valleys. Yet in their sacramental function they refused to mimic the hierarchical traditions so often associated with all priesthoods. Instead, in this time of democratic explosion and expansion, grace flowed like fountains from below.

For instance, with all the unpredictable power of a democratic outpouring from a substratum people, one of the most broadly located statements of the hour came from a pop singing group, The Impressions. Moved by the southern-based freedom struggles, they created the song, "Keep on Pushing," song of the inhabitants of the socially defined lower dep⁺hs who were re-visioning their own being. So Curtis Mayfield (a musical genius) and the group sang out,

> I got to keep on pushin', Can't stop now.
> Move up a little higher, some way, some how.
> 'Cause I got my strength,
> don't make sense; Keep on Pushin'!

As some of our students will remember, the song swept through the life of the Black communities of America. It seemed to speak for a people who would not be turned away from the transformative sense of vocation that appeared to be filling them more completely each day. In a way, "Keep on Pushing" became a northern, rhythm and blues version of "Ain't Gonna Let Nobody Turn Me 'Round," a modern statement of "We Shall Not be Moved":

> Look a look a yonder: what's that I see?
> Great big stone wall standing straight ahead of me.
> But I've got my pride, move the wall aside:
> Keep on pushing"

Perhaps this was an earlier version of Public Enemy's "Fight the Power,"[16] but whatever its relationship to the past and future, when students hear The Impressions, it may become clear that in those movement days of the 1960s "Keep on Pushing" was a major statement of the African-American struggle for a new, more democratic society, based in lives that were being lived out of a sense of "strength."

Surely that is worth consideration. For nothing could be more democratic than the action by the people of the substrata to reposition their vision and their own existence, gathering up all the traditions that had created them and working to change themselves in order "to change the world," to fulfill the best dreams of their ancestors. When the bottom level moves we are all affected. So the song ended with its "sacerdotal" connections becoming ever clearer, its democratic urgency even stronger, its powerful beat even more suggestive of the dances of the free:

> Maybe someday, I'll reach that higher goal.
> I know I can make it with just a little bit of soul.
> 'Cause I've got my strength, don't make sense;
> Keep on Pushin'!
> Ha-al-lelujah! Ha-al-lelujah!:
> Keep on Pushin'!
> Keep on Pushin'![17]

In the same way, many other soul groups and soloists were engaged by and lent their great gifts to the outpouring of protest, hope, and rage that marked this struggle for democracy, this attempt "to redeem the soul of America." Aretha Franklin's "Respect" was another powerful statement of a people's deepest longings, in which the personal and political were unobtrusively joined. The Staple Singers also spoke for everyone when they revived an old church song and cried out, "If I had my way/I'd tear this building down." And Nina Simone, not accidentally known as "the high priestess of soul," gathered much of the experience of the time into her own gifted performances, with songs like "Mississippi Goddam" and "I Wish That I Knew What It Means To Be Free." It was she, too, who spoke for a people and a nation after the assassination of Martin King as she sang, and asked, "What's gonna happen/Now that the king of love is dead?" In spite of, because of, all the questions and struggles and affirmations of those days, it was also Nina who expressed most fully the convictions of many African-American musicians (and other artists) when she told a sensitive Black interviewer in 1968, "I hope the day comes when I'll be able to sing more *love* songs, when the *need* is not quite so urgent to sing protest songs. But for now, I don't mind."

Then she went on to make it clear that the pro-democratic agenda was her first priority in those times. Joining Hughes and Whitman (without needing explicitly to acknowledge them), she said that for her as an artist

There's no other *purpose*, so far as I'm concerned, *for* us except to reflect the times, the situations around us and the things that we're able to say through our art, the things that millions of people *can't* say. I think that's the *function* of an artist.

Perhaps it should be very clear to our students that this was not simply a duty or a burden for Simone. It had become a source of life. "It's good to be alive," she continued, speaking in the heat of the Black movement for the expansion of democracy and the transformation of America, in the face of assassinations and subversions. Indeed, like others at that moment in history, the singularly gifted singer testified that "I feel more alive than I *ever* have and this is true for many . . . black people."[18]

Bringing life, abundant life, to the struggle for freedom, finding life as it luxuriantly informed the sometimes dangerous quest for authentic American democratic art—in this revivalist movement the musicians surely share a central place with the poets. (Actually, they shared the same stages and recording booths, and the poets regularly paid homage to their artist companions in their works.) And an artist like Simone, who combined several genres, makes it possible for us to explore the likelihood that the musicians who carried the struggle for new forms to the deepest (and ultimately most democratic) levels were the geniuses of African-American classical music, the great jazz artists of the post–World War II renaissance. For it was they, more than any others, who boldly took up the challenge put forth by Whitman and Hughes, the challenge of creating distinctive new democratic configurations in their art, often "displacing all that exists." It was they who boldly faced the primeval experiences of sound and silence and sought to de-structure much that had been known, defined, and worshipped as the good, the true, and the beautiful by European and Euro-American creators of categories—all in order to open new space, to hear new music, to bring new and previously unimagined realities into existence. These creative Black giants, often rising from what were considered the underground places of America's white supremacist landscape, dared to take saxophones and trumpets, pianos and organs, drums and bass fiddles, with other inventive additions, and transform them into weapons in the struggle for a new nation. (Just as sisters like Sarah Vaughan, Dinah Washington, and Billie Holiday before them had used their voices in magnificent cries and celebrations.) Beginning with the most democratic of American music, jazz, they created what was sometimes called new wave, bop, post-bop, or avant-garde music, but what was also more than music. As one contemporary observer wrote, in the course of their work these astounding Black alchemists opened up "the floodgates of passion, anger, pain and love, and aroused that fury for liberty which is the essence of the new black art."[19]

(In keeping with his far more prosaic and very wise ways, Langston Hughes's character Simple described the phenomenon in these words: "That is where Bop comes from . . . out of them dark days we have seen. That is why BeBop is so mad, wild, frantic, crazy. And not to be dug unless you have seen dark days, too. That's why folks who ain't suffered much cannot play Bop, and do not understand it. They think . . . it's just crazy crazy. They do not know it is also MAD crazy, SAD crazy, FRANTIC WILD CRAZY—beat right out of some bloody black head! That's what Bop is. These young kids who play it best, they know."[20])

Obviously, once we free ourselves from our obsession with "civil rights" as the essential process and goal of the post–World War II freedom movement, we are able to move with our students to a direct encounter with the artists, especially the musicians, whose "fury for liberty" is so central to an accurate sense of this period. Approaching the efflorescent jazz community of those years we discover dozens of persons (often with bloody heads) who might become our guides into the world of these Black magicians. Some of the best-known instrumentalists and experimentalists among them were Charlie (Bird) Parker, John Coltrane, Dizzy Gillespie, Charlie Mingus, Miles Davis, Albert Ayler, Milford Graves, Pharaoh Sanders, Marion Brown, Max Roach, Thelonius Monk, McCoy Tyner, Ornette Coleman, Herbie Hancock, Eric Dolphy, Elvin Jones, Archie Shepp, Alice Coltrane, Sonny Rollins, David Murray, and Rahsaan Roland Kirk. And there were many more.

Even on so limited a list, each of the names represents a

treasure house of rich and multivocal expressions of the freedom renaissance. But for here and now it is only possible to mention most of them briefly, to suggest recourse to an important resource like the *New Grove Dictionary of Jazz*,[21] and then to encourage all of us to explore as many worlds as possible in this Black universe of liberating musical power, taking our most adventurous students with us. Whether it is works like Coltrane's "Reverend King," Shepp's "Going Home," or Roach's "Freedom Now! Suite," or dozens of other creations that explicitly picked up the themes of the freedom movement, or if our explorations simply carry us into the fundamentally improvisational and democratically shaped form of jazz itself, there is much to discover.

For our purposes, though, the ultimate jazz witness to the "fury for liberty" and the search for radically new possibilities was the life and the art of John Coltrane, an American genius. Here was an artist as liberator, as democratic hero/prophet for our age. Sensitively encountered, this man, who was often called "the most influential jazz musician of his time," becomes a special gift to our students. With careful guidance they will discover in Coltrane a man whose life and work were equally spirit-possessed. Listening, watching closely, they will meet in him that dual tendency which marks the lives of all seekers after new realities—the prophetic urgency to break open possibilities and vistas not yet explored, and the priestly longing to carry out "the healing of the fractured communal will."[22] Fortunately, it is likely that they will also recognize in "Trane," especially in his last decade, not the popular stereotype of the dissolute and morally undisciplined jazz artist, but a man—like many others— who was ascending the spirit's mountains, determined to meet and submit himself to the Source of all, committed to "sing all songs to God."

When they first hear some of those songs (like "Ascension," for instance), it may well be difficult for unprepared students and teachers to meet Coltrane, to sense his meaning for the great African-American freedom struggle. But let them also listen to some knowledgeable commentators who seek to help us hear Coltrane, who, like Phyl Garland, tell us that he abandoned the song as a necessary point of departure and opened up the music, enabling it to move in all directions, filling the spaces with incredible flurries of notes not always related to any set pattern or form. As his voice called out for a new freedom, others were impelled to answer their own inner voices.[23]

That was a key. In plunging, excavatory movements he tunnelled toward the core of the music (of the life). With unborrowed wings he flew toward the sun, in search of a "new freedom," one that Whitman likely could not have imagined, but one that opened the ears and voices of other seekers of his own generation. For his fellow artists realized that this man was trying "to liberate melody as well as tempo from the harmonic prison," in Garland's words. This was the musician as sometimes misunderstood liberator: "The near-frantic, yet ever-controlled flights through the register, from the growling lower to the screeching upper regions, were the exultant shouts of this newfound freedom." And who with soul could not respond?

So we take the students to this lover of freedom because he cherished it not as a private, selfish end in itself, but because his life joined the lives of all the world's best freedom workers in their recognition that freedom is fundamentally a *means* to humane development. We take them to meet this man because it was rightly said that "what he was fighting for, as do all Afro-American artists, was an expanse sufficient to contain natural expressiveness, 'living space' (to borrow the title of one of Trane's most intrepid late explorations) for a new race of men, yet unborn." Was Margaret Walker one of Trane's muses? Did he hear the Black southern sister more clearly than the other brothers? "Let a second generation full of courage issue forth; let a people loving freedom come to growth."

Whomever Trane heard, we must hear him. We encourage young and old to listen patiently to "a music more powerful, more anguished and celebratory than any in recent memory." We sit with them in the presence of this shaman and his side healers, listen to them speak in tongues, submit ourselves to his restorative silences, enter into his "ritual of restitution" on behalf of us all. Then we invite the gathered circle to hear Coltrane's response to the summons of Whitman, Walker, and Hughes: "There are always new sounds to imagine," he said quietly, "new feelings to get at. And always, there is the need to keep purifying these feelings and sounds so that we can really see what we've discovered in its pure state."[24]

Consider: The artist as seeker, as purifier. Consider the artist whose wife, Alice, another artistic and spiritual genius, later said, "He never stopped surprising himself." Pondering his capacity to surprise us, to challenge us to new thoughts and feelings about the inner meanings of the African-American quest for the purification of American democracy, we take Coltrane to our students and let him explain to them: "My goal in meditating on the unity in life through music remains always the same. And that is to uplift people, as much as I can. To inspire them to realize more and more of their capacities for living meaningful lives."[25]

Out beyond the conventional boundaries of politics and music he ranges. "To see more clearly what we are," to realize our "capacities for living meaningful lives." Let the people say, Amen! Clearly the artist of the new democratic vistas is exploring the depths of the "religious and moral character," which Whitman deemed absolutely necessary for the undergirding of the house of democracy. That is why we share Coltrane with our students. He was a democratic hero and a transcendental genius who was also described by one of his fellow musicians in this way:

> There was love that he emitted that is rare to find, a thing you recognized immediately on meeting him. He lived the way of the things he wrote or said. There was something sainted about him.[26]

Saint John. Here was one of America's most munificent gifts to the nation and to the world, one of the nation's unsung—but constantly singing—democratic liberators. Such are the lives that inevitably rise to the surface of great freedom struggles. Such are the lives that consistently feed the movements with their own best energies, visions, and loves.

Saint John Coltrane. He becomes a rich resource when we

seek new models and heroes for our own time. For though he
died young (like so many heroes!), when he was only forty years
old, his wife could say of him, "He was such a beautiful man
and I guess those kind of people don't stay here too long. They
come here and do their work and then they leave."[27]

By the time they absorb some of the distinctive creative energies of John (and Alice) Coltrane, and as they understand how
much the African-American freedom movement was really
about the discovery, release, and transmutation of such transformative power, our students may well anticipate Alice Coltrane's revelation. They will probably not be surprised that
shortly after John's death she should say,

> We had thought of setting up a center that would be like
> a church—we wouldn't call it a church, because it might
> frighten people away and they might wonder what kind of
> church it was, but it would be a church in that it would be
> a place for music and meditation, and maybe someone
> would feel like praying. It would bring others a kind of
> fellowship based on music, because he thought music was
> a single universal force and that there could be no dividing
> lines or categories.

Surely Whitman and Hughes, Martin and Malcolm, Fannie
Lou and Angela would all have been marvelously unfrightened
in this church, this democratic temple, created from the depths
of blackness to become the foundation of the nation's most
enlightened visions. Indeed, in such a place, each in his or her
own way might even have felt like praying, like praising, like
giving thanks for "A Love Supreme." For they knew, as we must
surely know by now, that the creation of a new, more compas-
sionately liberated social order is not the work of social engineers, economists, lawyers, or political leaders alone. But at far
deeper levels it requires love, creativity, and great liberating art.

During the years of democratic cultural explosion in the Black
communities of the land, it may be that the poets and musicians
were the most spectacular creators, but there was much more
at work. In the limited compass of this essay it will not be possible to do more than mention other genres in which African-

American artists worked for the realization of the "new race," for the revitalization of the old, and yet they must be mentioned. Fortunately, many examples are available to teachers and students who seek them out. For instance, if we take the large company of African-American graphic artists as an example, they provide a set of memories and fascinating bodies of work to testify to their own participation in the newness of the cultural renaissance, as well as demonstrating the ways in which they, like Nina, Langston, and others, were deeply renewed in their own life and work by the powerful movements of their people.

Certainly, if we watch closely the work of such established masters as Romare Bearden, Jacob Lawrence, and Charles White during those years of democratic ferment, we are able to catch unmistakable signs of their own renewal, their own participation in the "fury of liberty" that marked the times. At the same moment we can call attention to a figure like Herman (Kofi X) Bailey, who returned to the United States in the mid-1960s after a decisive sojourn in Ghana, settled in Atlanta, and was literally embraced by the young people of SNCC. As a result of his close encounters with these shock troops of the southern movement, Bailey's work exploded with new life, perhaps most vividly marked by the great brown arm thrusting its way, with clenched fist, toward the freedom of the sky.

Looking in another direction, we are able to discover, as well, that this freedom movement time was a period of powerful and deeply felt vindication for an artist like Elizabeth Catlett. A sculptor, printmaker, and painter of extraordinary talent, Catlett had chosen self-exile in Mexico during the early 1950s when her commitments to democracy, peace, and freedom brought her into conflict with the anti-communist McCarthyite scourge of that era. But as the post-Montgomery movement began to transform Black America and the nation itself, though her studio was in the heart of Mexico City, it was clear that Catlett was profoundly moved and encouraged. And our students will surely catch some suggestion of her spirit, even if they are able to see only photos of the powerful prints and the monumental sculptures that seemed to emerge like great witnesses to her own continuing search for liberating space, her own wrestling with the angels of freedom.

Although the work of such individual Black graphic artists embodied much of the meaning of this period of democratic renewal, the visions of Hughes and Whitman were also fully realized in the great flowering of popular representational art that began to appear on the sides of buildings all over Black urban America. These "walls of respect," as they were called, were indeed "of the people, by the people, and for the people." Usually developed on the sides of buildings, often carried out as community projects by groups of trained and untrained artists of all ages, it was normal for their subject matter to consist of political, cultural, and athletic heroes of the local, national, and international Black communities. So the question of whose portraits should appear became one of the first occasions for the practice of democracy. But that was not all. For the blazing colors on the brick and mortared walls became a form of shouting, a loudly announced affirmation of the right of the people to create these murals, of the community's desire to develop self-affirming images of itself, its leaders, and its children (for children's portraits were constantly present). Most of the walls of respect are gone now (why?), but the extant photos and slides will show our students the regular presence of King and Malcolm, of Angela and Coltrane, Muhammad Ali and Aretha, and many others. It was a wonderful mix, and in its sprawling, blazing reality, from Watts to Harlem, a familiar message was being put forth: Through these positive self-representations a community was in search of its own definition, its own healing, its own resurrection. A community was pushing, moving, announcing the magnificent and awesome knowledge that its own redemption and the redeeming of the nation were inextricably bound. Not only were we/they reading the handwriting on the wall, we were the hands writing. So we/they were all becoming priest-artists, creating restorative images, lifting up the magical mirrors to Mari Evans's announcement, chanting with her, "Look on me and be renewed."

Other genres contained the same stories of transformative energies at work. We cannot deal with fiction, drama, or dance here, but there are great riches from this exciting time for students and teachers who open themselves to the gifts in all of these realms. For the moment we will attempt only to note the remarkable world of the essayists who persistently sent fiery tongues of light into the midst of the American darkness, and who were most dramatically represented by that master of the form, James Baldwin. If we allow our students to immerse themselves in nothing else than *The Fire Next Time*[28] and *Nobody Knows My Name*,[29] then we will have made a magnificent contribution to their lives, introduced them to one of the greatest of America's "sacerdotal" voices, delivered them into the hands of their priest.

Baldwin is known, at least in a relative way. So we will not dwell on him—indeed we cannot dwell on anyone. But there are two other brief examples of the kind of essay that soared out of this period and that are important for us to encounter.

The first essay our students might sample is "The Spiritual Victory of Muhammad Ali," by Quincey Troupe. It appeared originally on the pages of what may have been the most important journal of the Afro-American renaissance of the 1960s and 1970s, *Black World* (formerly *Negro Digest*). Writing shortly after Ali's come-back conquest of George Foreman in 1974, the poet-essayist Troupe, carrying out a familiar function of the artist in those times, offered the Black community an interpretation of the meaning of their hero for their life. He wrote,

> African-Americans recognize in Ali our own struggle for dignity, beauty and survival in a hostile America. He has been a mirror image of our own collective struggle for freedom and dignity in this racist-to-the-bone, hypocritical country. When he won, we all won, much in the same way that Joe Louis won for all of us during the Thirties and Forties.[30]

Expanding the arena of victory beyond Black America, cultivating the international and spiritual vision that has always been part of the best artistic insights of the freedom movement, Troupe declared,

> If Muhammad Ali represents anything, it is those new and spiritual forces that will not give way in the face of tremendous adversity. In regaining the Heavyweight Cham-

pionship of the World by defeating a supposedly invincible George Foreman, Muhammad Ali not only claimed a great and significant victory for himself, but also, in winning, he spiritually and symbolically represented millions upon millions of people who, also in the face of heavy odds and during crucial times throughout the world's history, had said, "No," and in the end had had the remarkable staying power not only to survive, but to emerge from the struggle with a glorious and significant victory.[31]

In a sense, Troupe was being faithful to the vocation that had been set forth several years earlier by Larry Neal, a powerful cultural force in those times. Writing an Afterword for *Black Fire*, the exciting and significant anthology he edited with LeRoi Jones/Amiri Baraka, Neal offers our students a chance to recapitulate one of the major themes from that period of tremendous democratic ferment. Sounding very much like his comrade Askia Muhammad Touré, he wrote, "We must make literature move people to a deeper understanding of what this thing is all about, be a kind of priest, a black magician, working juju with the word on the world." Neal's final word—appropriately enough the last paragraph of *Black Fire*—is a testimony to one of the basic realities he and other artists were seeking to wrest out of the post-Montgomery explosion of Black Arts. To hear him seriously is to hear all the voices we have opened in this chapter. To hear him well is to journey far beyond civil rights:

The artist and the political activist are one. They are both shapers of the future reality. Both understand and manipulate the collective myths of the race. Both are warriors, priests, lovers and destroyers. For the first violence will be internal—the destruction of a weak spiritual self for a more perfect self. But it will be a necessary violence. It is the only thing that will destroy the double-consciousness— the tension that is in the souls of the black folk.[32]

But there were many necessary things in this time of imperatives, and it was surely appropriate that a Black woman, Gerene

Freeman, sent a poetic reminder to all the flaming masters of art, reminding them of one simple and human calling:

POEM[33]

To:
nikki, sonia, don
and all the poets
who don't write
of trees

because

they say there
are none
in Harlem,
westside Chicago,
and Watts

but
they're wrong
the trees grow all
around us
they are our youth
spreading their
limbs toward
the Black Sun—
Freedom

But we're
not tending properly
to our trees
the limbs are
weak and diseased
they cast
distorted
shadows

one small breeze
befalls them
lifeless
lacking roots
we in our failing
have allowed
pollution of their
souls;
their minds,
of their very bodies

they enter the jungle
seedlings
unprepared
we must not forget
our trees
we must care for
and replenish our
trees
water them
renew their history
feed their souls
open their minds

they are the guardians
of gardens to come
what will the
future reap?
                              desert
OR
                              oasis?

There is something almost eerie in this anticipation of the call from Tiananmen Square, the plea for the watering of the trees of enlightened democracy. It will be fascinating to explore with our classes how and why such themes and words return—in this case after almost two decades of separation and what seems like a world apart. While we reflect on such matters it may be even more important to call our students' attention to the fact that certain powerful moments of history produce trees that refuse to wait passively for the water. So even as Gerene Freeman was addressing her justifiable concerns to Nikki, Sonia, and Don, the young people (often in workshops with Nikki, Sonia, and Don—and June and Lucille and others) had already entered the spirit of the times. They were writing, watering, giving eager witness to their own "fury for liberty," touching familiar themes. For instance, Michael Gill was thirteen and Linda Curry was fifteen when they wrote these:[34]

THE JAZZ WORLD   FOR NINA SIMONE

Full of colors   wherever You are
Flashing popping   The great
Coming from everywhere   singer
Jazz is love   Nina Simone
Coming from the inner   Fills your heart with soul
mind   she makes your brain rock and
Sweet and soft   roll
I wish Jazz was   makes your mind forget
here   the question that is
    ALL   unanswered
   The Time   Go ahead Nina bring
    —Michael Gill   out all of your black soul
                 Just sing it
                  hit it to the
                  white man eyes
              Make him realize
              that a black woman voice
                 will never
                    die
                    —Linda Curry

Still, certain themes and certain people will not rest, and we are not permitted to forget the costs of democracy, even among the poets, perhaps especially among the youngest poets. So it will be understandable if our students wonder what happened to Glen Thompson, the manchild from Brooklyn who was thirteen years old when he wrote "Drums of Freedom." Did anyone water his tree? Did he know he was standing with Malcolm X, Martin King, and Nat Turner, and with thousands in Tiananmen Square when he announced,

>Some of us will die
>but the drums will beat.
>We may even lose
>but the drums will beat.
>They will beat loud and strong,
> and
>   on
>   and
>   on.
>For we shall get what we want
>and the drums will beat.[35]

Rising from the heart of Tiananmen Square, a generation later the drums respond:

>At present we are all fainting, we may fall any moment,
>But soon trees of enlightenment will grow up where we fall.
>Cry not for me, mother. Shed no tears.
>But slacken not to water the trees with your loving care.
>Surely God will bless the growth of enlightenment in China.
>   That soon it will shelter all its people.[36]

Chanting songs, beating drums, watering trees, redeeming a land. All the work of artists in the struggle for democracy, in the quest for new life. Perhaps our students will remember that such work is never complete, often has to begin again, and again. Perhaps they will realize that they are more than observers of a distant past (or aggrieved complainants against some disconnected and defeated warriors). Perhaps the "Creation Spell" of

Ed Bullins—one of the foremost poet-playwrights of the renaissance—will bring our times, our lives together, will join the living
and the dead with democratic seekers everywhere, beginning
here, again:

> Into your palm I place the ashes
> Into your palm are the ashes of your brothers
> burnt in the Alabama night
> Into your palm that holds your babies
> into your palm that feeds your children
> into your palm that holds the work tools
> I place the ashes of your father
> here are the ashes of your husbands
> Take the ashes of your nation
> and create the cement to build again
> Create the spirits to move again
> Take this soul dust and begin again.[37]

But where is Glen Thompson? And all his sisters and brothers—and his children? Have you seen them, heard them, Dear
John, Dear Coltrane? Are the drums still beating? And where
is the water? Take us to the water.

8

Doing the Right Thing in Mississippi and Brooklyn

How Shall We Connect?

At the end of the 1980s there appeared on the national scene two feature films based on very different approaches to the African-American struggle for justice and democracy. Alan Parker's *Mississippi Burning* and Spike Lee's *Do the Right Thing* could not have been more directly opposite in their settings, approaches, and characters, but the powerful waves of debate that accompanied both films offer us important lessons to ponder and develop in our teaching.

Aside from all else, it was fascinating to follow the films and their controversial receptions in major newspapers and journals, to witness their dissection on television programs as apparently disparate as *Nightline* and *Oprah Winfrey*, to sample the wisdom of Black barbershops and predominantly white cocktail parties, to imagine all the kitchen-table discussions and debates. This heated engagement surely testified to the continuing, absorbing power of race, racism, and racial issues among us. On the harshest national level we saw again that race is like a bone stuck in our throat, refusing both digestion and expulsion, endangering our life. But from another perspective this excitement about the films (especially Spike Lee's creation) testified to the unmistakable need and desire of our nation to deal with its terrifying and compelling history, to exorcise the demons of our racial past and present, perhaps even to discover the healing possibilities that reside in our many-hued and wounded variations on the human theme.

None of us who teaches in the United States can miss the presence of this often repressed force among students of every kind, from children to the elderly. Usually it is only after initial denials, feigned lack of interest, or attempts at liberal glosses that the subjects of race, racism, and relationships across racial lines open powerful and sometimes frightening hidden reservoirs of energy, curiosity, and rage that dwell deep in the hearts and lives of our students. It is then that we realize again that all of us, students and teachers alike, are in need of time, unthreatening space, and ample communal and personal opportunities to expose these hidden places to the light. For we have all been wounded and deprived in one way or another by the terrible visitations of America's racial nightmare. So there are few aspects of the teacher's role more important than our calling as wounded healers, hesitant, groping shepherds in the nation's absolutely necessary movement through the terrors of racism toward the wholeness of a mature, humane, and variegated community.

In their opposite, fascinating ways *Mississippi Burning* and *Do the Right Thing* not only make available the opportunity to air our deepest fears and hopes, but they remind us of how essential a role the visual media have come to play in the teacher's world. Ultimately, of course, these films return us to the theme of this work: the centrality of the African-American freedom struggle in any educational setting where human values, profound aspirations, and deeply moving inner commitments are explored and encouraged. With such considerations in mind, it may be helpful to examine some of the ways in which such films could be used as critical resources in our exploration of a few of the central lessons of the African-American struggle for freedom.

It would be fascinating, for instance, to compare *Mississippi Burning* with the Mississippi episode in the first *Eyes on the Prize* series. To do so creatively would be to raise such questions as:

1. Why was Mississippi so important in the America of the

1950s and early 1960s? What was its special meaning in the struggle for the expansion of democracy?

2. Where are the Black heroes in *Mississippi Burning*? What happened to Medgar Evers, Fannie Lou Hamer, Amzie Moore, Bob Moses, and many other persons of courage and commitment who overflow the frames of the *Eyes* approach to Freedom Summer and its story of the martyrdom of Chaney, Goodman, and Schwerner?

3. Indeed, where is the historical Freedom Summer in the Hollywood story? Why are we not given any serious part of that powerful epic of a people organizing themselves to challenge the terrors of their state, the resistance of their national leaders, and the centuries-old fears of their own hearts? Why are so many of *Mississippi Burning*'s Black characters seen only as victims, and cardboard ones at that? (The director claimed that a Black-focused film wouldn't have sold. How much of that conclusion was his personal reflection of America's familiar racist bind, refusing to make space for white people to move beyond their restricted history?)

4. Why is the FBI given so prominent a role in *Mississippi Burning* when the *Eyes* film (and many other scholarly sources) documents the continuing reluctance and refusal of that agency's director to offer any protection to freedom workers in Mississippi and elsewhere? Is the casting of the federal agents as the flawed but definite heroes of the story part of a continuing mainstream American fantasy, or was it willful blindness?

5. In light of the known facts of the case, why does *Mississippi Burning* need two Hollywood standbys—sex and violence—to explain the breaking of the case against the murderers? (There is much reading material available to any of our students who might exhibit serious interest in the real story of that investigation.) It is especially fascinating to ask why the Black FBI agent was invented to carry out the totally fictional (but stereotypical) role of threatening to castrate the key white witness. Considering the gruesome history of castrations suffered by Black men in the South, this was a strange turnabout. Or was it a return to the terrible, ancient nightmares suffered by those who engaged in—or too long condoned—such racially motivated crimes?

Reflection on questions like these may allow us to explore with our students the possibility that the filmmakers of *Mississippi Burning*, and many Americans with them, simply were too impoverished in faith and imagination to do the right thing (to borrow a phrase). For instance, it may well be that they could not imagine a successful attack on a violent system of injustice like Mississippi's being carried out by a basically Black and essentially nonviolent army of courageous freedom fighters. Even though the martyrdom of three members of that army was the purported jumping-off point for the film, the creators apparently did not understand the meaning and function of martyrdom in human struggles for justice and truth.

In the climate of our times, where white and Black people, and others, still find painful reasons to doubt the possibility of a humane common ground for us all, it is especially important to probe the message of the organizers and the martyrs who helped to deliver Mississippi (and much more) from its worst self. For what we begin to see in the *Eyes* film, and what is denied to us in *Mississippi Burning*, is the story of a group of Black native daughters and sons, encouraged and abetted by a very small band of predominantly Black organizers from SNCC and CORE, whose life-risking commitment to freedom actually drew white allies from all over America to come and stand with them, offering their lives together as a sacrificial bridge toward a new society.

At the center of this compelling Mississippi story stands one of the archetypal native daughters, Fannie Lou Hamer of Ruleville. When we follow her life and the lives of her comrades in struggle, and recognize the flame that burned so brightly within them, we can understand the liberating effect they had on so many others. We can help our students to grasp the significance of the exchange that took place toward the end of the summer of death and victory between Rita Schwerner, co-worker and wife of one of the white martyrs, and her Black adopted Mississippi grandmother, Mrs. Polly Heidelberg. Mrs. Heidelberg later recalled how it was after Mickey's body was found and Rita was preparing to leave all the co-workers and extended family she had come to love. "You never saw a lady weep like Rita Schwerner when it was time for her to leave," Mrs. Heidelberg said. "When we were packing her things, she told us she loved us and our children. She said, 'Miss Polly, you were the light in my path!' I said, 'Rita, you were the light I held,' and we held each other and cried."[1]

In our vocation of keeping hope and trees and memories (and therefore life) alive, we can also share with them the scene in the film biography of Mrs. Hamer, *Never Turn Back*, where women and men from all over the nation gathered for her funeral and memorial service in 1977. For only as they understand the role of the militant Black healers, the nonviolent liberators, can students appreciate the deepest meaning of the moment in which Hodding Carter III, scion of one of the most influential white Mississippi families, holds back tears to testify about what Mrs. Hamer and the freedom movement did for Mississippi: "And I think that history will say that among those who were freed most totally by her were white Mississippians, who were finally freed—if they had the will to be free—from themselves, from their history, from their racism, from their past."[2]

Are there still men and women whose hearts burn with great annealing flames on behalf of a new and just America? Are there young students, middle-aged people, older people, who are still prepared to take great risks to create a more humane world for children not yet born? Are there Black people who still have the energy, the hope, and the courage to open a path for whites who *will* to be free? Are there white persons with such a will? And are there still common grounds of struggle and hope where all of our newly emerging American rainbow tribe of justice and peace seekers may discover their purpose and their most authentic identity? Of course, as they consider these questions our students of the 1990s may well want to know if the common grounds of this generation are located anywhere near the deserted mines, the polluted rivers, the AIDS wards, the inner city and suburban crack houses, shelters for the homeless, anywhere near the abused women and children of our land.

Yes, I know: It is often assumed that children and young people are not really interested in such questions, just as we too easily believe that adults are too cynical or preoccupied to take similar queries seriously. But what is there to lose in raising the issues, in testing the waters of our souls? And what context is more inviting than the study of our nation's great Black-led freedom movement, especially as it is revealed, or obscured, by such films as the *Eyes on the Prize* series and *Mississippi Burning*. For while there is nothing to lose by testing these waters, we will have failed ourselves and others if there are, indeed, young people and their elders who are secretly longing for a chance to wade in the waters, and we deny our calling as teachers by failing to encourage their best selves to venture forth. In my experience, every group faced with the story of the freedom movement has produced children, youth, and adults who are ready at least to consider the experience as a call to the expansion of their own lives. Something seems to tell them that they can, if nothing more, be the water for the trees of enlightenment and hope.

Although it took on different forms, a similar openness, a search for personal — as well as collective — meaning, constantly emerged from the discussions that erupted out of *Do the Right Thing*. In direct contrast to *Mississippi Burning*, this was a film by a perceptive, creative, young Black filmmaker who was willing to take risks, and who knows how to laugh. Deep in his heart is the desire to tell the story of his people's life and times as richly and as fully as possible. (Expressed in 1980s northern argot: "I'm on a mission to bring our shit, undiluted, uncut, to the screen." Before wincing at the language, it is important for students of all ages and colors also to hear Lee saying, "I want, always want, my work to have some spirituality about it. It shouldn't be overt but it should be there nonetheless."[3]) For the work of this film his base of operation was a block in the Bedford-Stuyvesant section of Brooklyn, New York, a contemporary, hyper-northern variation of some of Mississippi's woundedness, of Alabama's pain.

In spite of the differences in styles, language, and milieu, it was not hard for many viewers to recognize that there was some kind of connection between Lee's provocative creation and the experience of what we have called the freedom movement. From the outset of the film we are almost literally hit with a rich and fascinating but sometimes unnecessarily ambiguous mix of sights and sounds, set to the theme music of the experience, Public Enemy's "Fight the Power." With the title of the film and the

choice of his musical theme, Lee has opened to us another powerful, filmic pathway into the heart of America's great obsession:
race. Certainly Lee's path is one that none of us can afford to
ignore as we attempt to engage ourselves and our students—of
every age and setting—to wrestle with the darkness and the
light, the humor and the rage of a divided America.

Throughout the high-energy movement of the film Lee gives
us handles (or is it hands?) to hold, questions to grapple with,
and it is fascinating to offer and raise these in our teaching. Of
course, near the center are the natural questions: What is "the
right thing"? In the film, in our lives, what is it? How do we
know what it is, and even if we think we know it, how do we do
it? Is this simply a personal, intensely private matter? If so, how
can it be of importance to the life of Spike Lee's Stuyvesant
Avenue or all the Stuyvesant Avenues we know?

The questions spurt up like a playful, serious, sometimes dangerous geyser. Is there a "right thing" for Black people and a
different one for Hispanics, Euro-Americans, Asians, and others? Does the "right thing" for one group necessarily conflict
and collide with the right thing for another group, another person, another time? Without naming them as such the film is
obviously introducing us to, reminding us of, the liveliness of
profound ethical issues, suggesting that all life—in Mississippi,
Bed-Stuy, or China—may well be based on our perception of
and responses to such crucial questions. Who dares avoid them
in a serious process of education?

It is to Lee's credit that he has provided a most accessible
opportunity for dealing with issues of great moment in such an
audacious, inventive, and sometimes raucous manner. Whether
he was always able to keep his eye on the prize is another, and
very important, question. As might be expected, I am especially
concerned about the film's connection, and lack of it, to the long
history of the African-American struggle to "fight the power"
that has sought to enslave us, dehumanize us, exploit us, ignore
us, discourage us, miseducate us, and when all else fails, to
deracinate and remake us into some of the worst of white
images. (So it was disappointing to read the words in Lee's journal that seemed to come out of a certain historical disconnec-
tion: "The days of twenty-five million Blacks being silent while

our fellow brothers and sisters are exploited, oppressed, and murdered, have to come to an end."[4] Does he know that every generation has produced breakers of that silence, some of the loudest in the 1960s? Or is he referring only to now? Can there be a "now" without constant reference and connections to our other days of struggle and unsilence?)

As our students need continually to see, these links are critical. Indeed, the more grounded we are in that centuries-old history of fighting "the power(s)" the more fascinating and compelling are the questions students and teachers may raise with the film. For instance, what is "the power"? Is it all white people, or some, or "the government," or leading white racists everywhere, or white racism, or the racist-capitalist system? Or is it deeper, broader, more pervasive than any of these? Is it the same now as it was in the 1950s and 1960s? Could it be, as one Black college student recently suggested to me, the power of ignorance which threatens to destroy us all?

Such an insight moves us to another level, encourages us to take seriously Spike Lee's commitment to the place of spirituality in his work. As a result, it seems right that we dive even more deeply into the issues raised by his fascinating film. Can we encourage students to ask questions like these, or will they be ahead of us in asking, is "the power" that damages us, that binds us, that destroys so many of us, solely external, or do we find it at deep levels of our own hearts and minds? And if it is there, how do we fight it from within? Are there any veteran freedom workers, long-distance runners who have fought both external and internal forces for a long time, who might help us here? Isn't this part of the reason we need to explore and nourish our connections with the past?

None of these questions is limited to Black people, of course. Lee has made very clear his conviction that all of us, in our many-splendored colorations and ethnicities, have been partly devoured or at least wounded by the beast of racism (is that "the power"?). Who then does not need to fight "the power"? And here we return to one of the original questions of Lee's important film, and one of the historic questions of the Black-led struggle for a racism-free America: Does every person, every group have to carry on a separate struggle against the external and internal, destructive, anti-democratic "power"? For instance, is "the power" fundamentally different for women than for men? Let us and our students wrestle with such questions, in schools and synagogues, in churches and community centers, in the privacy of our living rooms, in the solitariness of our hearts. Spike Lee is good for us, very good.

Recognizing that important fact, perhaps we can then be free enough to ask Lee, and ourselves, what "the power" had to do with the death of Radio Raheem. Ask him and ourselves how "the right" response to Raheem's murder might be related to a trash can tossed through a window after the legalized murderers have run away, or how it is connected to a pizza parlor burned to the ground? Or is the dialogue that continues between Mookie and Sal amidst the rubble really part of "the right thing"?

For those students and teachers who have begun to examine the history of the centuries-long, Black-led attempt to "do the right thing" and to "fight the power" inside us and around us, it may be that Mookie's sister, Jade, comes closest to home. For Jade is the only one in the entire film who—in a partly improvised, less-than-thirty-second statement—is given the chance to suggest that effectively fighting the power can only be done by the community organizing itself internally and externally and carrying on a creative, "positive," empowering struggle for clearly defined goals. Perhaps we can wonder aloud why *this* version of "the right thing" was given so little time and attention in the film. And that is not an idle question, for the fact is that Jade's briefly stated organizing vision may be the central link that really ties the people of Stuyvesant Avenue most closely to the organizing people of Montgomery, to the courageous organizers of the Mississippi Freedom Democratic Party, to the constantly organizing young people of the Black Panthers, to the organizers of the campaigns of Harold Washington and Jesse Jackson, to the lives of Bob Moses and Diane Nash, to the memory and meaning of Ella Baker, Medgar Evers, and Fannie Lou Hamer, master organizers all.

I think it is an important question for our students and the thirty-two-year-old Spike Lee to engage. It is partly a matter of developing generational links, of making life-giving struggle connections. For in his journal Lee suggests that he saw the relationship between the southern struggle and the folks on Stuyvesant Avenue most clearly when he envisioned the scene of the Brooklyn firemen turning their hoses on the enraged community people as the pizzeria burned. This reminded him of Alabama, he said. (He mentions Montgomery, but probably meant Birmingham and the 1963 fire hose attacks on the marchers there.) Unfortunately, what Spike points to as a crucial connection is the experience of the black crowd as victims, as objects of the firemen's actions. But that was only a part of the story in Birmingham. There, the firemen were facing a freedom-seeking, segregation-attacking, organized, Black-led movement whose participants had been mounting their carefully orchestrated challenges for weeks and who had been planning for many weeks before that. Most important, the Birmingham fire hoses did not stop the freedom fighters. They came back again and again. They maintained the initiative. They refused simply to be victims. In the long run, at costs even greater than the one paid on Stuyvesant Avenue, they broke the back of official segregation in Birmingham and set the groundwork for a challenge to the federal government itself.

Neither Spike's journal nor his film caught the major difference in those two fire hose scenes. It is important that we all see it, especially our students. For what an organized movement does is not simply offer sporadic, enraged reactions to murderous provocations, but carefully develops within its own forces a new power, one that must create a new reality, both within its participants and within the space where their battle is carried on. Can we either understand or do "the right thing" if we ignore the lessons, the sacrifices, and the wisdom of all who have fought before us?

In a sense, Smiley, the speech-impaired hawker of the Malcolm and Martin photos, was probably meant to be another representation—with Jade—of this connection to past struggles. But a young woman who questioned Lee on a television talk show asked a profound question when she wanted to know why it was that Smiley, the one person who seemed to have integrated the relational meaning of King and Malcolm, was cast as almost a buffoon and not a person of wisdom. Lee admitted that the Smiley character was really an afterthought and had not been fully developed. It was good of him to share that, good for us to recognize how much can emerge out of spontaneity and improvisation, but now Lee and the rest of us are obliged to probe more deeply, more systematically, into his best resources. We need as much coherence, as much connection, as much wisdom as we can muster for the time ahead—always resolving never, never to leave the Spike Lee laughter and creative genius behind.

Of course, we cannot deal fairly with our students' current experiences without at least acknowledging the major topic that Spike Lee considered including, but then felt unready for—the deadly presence of drugs in the Black community. Indeed, some viewers—Black and white—claimed that the film was less authentic than it could have been because they didn't see pimps and prostitutes, junkies and dealers. My response and my need was of another kind. It might be helpful to test it on ourselves and our students.

As I've already suggested, what I missed in Lee's creative approach to a cross-section of the African-American community on Stuyvesant Avenue were models of the women and men in our communities who are seriously, continually struggling for change today, often at great risk to themselves and to their families. (One such Brooklyn man recently lost his wife to a hail of bullets poured into the window of their home, clearly in response to their fight against the neighborhood drug trade.) I wanted to see the urban organizers who now carry the mantle of those heroic sisters and brothers from the Mississippi and Alabama roads. I needed to see the same manifestation of pastors, teachers, social workers, Fruit of Islam,[5] organizers of one kind or another, coming out of churches, schools, community centers, and mosques in the North. I needed to see them, pitting their tough, compassionate lives against "the power," seeking to draw others into the disciplined, sustained struggle for new power, for profound change. I needed to see them partly as a way of helping our students—and ourselves—to know that we are not simply victims of materialism, exploitative social structures, apathy, or unfocused rage. We needed (without preaching, Spike!) images of those who take initiatives, who organize blocks, who seek to empower themselves and others, who go far beyond sporadic protest to explore and create undiscovered or untapped sources of power, internal and external. That was what both Malcolm and King were about at their best.

Both of them, for instance, would have agreed with Lee's journal notation: "The drug epidemic is worse than the plague. Entire generations are being wiped out by drugs. If drugs aren't getting them, then the guys shooting over the drugs are."[6] Both King and Malcolm would have known that crack and other drugs are now more devastating to the Black community than segregation and direct racism ever were. Especially when the drugs and the related violence are combined with economic and social isolation, the failure of educational and political systems, the steady erosion of familial and community structures of support, they are surely worse than the plague. Though both men would have understood the burning of a pizzeria, they would surely have pressed on to deeper, higher levels of response.

Of course, Lee's film encourages us to recognize that the question now is not simply the responses of Malcolm and Martin, Ruby Doris Robinson or Ella Baker, Mookie or his friends, but ours, and our students, and all who sense the need to fight both plagues and powers for the lives of a generation of children, and for generations after them. So we thank Spike Lee, even as we disagree with some of his approach, even as we ask him for more, for greater depths, we thank him. If this is his work at thirty-two, as he keeps his pledge to continue working and learning we may expect great things. Meanwhile, we thank him for pressing us to ultimate questions, for helping us to ask how we may learn and do the right thing, how we may fight the old power while creating a new power within and around us. Perhaps we can all expect great things, right things, even in the midst of plagues, even from ourselves, from our students, from our world. Let's see.

9

In Search of the World

A Geography of Freedom

When the decade of the 1980s closed in a spectacular and unexpected burst of people's movements across the globe, demanding new beginnings and manifesting new hope, we were faced again with an old and all-too-familiar lament from the world of American education. As the names flashed on TV screens and leaped up from newspaper and magazine headlines—Beijing, Budapest, Leipzig, Berlin, Prague, Capetown, Lithuania, Azerbaijan—they testified anew to our fundamental geographic illiteracy. Apart from the large general spaces represented, for instance, by China and Eastern Europe, and the availability of terms like *Communist, Iron Curtain,* and *apartheid*, there was little that most of our students of every age and setting could say about the location, condition, or history of these places. Indeed, the more spectacular the events in such cities and nations, the more vividly they testified to the major gaps in our awareness, especially when compared to the geographical knowledge of other modern, industrialized peoples.

So in a world that is constantly being contracted and condensed by the technological marvels of our time and drawn together by a series of global-sized political, economic, and environmental challenges and crises, our students, our citizens, often seem unprepared participants. Despite the fact that we are now, more than ever before, a marvelously diverse nation of many nations, neither the history, language, and cultures of other nations nor the variety of relationships we have had with them take high priority in our education.

Breaking out of so dangerous a cocoon is not easy, but it is surely necessary, especially in light of the kinds of potentially dangerous power Americans continue to wield in a world that we cannot dominate. When we consider that people of color are the world's overwhelming majority, it should not be surprising that our engagement in the story of the African-American freedom movement again provides significant opportunities for us all to develop connections to and helpful comparisons with the rest of humankind. In the sharing of this unique domestic story many important doors are opened to the world. For instance, Africa has always been present in the minds and hearts of members of the Black American community. For ever since the bitter years of the slave trade, the children of Africa, a fundamental part of our nation, have been firmly tied to the second largest continent in the world. Sometimes the relationship came only through dreams and fading memories; at times it was preserved in songs and colors and skilled artisanry, in the sounds of drums, the folk wisdom of religion, and in loving connections to the earth. At other moments, for a variety of reasons, the connection was denied, minimized. Periodically the relationships were so infused with burning movements of hope that shiploads of African-Americans created ingenious means to go back home. In addition, there have always been men and women, bound to these shores, who expressed their abiding commitment through politically conscious efforts to aid and comfort the besieged and occupied motherland.

This story of international connections, especially African ties, is central to the development of the African-American freedom movement, and a fascinating mixture of persons helped keep the relationship alive. Students should meet them. They include a powerful, too-little-known African Methodist Episcopal bishop and political leader named Henry McNeill Turner; a charismatic, Jamaica-born visionary and organizer of hundreds of thousands (perhaps millions) of Africa's scattered peoples named Marcus Garvey; an erudite scholar, artist, and creator of Pan-African networks named W.E.B. Du Bois; along with scores of Black women missionaries and shiploads of African-American pilgrims singing songs of hope as they set out for the Promised Land of their ancestors. The account of these connections is full of magnificent, though often tragic, stories, well-suited for introducing young people and adults to a world they never knew. (Sometimes I wonder: Is knowledge really power? Does this knowledge, sensitively shared, have enough power to help rescue some of our lost and purposeless young people? Sometimes I wonder: Who will tell the story?)

Eventually, of course, the exploration of such ties leads to the southern tip of Africa, takes us by way of Black American consciousness into Mozambique, Angola, and Zimbabwe, moving us with maps, recordings, movies, and computer geography programs. Guided perhaps by the music and spirit of Miriam Makeba, finally the vector enters South Africa. In the burning light of those struggles we come to recognize a resurgence of Africa-consciousness in Black America by the end of the 1960s. We see a new traffic between the children of Africa in America and the homeland, focused at first in Ghana with the encouragement of the inspirational Kwame Nkrumah, then later in Tanzania, as many of us were drawn to the quiet integrity and attempts at revolutionary self-reliance that marked the leadership of President Julius Nyerere.

Why was there this rise in connection and commitment to Africa and its struggles in the heart of Black America at that time? What forces drew thousands of marchers out into the streets of Washington and San Francisco in 1972 for the first national African Liberation Day events? Why had the Black Power conferences of the late 1960s evolved for a time in the early 1970s into the Congress of African People? Where did the great flowering of African-styled clothing, jewelry, hairstyles, and educational studies come from? All these questions flow out of our attention to maps and to movements, reminding us that all maps are simply an invitation into the experiences and explorations of human beings. So we tell the story, lift up its music and drama, and students may well be drawn to the fascinating geography behind it.

The story, of course, is also the story of our own time. It is the story of the Congressional Black Caucus giving leadership in the 1980s to a new set of challenges to the Republic of South Africa and to American policy toward that essentially illegitimate white supremacist government. It is the story of Martin Luther King's oldest daughter, Yolanda (Yoki), experiencing jail for the first time as part of a protest at the South African embassy, taking her father's spirit where he would have gone himself. It is the great thrill that swept through our hearts when Nelson Mandela walked out beyond the prison gates, reminding our students again that maps are often best read as stories of great human struggles.

But the ties to the African continent, while dominant, are not the only international connections that rise naturally out of the history of the Black freedom movement. For ever since the establishment of this nation the children of Africa here have lived with a consciousness of the African diaspora everywhere, especially in this hemisphere. So when at the end of the eighteenth century the enslaved Black peoples of Santo Domingo (eventually called Haiti) rose up in the first slave revolution of the Western Hemisphere, African-Americans all over the young United States heard and felt the chants and drums. When England was forced by Black resistance and white internal politics to end slavery in its New World West Indian colonies in 1837, Africans in the United States not only knew it, but wherever they were free to do so they went on to observe the anniversary of the emancipation of the West Indian kinfolk with elaborate celebrations each year up to the Civil War.

After slavery ended in the United States and our native white supremacist racism extended its international manifestations, African-Americans raised powerful voices of concern whenever their expanding, white-dominated nation claimed to be concerned about the rights and freedoms of other peoples of color. So at the turn of the century, Black people protested against our government's act of aborting the Afro-Cuban revolution on that nearby Caribbean island. Later, during the Pacific Ocean phase of the Spanish-Cuban-American war, Black soldiers deserted the U.S. Army in the Philippines to fight on the side of the independence forces there, risking their lives to oppose the racist Manifest Destiny proclaimed by their government. As the United States expanded its economic, political, and military power into Central and South America, there were consistent objections from important segments of Black America who suspected the nation's motives in any dealings with peoples of color—whether in Nicaragua, Panama, or Haiti. Then, by the end of World War I there was a rising tide of Black immigrants arriving in places such as New York City and Boston from all the islands of the Caribbean, especially the English-speaking ones, establishing an important set of new connections.

Simply to seek and find these places of the African diaspora on a map or globe, or with a computer geographic information system, would be a significant beginning. Then, moving beyond beginnings, we would soon discover that the exploration of these hemispheric developments through the eyes of Afro-American freedom workers provides an important point of view for those who wondered why there was—and is—so much distrust of "the Yankees" among our southern neighbors, and why there continues to be so much disdain up here for the "Banana republics" of the peoples of color in "our back yard."

At the same time, our classes should certainly be exposed to another intriguing side of this story, one that is manifested in the persistent search by African-American artists in the United States for their diasporic roots here in our adopted hemisphere, as well as in Africa. Of course we know that such a quest is an unmistakable element of the familiar struggle for liberation, for freedom from the ravages of deracination, amnesia, and cultural shame that slavery and its various successors have sought to impose on the children of Africa. Within that context, we may help students discover the carefully, anthropologically informed research and masterful choreography of scholar-artists like Katherine Dunham and Pearl Primus, as these women of power reflect such Afro-American cultures as Haiti, Brazil, Cuba, Jamaica, and Trinidad in their magnificent dances and eloquent lectures. Viewed on videos and in movies from earlier times, encountered in person now, such lives provide another means of demonstrating the ways in which the world of African peoples has found connective expression in bold, evocative creations.[1]

A similar testimony is available in the work of the poet Langston Hughes, who anthologized and often translated from Spanish and French the contributions of African writers based on the home continent and in the Caribbean. And students will also be fascinated if they listen carefully for one of the most significant developments in the post–World War II evolution of African-American jazz, the inclusion of Afro-Cuban rhythms, instruments, and musicians—to say nothing of the later rise of West Indian reggae in this country. To experience and explore the places and people who inspired such creative reconnections is to discover a stimulating setting for the world of geography.

Just as culture and geography are inseparable, we also know that history and geography must be approached in tandem. So it will be helpful to introduce our students to some of the ways in which the events and developments surrounding World War II opened the global arena in a decisive way for the Black freedom movement in the United States. Here again, our students of all ages would gain a fascinating angle of vision on the world if we used the evidence of African-American newspapers, journals, memoirs, and other published works to see through the eyes of Black folk, especially to see the world that the war was helping to create. (Indeed, if we follow the African-American story closely it takes us into wartime Europe even before the official onset of World War II. For one of the most fascinating developments of the 1930s was the organizing of the Abraham Lincoln Brigade, the independent group of United States civilian volunteers who fought in the Spanish Civil War on the side of the Republic against General Franco and his German-aided fascist revolutionaries. The Black men and women who served in the unofficial brigade of several thousand United States citizens were participants in the first racially integrated American-based military force. That was only one of the ways in which they were before their time.)

Parallel to all the chilling contradictions embodied in the fact of hundreds of thousands of Black men and women serving a segregated nation in segregated military units in a war against Hitler's deadly racism, the conflict also presented new vistas to explore. The Black soldiers of World War II received an important exposure to the world through their military service. They were scattered on duty throughout Europe, into North Africa, to the borders of India, Nepal, and China, on to all the war-torn islands of the Pacific Ocean—and their eyes were opened, both to the ways of non-American white people and to the variegated worlds of color. The accounts of their experiences, which appeared regularly in the African-American press, are simply fascinating, providing entry into a universe that many of our students have only vaguely been aware of, offering motivations for deeper probing, seeking.

This was a world that the Black servicemen never forgot. (A good many of them are still alive. They might make a major contribution to a classroom experience.) Nor did they miss the ironies of their presence, along with Africans, West Indians, Vietnamese, Indians—all colonized (or semi-free) peoples of color, fighting on behalf of the supposedly democratic "mother" countries who could not share the riches of democratic equality with their nonwhite "subjects" and second-class citizens during peacetime.

So, our guides, the Black servicemen, were present and often very aware when the uncontrollable fires unleashed by World War II began to attack the foundations of white Western colonialism. Indeed, many of the African-American soldiers and their people at home recognized the dawning of a great new time, the reshaping global realities, the creation of a new geography. Thus they saw more in China and Vietnam in the 1940s than communist takeovers. For them, peoples of color were taking responsibility for their destinies, often at stunning costs. From the perspective of African-Americans and their freedom struggle, the rumblings in postwar African colonies were tied to the new resolve in the hearts of so many Black American soldiers who had returned to the United States determined to make democracy more than a slogan, to make America more than a white man's country.

Eventually, many of these returning veterans became some of the most important grassroots leaders in the southern freedom movement. So the story that takes our students to the borders of China eventually returns to more familiar ground. (Of course, even here, at home, our geographical knowledge leaves much to be desired, and there is ample opportunity to introduce entire classrooms to such places as St. Augustine, Florida; Greenwood, Mississippi; Selma, Alabama; Albany, Georgia; Opelousas, Louisiana; and Danville, Virginia—to mention only a few important battlegrounds of the southern freedom movement.)

Teaching about our international connections from the perspectives of such pro-democracy leaders as W.E.B. Du Bois, Paul Robeson, Adam Clayton Powell, Jr., Ella Baker, Malcolm X, and Martin Luther King, Jr., provides a very special way of seeing the world and our nation's place in it. For in this setting the post–World War II Afro-American freedom struggle becomes part of the larger world movement, a hard but beautiful and necessary transformation in which the peoples of color, the global majority, begin to rediscover their vision and their voice, move to establish their rightful place in this world. From that perspective everything takes on a different cast, from the Cold War to the United Nations to the meaning of Vietnam, Nicaragua and South Africa, again drawing history and geography together. Perhaps we may even send our students back to the recently, temporarily aborted pro-democracy revolution in China, showing them again the "We Shall Overcome" signs, suggesting that they use maps to follow the trail of the song across continents, helping them to understand the common threads of human aspirations that eventually tie together all the far-flung places, especially all the battlegrounds for democracy, all the meeting grounds of human hope.

Approaching the world from this angle, we understand much more fully the deepest roots of Dr. King's historic statement in Riverside Church on April 4, 1967, calling his nation not only to end its war against the Vietnamese, but urging us to "get on the right side of the World revolution" of poor, nonwhite peoples. Standing on this ground our students can hear Stokely Carmichael (now Kwame Turé—why, let someone ask, would he choose a name like that? Let them explore and discover.) more clearly as he raised the late 1960s cry, "Hell, no. We won't go!" We can see Muhammad Ali (and what of *that* name?) as an unexpected source of wisdom and history when he refuses military conscription and exclaims, "No Viet Cong ever called me Nigger!" Ultimately such explorations of movement-grounded historical geography are joined to politics and economics when Martin King declares, six months before his assassination,

The storm is rising against the privileged minority of the earth from which there is no shelter in isolation and armament. The storm will not abate until a just distribution of the fruits of the earth enable man everywhere to live in dignity and human decency. The American Negro . . . may be the vanguard of a prolonged struggle that may change the shape of the world as billions of deprived shake and transform the earth in the quest for life, freedom and justice.[2]

If we accept the tutelage of the Black freedom movement in our quest for international connections, no one can be too surprised if the search eventually carries us into the presidential campaigns of Jesse Jackson. A serious examination of his comparatively bold and sweeping international policy proposals and initiatives reveals a definite set of connections to the long history of Black concern for and commitment to the world outside our borders.

Interestingly enough, our exploration of that history and geography may also suggest a remarkable prescience on the part of the Black visionaries of the past as they established positions far in advance of the white American political mainstream. Though initially condemned, these beachheads on the future would eventually be claimed by conventional wisdom. Examples of such insight can be found, for instance, in the role of Robeson, Du Bois, and later King calling in the 1950s and 1960s for the United States to abandon its unenlightened policy of hostility to mainland China (especially concerning its reception into the United Nations). Or it can be seen in King's stance on Vietnam, or in Andrew Young's and later Jesse Jackson's call for United States conversations with representatives of the Palestine Liberation Organization. (By the way, wouldn't it be fascinating for our students not only to discover where the Middle East is but to learn why it is called by that name, or why the Far East was far, or the Near East near?)

At the same time, we cannot let our students forget that these international connections of African-Americans were never one-directional, a fact that only adds to the excitement and humanity of the issues. So they can learn of Ho Chi Minh's residency in

Harlem in the 1920s and his special concern for the situation of Afro-Americans from that time on. They can hear the stories of how the Black people of South Africa stormed out into the streets in victory celebrations each time their radios brought news of a Joe Louis victory in the ring (yes, those battles of "The Brown Bomber" were also part of the freedom movement!). We can assume that Chairman Mao's words of encouragement to Dr. Du Bois and other Afro-Americans in the 1950s and 1960s were more than propaganda blows, and sought to demonstrate a genuine feeling of solidarity.

Our students need to understand how the southern-based Black freedom struggle and the later widespread urban rebellions and the Black Power movement inspired other freedom fighters all over the world, from South Africa to Korea, from Europe to Central America. Let them know, for example, that Nicaraguan Sandinista leaders say they carried King's book of sermons, *Strength to Love*,[3] into the mountains with them in their struggle against the Somoza dictatorship. Indeed, the foreign minister of Nicaragua, Miguel D'Escoto, a Roman Catholic priest, now calls King "my patron saint."

In the same vein, perhaps they could view parts of the documentary film on the freedom movement anthem, "We Shall Overcome." When they see and hear it sung across the globe in dozens of languages, on many grounds of struggle and hope for peace and justice and nuclear disarmament and ecological responsibility, then students may recognize again how we are all connected, how this American freedom movement has helped to move the world to a higher ground. Of course, as we have seen, they must also remember the costs that have been paid. Perhaps it will be enough for them to see the Chinese students, fasting in Tiananmen Square, carrying their signs, wearing their shirts with the words, "We Shall Overcome." Perhaps that will be enough for them to understand the costs that some must pay—under the glare of television lights or hidden in dark cells or buried under the woods of Mississippi and Romania—to create higher ground for us all.

At such a time we need to be careful, for our students may wonder aloud if they are possibly seeing in these scenes what should be the real purpose of all our international connections—

not to dominate, threaten, destructively compete with, or sub-vert, but to help each other on to higher human ground. Then a new conversation may need to begin — about international relations and geography, yes, but also about the purposes of human life, wherever it is found. They may initiate a deeper search concerning the possibilities of human community across all geographical lines, and inquire about the education that best prepares us for higher ground, for connections. Perhaps some students will even want to explore the difference between the international search for cheaper goods and wages and the quest for higher ground. (What a reward for teaching!)

Under those circumstances what they will likely hope for from us are not answers, but a recognition, a confirmation that these are right and necessary questions for this time. Indeed, our best response may be nothing more than to join them in watching the video and singing the sometimes sentimental (and very hopeful) song, "We Are the World." But as we do it together it will be most helpful if we can remind ourselves again of the costs of such apparently romantic convictions, even discover that they are more than romantic. For this may be the point to bring geography, music, politics, and history together as we remember the South African children who were brutally whipped in the streets for daring to believe and to sing "We Are the World." And still they sing, and still they act. And now Mandela's voice can be heard with them. Let scrapbooks be kept of these children. Let maps be drawn toward them. Let all in the room memorize the words of the great Afro-Caribbean poet-politician Aimé Césaire: "The work of humankind has just begun. . . . There is room for all at the rendezvous of victory."[4]

Perhaps it is only fitting that a study of human geography that grows out of one people's freedom movement should eventually return, via the mappings of our hearts, to the higher ground that bears our common struggle, our deepest human hope. Even the youngest of our students will likely understand that path.

10

Is America Possible?

The Land That Never Has Been Yet

Some years ago I came across one of the most intriguing book titles that I have ever seen. It was set forth in the form of a question: *Is America Possible?*[1] Even without delving into the contents, I was struck by the playful seriousness of the inquiry, the invitation to imagine and explore the shape and meaning of a "possible" America, an America still coming into existence. The idea itself, of course, was not new, simply its formulation. But since then, everywhere that I have paused to reflect on the powerful, flooding movement of the Black struggle for freedom in America, I have been called back to that title, to its query and challenge. For it is a question that has always been at the heart of the Afro-American quest for democracy in this land. And wherever we have seen these freedom seekers, community organizers, artisans of democracy, standing their ground, calling others to the struggle, advancing into danger, creating new realities, it is clear that they are taking the question seriously, shaping their own answers, testing the possibilities of their dreams.

Is America possible? Yes, they say, sometimes testifying to their vision with great eloquence: "I have a dream that one day . . ." Sometimes joining their vision to the magnificent Biblical images, they proclaim, "I've been to the mountaintop. I've seen the Promised Land." Or, in the marvelously mundane messages of their freedom songs, expressing great hope: "If you

177

don't see me at the back of the bus / And you can't find me nowhere / Just come on up to the front of the bus, / and I'll be riding up there." Envisioning very specific expressions of America's possibilities they sang, "I'm gonna eat at the Holiday Inn ... one of these days." And the great hope and vision were ultimately caught up in the anthem of the movement, in the stanzas that came from the past, as well as in the ones forged in the heat of the post–World War II struggle. "We shall overcome. ... We'll walk hand in hand. ... The Lord will see us through. ... The truth will make us free. ... Black and white together. ... Our children will be free. ... The whole wide world around."

Somehow, in a time like our own, when the capacity for imagining appears to be endangered, both by the technology of television and by the poverty of public dreams, it seems especially crucial to introduce our students to the meaning of such a question as "Is America possible?" And it is absolutely necessary that they discover the significance of the Biblical text: "Where there is no vision the people perish." Indeed, it is precisely in a period of great spiritual and societal hunger like our own that we most need to open minds, hearts, and memories to those times when women and men actually dreamed of new possibilities for our nation, for our world, for their own lives. It is now that we may be able to convey the stunning idea that dreams, imagination, vision, and hope are actually powerful mechanisms in the creation of new realities. Especially when the dreams go beyond speeches and songs to become embodied, to take on flesh, in real, hard places.

This is why we turn to the world of dreams and visions that became flesh and blood in the Afro-American freedom movement. This is why we return to Rosa Parks and wonder aloud what visions of Black and white together were in her mind and heart as the bus approached her stop on December 1, 1955. This is why we listen and laugh when her friend and mentor E. D. Nixon tells us that his dream of a new America for his grandchildren had eventually changed to a vision of a new nation that he could see and feel and experience in his own lifetime. It is in search of that power of imagination and action that we approach Malcolm X, realizing that the best heroes of democracy's shaping were constantly opening their dreams and visions to change, and were never satisfied to get high on dreams alone. So, too, because we need new dreams in each generation, new visions for each time, we ask ourselves and our students about the dreams that moved fourth-grade-trained Mrs. Hamer to challenge an entire political party and its presidential leader. We seek to know more about the visions that kept her working for the poor and the left out until she died. Because we believe in the power of imagination, especially when linked to committed lives—even when the lives and dreams go astray—we look deeply into the eyes of Huey Newton and understand why a long-time resident of his community, shocked by his murder in 1989, could nevertheless say, "To us, Huey Newton was a hero. The Black Panthers were a thing to identify with, along with Malcolm X and Martin Luther King."[2] What a gathering of dreamers!

If we dare, it may still be possible to encourage such audacious—and necessary—dreaming on behalf of a more just and humane America today. With some encouragement, our teaching may yet find the way to engage the centers of imagination and open visions of a possible America in places where no one ever expected to find them. (Can any good thing come out of Dorchester?) As we have seen, we could do this through entering the dreams of those visionary workers who have gone before us, hearing and speaking their words, singing their songs, exploring the hope that moved their lives, finding the mysterious connections that exist between them and our own centers of creativity.

Or, at times we might try another path. Exploring the world of the Afro-American freedom struggle, we might grasp firmly one seminal statement of vision, one powerful answer to the key question, "Is America possible?" and walk with our students into the depths of that experience. Considering Octavio Paz's description of poetry as "the bridge between history and truth," it would be exciting to explore a classic poetic statement of the archetypal African-American dream of democracy and see if it can help to bring some fundamental truth and hope to the life and times of our students, especially in this decade of awesome transitions. If I were to choose such a vehicle it would be Langston Hughes's magnificent poetic summons, "Let America Be America Again." Such a work could easily occupy us for days or weeks, as we touch all the levels, enter all the hope, receive with gratitude all the visions shared by Hughes more than a half century ago.

To provide a setting, to mix poetry with biography and history, someone (not necessarily the teacher) might explore what America was like in 1935 when the poem was written. What was it like to be Black in New York, or on lecture tours through the South, or on troubled waters somewhere, far from tours and cities and help? In the midst of a national Depression how could a Black man dream? Indeed, we are pressed by this initial investigation to raise the larger question: What is it that makes for dreams, for visions, for some audacious movement beyond the "is" to the "ought" even in the midst of the most desperate and dangerous situations? But returning to the specific object of our attention, to the keeper and singer of some of the nation's most important—and most ignored—dreams, we can best respond to the search for sources by looking more closely at Hughes himself. We see his Harlem-based, world-traveling life; we grasp the remarkable span and fidelity of his work. And everywhere we recognize his firm belief in the life-giving purpose of dreams, as well as his sense of responsibility for sharing that belief with those who were younger than he. In a thousand ways throughout his work we hear him say, as he did in "Dreams":

> Hold fast to dreams
> For if dreams die
> Life is a broken-winged bird
> That cannot fly.[3]

Against that background, we approach the larger poem, "Let America Be America Again," again allowing our pedagogy to free us from older academic categories, to strengthen our own wings, to speak to our students in songs. And as we use the half-century-old poem to encourage an experience of flight in us all, it may be good to go right to the heart of the work, to experience its last stanzas together. Invariably I have found students of all ages responding fully to this poem, opening themselves both to its larger vision and to its implications for their own apparently dreamless lives. Sooner or later it becomes clear that they have not been encouraged in the nurturing of dreams and visions. Or they have closed themselves against the exposing of such personal levels of their being. Even more frequently, they have been taught by words and examples that they have no role in the dreaming of America, in the storming of the impossible. Once they feel permission, once the life-giving power of their own imagination is touched at some vital point, it is amazing how quickly and how well they find their voices and their visions.

Of course, my own experience is not a substitute for each teacher's own path of discovery; rather, it is simply offered as a word of encouragement. So, too, the brief reflections on the poem outlined here provide only an idea of what has often proved helpful in the settings where I have shared Hughes's call—from maximum security prisons to Sunday school classes. In many ways, the poem is its own commentary and encouragement, its own faithful reflection of the central dreams of so much democratic struggle in this land:

> O, let America be America again—
> The land that never has been yet—
> And yet must be—
> The land where *every* man is free.[4]

So we begin with a marvelous and stimulating set of ideas and images for our students to explore (rather than focusing on literary criticism). What does he mean by these two lines?

> The land that never has been yet—
> And yet must be—

Already we are offered the sense of vision, of hope, of dream, of a land that does not yet exist. It is on one level a familiar approach to the entire American hemisphere, as dream, as that which is conjured up within the minds and hearts of those who have come here, voluntarily or enslaved. But Hughes takes it further than the usual semi-passiveness of inner dreams. For he encourages us to recognize that this nation is still in process, still coming into being, still on its way to the fulfillment of its best self. And once that image is suggested, then the natural questions flow: What would America's "best self" be like? Earlier in the poem Hughes referred to the essential dream of founders, immigrants, and slaves, of building a "homeland of the free" on these shores. In this latter segment of the poem he opens up the vision, looks for a land "where *every* man is free." Of course, we stop to ask if Hughes would use the word "man" today. And it is more than academic for us to press on to the question: What does it mean to be free, in America, in the 1990s? Constantly tantalizing, nudging, calling forth, we might inquire: What would this country be like today if we were all "free," free to become our best selves (and who might *that* be), free to create a more perfect union for us all?

Such questions only begin the conversation, suggest directions for the imagination, invite a variety of sometimes conflicting dreams. Hughes goes on to contribute more concrete images when he writes of

> The land that's mine—
> The poor man's, Indian's, Negro's, ME—
> Who made America

His owners of America are a fascinating group, similar to many that we have seen in places like the Poor People's Campaign and the Rainbow Coalition. Indeed, there is almost an echo here of the classic, prophetic, justice-obsessed strands of the Hebrew and Christian scriptures. Hughes envisions the land, God's land, as belonging to the outcasts, the workers, the unexpected. Are these really the ones who *made* America? And if that is so, what are the implications of such truth for the future of the nation? How should it be shaped and directed and governed and cared for if our country really belongs to poor people, Native Americans, African-Americans, and all the laborers "who made America"? What would a country be like that gave its greatest attention, care, and concern to such people? What would a country be like that took its major leadership from such owners?

Even as we attempt to play with such ideas and visions, it becomes clear that they may not present the greatest challenge to our capacity for seeing the unseen. For it is possible that the most arresting aspect of Hughes's dream is not a matter of who owns America, but his assumption that the primary owners also have primary responsibility for fulfilling the original dream of a "homeland of the free." Isn't this the essential message in the words

> Whose sweat and blood, whose faith and pain,
> Whose hand at the foundry, whose plow in the rain,
> Must bring back our mighty dream again.

At the center of the vision is a dream of a land that does not yet exist, and a vision of its creation placed in the hands of very ordinary, non-elite men and women. What do our students— and their teachers—think of such a vision? In other words, who do we think America belongs to, and who has the essential responsibility for its future? Are we prepared to abandon the cynically safe responses to those questions, responses like, "It belongs to the people with the most money, the best lawyers, and the greatest access to the levers of political power"? Do we know that such supposedly realistic responses eventually stunt and finally destroy all the dream ports of our spirit, break all the wings of our hearts—and that they warn our students against ever dreaming, ever believing that they can fly?

Eventually Hughes also insists that we confront one of the most daunting realities of all dreams concerning the creation of a more just society, of an America more faithful to the truth of our joint ownership. As we have seen throughout the Afro-American freedom struggle, and in other movements for the expansion of democracy, all visionaries must count the costs. And Hughes's next stanza reminds us of the ever-present opposition which sets itself against dreams of hope and flights of freedom.

> Sure, call me any ugly name you choose—
> The steel of freedom does not stain.
> From those who live like leeches on the people's lives,
> We must take back our land again,
> America!

Do we know (perhaps from our own hard experiences) or can we recall or imagine some of the names that women and men who nurture such dreams have been called? Communist? Unpatriotic? Crazy? Naive? Unrealistic? Troublemaker? Agitator? The list is much longer, of course, and if the responses were confined simply to name-calling they would be easier to take. But as we have seen, in this country and abroad, anyone who vows seriously, publicly to "take back our land" from "those who live like leeches" off the lives of ordinary people is mounting a significant challenge to the status quo. It would be helpful to have our students reflect on what those words might have meant to Hughes when he wrote them (and later on when he was "investigated" by a congressional committee), what they might have meant to Martin Luther King, or what they mean now to Diane Nash, Bob Moses, Zoharah Simmons, Jesse Jackson, or those unknown, endangered, and courageous people who have vowed to fight the scourge of drugs in their local communities.

Whatever the meanings, it is likely that many of those people who have worked for the expansion of democracy and freedom in this land would feel the resonance of Hughes's powerful affirmations:

> O, yes,
> I say it plain,
> America never was America to me,
> And yet I swear this oath—
> America will be!

In many ways, the first, accusatory pronouncement has always been easier to make for those who have fought against injustice, segregation, and exploitation. They (we) have seen the great distance between the nation's magnificent potential and its present reality and they (we) have announced it loudly, "America never was America to me!" But Langston and the subsequent history of the movement for freedom and democracy have continually made it clear that while such an initial declaration is surely necessary, it is not sufficient.

Always, everywhere, the second statement, the more difficult

commitment, must follow: "America will be!" And this is precisely the point at which our students and all of us who sense
the inadequacies and injustices of the present and past must be
encouraged to cultivate not only indignation and anger, but
vision and hope. There is no humane future without them. So
Hughes is able to predict the coming of a more just and democratic America partly because,

> An ever-living seed,
> Its dream
> Lies deep in the heart of me.

The dream, the seed, the inner vision of a new nation are crucial.
And all of us who are willing to hear the call are challenged to
be the bearers, the nurturers, the waterers of the seed, the tree
of democracy that grows deep within our hearts.

So the question becomes more urgent: What is the America
that we dream, that we hope for, that we vow to help bring into
being? If Langston (and there are many Langstons) is right, then
ordinary people, whose lives still carry the life of all the early
workers and makers of America, bear the central responsibility
for the re-creation of the nation. And in the 1950s and 1960s,
while Langston was still alive, a generation of African-Americans and their white allies took up the challenge, crafted their
own versions of the dream, and committed their lives to its fulfillment. Indeed, the work was carried out with such fervor and
fullness that one of Langston's Harlem-based contemporaries,
Congressman Adam Clayton Powell, Jr., could stand in the midst
of that movement and declare, "We are the last revolutionaries
in America—the last transfusion of Freedom into the blood
stream of democracy."[5] What do our students know of all this,
think of all this? (What does the name of Powell or the Abys-
sinian Baptist Church mean to them?) What shall they do with
the idea of an America in process, an America that is not a
finished block of white granite, but is instead a malleable, mul-
ticolored gift of clay, still seeking, taking, giving shape, purpose
and direction? Even more important, how shall our students
respond to the challenge of Langston's dream, Langston's hope,
Powell's audacious declaration? Is it too old and out of style,

this call for dream keepers, reality shapers, life-giving revolutionaries? Is this a time of permanently broken wings? Are we in a place without healers?

Clearly neither Langston—sainted poet of democracy—nor any of those who made the movement that helped to transform the last years of his life, would settle for broken wings, aborted transfusions. Rather it is fascinating that Hughes, ending his poem in the 1930s, and the SCLC founders, opening their campaign in the 1950s, used the same religiously charged imperative—to *redeem*. In this supposedly more secular age, when we tend to be uncomfortable with the age-old memories of a religious spirit that "can make a way out of no way," we are still faced with Hughes's last words, his repeated challenge, his call for something resembling a religious fervor to rise up in our ordinary lives:

> We, the people, must redeem
> Our land, the mines, the plants, the rivers,
> The mountains and the endless plain—
> All, all the stretch of these great green states—
> And make America again.

Now, in the last decade of this amazing century, when the "impossible" has sprung up live among us again and again, it may be possible to rescue such words from mere sentimentality, to let them call us and our students from temptations toward nihilism and indifference.

How? Perhaps we begin simply by listening together to the incantatory "We, the people," allowing its vibrations to inhabit us, asking each other about its original source and its meaning in this setting. Gathering to struggle against our hesitation to dream "a more perfect union," we may begin to play, to imagine, to dare envision some of what Hughes was (is) calling for. Gathered together, protected in the common circle of our common work from our own fears of exposure, we might ask each other what it would mean to redeem or rescue our land, mother earth—from its erosion, from our chemical pollutants, our nuclear waste, our garbage and our greed. How might the land be rescued from its concentration into fewer and fewer hands, further and further away from the ordinary owners that Hughes identified?

The challenge is powerful, especially when we absorb into our beings the ecological, economic, and political developments that have taken place in America since Langston wrote, since he died in the mid-1960s. For now we must place new meaning on saving our mines, recovering and remaking our disappeared and dilapidated industrial plants, rescuing our dying rivers and our denuded mountains. Indeed, one of the most important responses to the call of the poem would be the expansion of our imaginations into the twenty-first century, bringing together the older, valiant dreams with all that we have seen and heard and felt since World War II regarding the struggle for democracy in America and across the globe.

Because we have been given years that were not his, it may be that one of the greatest challenges of the poem is to dream beyond Langston, to recapture the best dreams of Ella Baker, Huey Newton, and Harold Washington, to join forces with the dreams of Angela Davis, Jim Lawson, and Myrlie Evers. We need these dreams badly. These are marvelous sources of "advanced ideas" about democracy. So it is likely they would ask us to nurture the living seed within us and imagine how our cities might become safe, rewarding, and nourishing places, especially for our children. They would ask us to look somewhere between the isolation of the suburbs and the desolation of so many inner cities to dream a way of housing our people in places worthy of human dignity. They would encourage visions of a health system that would care for the needs of all our citizens. They would invite us to dream of schools (and neighborhoods) where children of all races, cultures, and economic groups are taught together to become responsible, compassionate citizens in an ever-expanding democratic society.

Taking up Hughes's unmentioned concerns, those who lived beyond him in a struggle for a new America would ask us to envision a nation free from the scourge of drugs, in both our personal and our collective lives. They would nurture dreams of a society in which training for nonviolent peacemaking took priority over military preparedness. They would call us to see a time when our relationships with other nations became more neighborly, more mutually supportive in the great multinational tasks we have to accomplish, ecologically, economically, and educationally. Remembering King, we know these rainbow warriors would urge us to dream a world in which our country works with others to seek economic justice for all the basic-goods producer nations who are now broken and exploited, a world where the United States takes the path of peace with all who are now threatened by our immature and unwise search for military-based "security."

Of course, continuously, persistently, all the heroic voices of struggle join Hughes in the common message to us: The work of discovering, exploring, developing this true America is our work—we, the people. Is it too much to ask our students to consider their role in this life-seeking action, both as dreamers and as workers? Are there noncoercive ways in which we may invite them to live beyond their presently defined self-limits, to participate in the re-creating tasks, beginning with themselves and stretching out to all "the endless plains," and to the wounded cities of our land? To dream such dreams, to grasp such visions, to live lives anchored in great hope is certainly to develop ourselves and our students in the best traditions of the freedom movement, of all movements for justice, compassion, and democracy. Eventually we discover that it is also the path to our best personal humanity.

Once, in the midst of the African independence struggles of the early 1960s, I remember hearing a poet of that continent say, "I am a citizen of a country that does not yet exist." Perhaps this is the paradox into which we must allow Hughes to move us. Together with those we teach, we are citizens of the America we now know, but we are needed to give our greatest energies to the creation of the country that does not yet exist. Hughes calls us to envision it, to encourage our students to use all the magnificent but underdeveloped faculties of their imagination to begin to bring it into being, to share that work with those who have gone before us. Ultimately Langston spoke both for our personal lives and for our nation when he wrote

Hold fast to dreams
For when dreams go
Life is a barren field
Frozen with snow.

The message is for all of us who teach. We are the nurturers, the encouragers of all the dreams, all the seeds deep in all the hearts where the future of a redeemed and rescued land now dwells. So we hold fast and see beneath the snow, always calling others to recognize their own magnificent possibilities, to see and plant and join our hope with theirs. Singing, saying in our dreams and our actions, America (Langston's and Malcolm's and Ella's and all the marchers' and mourners' and organizers') is possible, is necessary, is coming.

11

One Final, Soaring Hope

Building the Campgrounds of Renewal

As an adviser to the filmmaking team, I was privileged to see some of the earliest working images of the *Eyes on the Prize* series. Ever since then, I've been obsessed, sometimes overwhelmed, by a relentless vision, a wild and soaring hope: What if we could get some of our young sisters and brothers off the most dangerous streets, out of the drug-related traps of quick, apparently easy, bloodied money, away from the flashy, destructive models (both human and automotive), apart from their lethal weapons and their beepers, out of the crippled and often crippling schools, freed from the brutalizing cycle of the criminal justice system. If, with the help of these films, we could create and discover together a new set of personal, family, and social options for their lives. If.

Yes, I think, if we could perhaps find a way to convince a dozen, or twenty, or fifty of them, along with their most supportive, least despairing grandmothers, uncles, parents—whoever is ready to risk a new beginning, to provide the needed support. If we could journey together with such a group to John's Island or to Lincoln University, or to a campground in the Maine or Michigan woods, or even to a monastery or retreat center on the Pacific coast. And there, here, wherever, if we could gather the young people and some of their family members, together with half a dozen other serious, centered, creatively mature women and men to play, to work (perhaps even to meditate and pray), and to watch *Eyes on the Prize*, it might be possible to begin to break the deadly cycle.

In such a setting, with the fresh air of life intoxicating us, with demanding work to engage and reward us, with time for play and quietness, it might be possible to discover together a set of new life-affirming possibilities for some of them, for some of us. Indeed, in such an unfamiliar setting we might even stumble upon new models of teaching, learning, and hope, and set them loose across this nation like dancing tongues of fire, networks of purifying flame.

But first, before the fire: After the first few difficult, exploratory days, I see us sitting together, watching one segment of *Eyes* each day, discussing the films in small groups, working with the images and messages formally and informally, during meals and work and play. I hear us, feel us, moving continually toward the key questions: What did these earlier, historic experiences mean for the people who lived through them, and what meaning can we make for ourselves now, and in the days that follow these, the daunting days when we must leave this hidden place?

(By the way, I think I would begin with a group of African-American young people. Part of my reasoning is based on the fact that so much of the trouble of the larger society bursts out harder, sharper, clearer among them. I would begin there, too, because they are often in greatest, most vivid need, with so few resources available to them. I think I would start there because so many of the role models on the screen become fully accessible, perhaps inescapable, for them. Of course, I would also begin among such youngsters and their families because my own life experiences as a child of Harlem and the South Bronx have so often brought me so close to where they are, and I simply cannot pass them by. And yet, having thought and said all that, I still hesitate, for I am not fully at peace with such logical conclusions. Rather, I see and feel the powerful arguments for a multiracial gathering on our campground of renewal. It might be predominantly Black, but rich in other experiences of struggle and hope, especially among peoples of color. So I continue to wrestle with this part of the vision. Meanwhile, I trust I have already made it clear in the earlier essays how many ways there are for us to use the same materials to open new possibilities for all young people and their families, whatever their color and condition. Regardless of where I begin on the campground, my basic assumption of universal application remains the same.)

This is not the place to try to elaborate on the discussions, debates, and profound explorations that I know would emerge from these workshops in the woods, these vacations from the streets. (I say I *know* only because, like some of you, I have spent time among young persons such as these, opened opportunities — occasionally with a segment of *Eyes* — for their voices, fears, hopes, and wonderings to be heard. And the depths to which they have taken the discussions have often been stunning.) But could we begin here to imagine some of the ways in which elements of both parts of the *Eyes on the Prize* series might be brought together in serious engagement with the hard realities of their lives?

Early in the process, whatever else happened, we would surely introduce them to Mose Wright, allow them to begin to imagine what Mississippi had been like for him, let our young friends and their families talk about his real alternatives when the killers came to the door for his grandnephew, Emmett Till, reflect together on the sources of this man's courage when he pointed to Milam and Bryant in the open court. For some of the older family members these scenes may dislodge harsh and hidden memories of their own southern-based childhoods, or of summers spent sequestered in the crevices between the beauty and terror of that land. Perhaps some of them will remember with loving appreciation their own Mose Wrights, men and women of great, rough-hewn dignity, caught in hard and threatening places, striving to maintain integrity, safety, and sanity. And what discussions of family and womanhood might flow out of the consideration of Mamie Till Bradley, and of *her* mother, and their firm determination to open their sorrow and indignation to the world?

In the same way it would be crucial for Rosa Parks (perhaps even in person) to be present for them, to help them learn — some for the first time — the meaning of living with and against Jim Crow, and the great risks and brutal costs that were necessary before its legal realities could be eliminated, just in time for them to be born (free from the terrible constraints that their foreparents knew, but now tragically imprisoned in lives that have not yet found anything to be free *for*). Let them watch King and ask why he left the relative security of his middle-class Baptist pastorate to risk his own life and the safety of his family to respond to the compelling, freedom-seeking call of the rising people. And certainly, we can begin to savor the kinds of struggles that could take place among us when we explore together King's stirring invitation to the way of collective nonviolent resistance, and his little family's early personal decision to give up the gun they had kept in their house for protection. Was that part of their own movement toward freedom? And what does such freedom mean now for the gun-filled streets of Dorchester, of Lawndale, of L.A.? Is there any place for courageous, persistent nonviolent soldiers in our own time?

The questions abound. Would our young people grasp the great daring and high hopes of the sit-ins and freedom rides? Could we introduce them to role-playing to demonstrate the disciplined courage that it took for young women and men to refuse to allow their opponents to set the familiar agendas of violence-for-violence? Who would play the roles of the courageous white students who came to risk their lives and shed their blood in the cause? It would be revealing to hear the discussion in the role-play groups concerning the decisions and commitments which finally led the Nashville contingent of college students who had given leadership to the 1960 sit-ins there to go forward again in 1961, determined to reclaim for democracy the brutal ground of the Montgomery, Alabama, bus station. The question of what our young people and their family members think they might have done later, with the mob surrounding the church, would certainly provoke intense and moving responses. At some point someone, perhaps one of the grandmothers present, could also call our attention to all those "square" Christian women in that endangered church building, many with their flowered hats and white gloves on, bravely singing "Leaning on the Everlasting Arms." What would they make of that? What do we make of it? (Remembering that powerful church scene, I can hardly wait to see who will volunteer to play the role of Fred Shuttlesworth, beaten and bombed in the freedom cause more than once, courageously, foolhardily, pushing his way from the outside, through the mob and the police, clearing the path for himself and James Farmer to join the beleaguered folks on the inside. How do you explain that from the South Bronx or from Grand Boulevard in Detroit?) Will there be anyone in the families to testify to the ways in which religion can empower, encourage, and discipline people to walk through fire on the way to freedom?

Then, for the young people who have asked us, seriously, sadly, "And who was Malcolm the Tenth, anyway?" this would present a marvelous opportunity. Here, perhaps, is a life that allows them (us?) no excuses, no escapes. Detroit Red, child of a cruelly broken home, experienced with destructive white enemies and paternalistic helpers, exposed to a wild life on the streets, dope user and dealer, immersed in crime of many kinds, with memories of seven long years in prison. And out of it all emerges a man transformed (one of a growing company for whom prison becomes a fiery furnace for annealing and conversion), a man who, in the words of poet Robert Hayden, "became much more than there was time for him to be."[1] What will they (we) do with Malcolm, with the Muslims, with the world of Islam, with El-Hajj Malik? More important, what will we do with *them*, the children of Malcolm, the offspring of Malik who gather with us in the woods? Will someone help them, guide them to receive all the gifts brought by *Eyes*, help them perhaps to claim for themselves the time that Malcolm did not have? Will they find tough, loving, compassionate teachers, as Malcolm eventually did? Will there be relatives to share new life with them? And who will answer the other questions: Does our society— and its teachers—look forward to the second coming of many Malcolms, many Martins, many Ella Bakers and Fannie Lou Hamers? And what is the future of this nation if there is no space, no time for the women- and men-children of the streets to find their truest maturity, their temporarily hidden redemptive purpose, identity, and hope?

Once more, questions abound, even as we imagine our young folks and their families watching the encounter between C. T. Vivian and Sheriff Jim Clark and his deputies on the steps of the courthouse in Selma. What empowers a Black man in 1965 to stand in front of a group of white law officers (with all the terrible history of such encounters written in his bones) and lecture them on the meaning of the Nuremberg tribunals and on personal accountability for their consciences? And how did C.T. get up again from the ground after taking a combination punch and billy stick blow? How did he stand, refusing to run, refusing to be quiet, indeed insisting on paraphrasing Winston Churchill ("What kind of people are you?") to the threatened, threatening keepers of Selma's old law and order?

What will be their responses when *Eyes on the Prize* helps to make it clear that C.T. rising from the ground, that the people returning to the Edmund Pettus Bridge, armed only with courage, to face again the officers who had recently beaten them to the earth, that Viola Liuzzo singing a freedom song as she saw the assassins' car approaching her vehicle on the road, that Jimmy Lee Jackson dying for his mother and his people—that these and many more are all part of the price that was paid for the expansion of their possibilities beyond the limits of the streets? (Of course, they will also see eventually that all these were part of the path of human courage, sacrifice, and hope that made it possible for their hero, Jesse Jackson, to have a podium from which he could speak to the world. Indeed, what we all eventually discover is that the same spirit, the same courage, the same sacrifice, the same hope also made it possible for Nelson Mandela to emerge from twenty-seven years in prison as the unofficial president of South Africa.) When they discover the costs that others have paid to begin to break open certain doors for them, will they begin to re-vision themselves and their best possibilities?

It may be that we will be faced with even more piercing, probing questions when we move with our young friends and their families into the *Eyes II* presentation of some of the northern phases of the great struggle for democracy. To share their responses to the fury of the white mobs of the Chicago suburbs, the burning of Detroit, and the rise of the Panthers will surely be worth all the effort it will take to develop the setting. For the opportunities those stories provide for ventilation, reflection, and powerful re-visioning are unlimited. The conversations across generational lines will likely be invaluable, both upsetting and healing. We may wonder, for instance, about what differences they will see between the defiance of the system that Fred Hampton of the Chicago Panthers represented and that of the leading drug dealers in their communities. Will they recognize differences between the guns of the Panthers and the guns of the gangs? Perhaps even more important, will they see the similarities? Do we?

Of course, the camp will not be complete without the marvelous scenes of Muhammad Ali. Perhaps it will be necessary to include a set of boxing gloves (very well padded ones, of course) in our equipment. If we are able to get past that stage, it will be good to see our young people, male and female, respond to Ali, absorb the significant levels of personal and racial meaning that flow beneath his marvelous humor. In fact, there may even be time to re-enact the earthshaking Ali-Maynard Jackson engagement from *Eyes II*. What better way for them to be introduced to the positive possibilities of inspired and inspiring electoral politics, to the world that the movement helped open up for Shirley Chisholm, Jesse Jackson, Harold Washington, David Dinkins, Douglas Wilder, and many more. If we could encourage them to add their own names to the longer list, if together we could imagine their faces on some future screen of honor, a great dream might begin to rise.

But there is one other segment of *Eyes* that must be seen at the retreat, one less dreamlike sequence for this quiet place of re-visioning. Attica. Here the intention will not be to frighten but to bring into focus for frank discussion the world of the prison and the role it has played in our lives as African-American people. It will not be an unfamiliar territory for some of our extended family, but it needs to be seen again. Perhaps Frank "Big Black" Smith could visit the camp, could be heard and seen and touched in discussions and basketball games. Perhaps he could simply tell his story, like a great big uncle whose love for them is palpable, who seeks to call them away from the paths of self-destruction to the unmistakably creative powers inherent in their lives.

Imagining the presence of our brother from Attica sets loose scores of other possibilities, suggests many other visitors. I wonder how our extended family would respond to the inspiriting, compassionate presence of Sonia Sanchez and Gwendolyn Brooks and others like them. Would the group understand the calls from Amiri Baraka, Angela Davis, and Haki Madhubuti, from June Johnson and Ben Chavis, calls to rethink the choices they have made, to consider far better uses for their lives? Who knows? June's powerful, dangerous, and courageous experiences as a teen-age freedom fighter in Mississippi, as a committed worker for democracy now, just may come through.

Perhaps when they hear the Last Poets and recognize some of the movement foundations for rap and hip-hop, perhaps they will respond to the calling from their roots, dare to write some poetry of their own, explore the deeper, hidden fountains of their humanity. Perhaps when our discussions of the series open them to Nkrumah and Nyerere, to Winnie and Nelson Mandela, and to the great world of explosive democratic aspirations beyond these shores, it may be they will find even more heroes, new models, new hopes. And what then? When the struggles engendered by *Eyes* begin to rage within the deep places of their lives, someone will need to be present for them. That is why we invited the families. That is why we came ourselves. Thus we are reminded that when we determine to explore the most profound levels of human experiences and possibilities, the role of the teacher is expanded in grand and awesome ways. We become part of the extended family, part of the healing company of witnesses.

Then, in the wildness of my dreams, after we have seen the entire *Eyes on the Prize* series together, the students would be asked to write letters to both the living and the departed makers of that history. They are asked especially to write to the people who meant something to them as they watched the films, to people who raised fundamental questions or great hopes for them. So hours would be given to the sometimes painful task, perhaps now made a bit more bearable by new motivation, a sense of great relevance, and the presence of compassionate teachers and supportive relatives. Letters to Mrs. Parks, to Angela Davis, to Medgar Evers, to Dr. King, to James Chaney and his courageous passengers in the station wagon, Goodman and Schwerner, to James Reeb, Huey Newton, Unita Blackwell, Fred Shuttlesworth, Mose Wright and the nuns on their way to

Selma (on their way to new freedoms and new challenges in their own lives), to Coretta King and Jo Ann Robinson, to the men of Attica, to Ella Baker and Fred Hampton, to Paul Robeson and many more. They would be asked to write letters from their hearts to the men and women who kept their eyes on the prize for themselves and for us. The only prescribed part of the letters would be an expression of gratitude for what the addressees did, gave, created, and envisioned on behalf of us all. The rest of the letter would be whatever they wanted to say, ask, present.

This is more than an exercise. It is meant to call the young people into communion with their Black and white ancestors in the struggle for a more humane American nation. It assumes that we are less than human when we do not acknowledge those who prepared the way for us, often at great cost, when we do not give thought to how we shall help clear the path for others yet unborn. Something tells us that one of the deep wounds of the life of the streets (indeed, these wounds are inflicted on streets and malls of many colors and classes in this nation) is that the young people have been separated from both their past and their future, leaving a vast and aching void, often to be filled with nothing more than the most destructive values of the society. *Eyes on the Prize* opens a way for such young people to re-enter the humanizing flow of history, to consider the possibility that there is purpose and meaning for their lives far beyond the terror and temptations of their immediate situation.

Actually, as the vision soars, the letters are answered by both the living and the dead. (Creative, sensitive teachers can often serve as exciting amanuenses.) As a matter of fact, as indicated above, I envision many of the long-distance runners of this post–World War II freedom struggle, the prize-seekers and creators, coming to where the young people are, listening to them, sharing with them, encouraging them to believe that there are real alternatives for their lives.

However, it may be that some of the most important letters, the most crucial encounters, will be closer at hand. Somewhere in the campground process, after we have tried to learn, teach, model, and encourage the uses of silence, the power of mediation, the many varieties of prayer and reflection, the therapies of gratitude, at such points new visions may arise. Some young people may make new discoveries concerning their families, will see in this setting great strengths and feel deep love that they had not been free to recognize before. Here, we would encourage not only letters of gratitude and rethinking, but specific acts of appreciation directed toward those family members who have come to share the experience, who have offered so much teaching from their own lives. Small gifts created and given, flowers presented, poems and rap songs composed and shared in honor of those who have stood by them. Letters written to those who wanted to come but could not. Actions that might have seemed unthinkable before may now be recognized as pathways toward the expansion of our hearts, toward the healing and building of our humanity.

As a result, as a cause of such actions, one other level of communion will likely open to us. We will probably discover together and alone the healing, empowering spirit that lives within us all, the force that is always with us, the great connective presence which eventually draws us to such deep levels of our being that we cannot easily escape our rendezvous with all other life and existence. For many of us on the campground, such discovery (or rediscovery) may lead to a new path, may allow us to recognize that we are all capable of the kind of magnificent lives that have flashed before us on the screen. In the presence of this discovery, poems and songs, letters and love dances to ourselves, to the divine within us, to the life force in the trees and skies, lakes and flowers, rocks and earth will surely and appropriately overflow.

This is the healing creativity that our fractured, searching world now exhibits and requires everywhere. As we begin to discover it in the midst of the extended healing family, as we experience restructuring of our selfhood along with others, hope begins to grow. As a result, coming to the end of the retreat, preparing to leave the campground, some of our young people and their family members may be filled with certain understandable questions and concerns about how and where they can best nurture the seeds they have newly discovered within themselves. Some members of the community of hope will sense a need for fresh beginnings. Perhaps they will want to find new settings where they may prepare themselves more fully for their eventual return to the streets of their youth, equipped with skills, courage, hope, and direction, ready to be present for others like themselves, already building new campgrounds in their minds.

And this may be the point at which the wildest hope of all rises out of the series. For I would think and dream that there might be women and men and families who are working on their own development and who see their present role in the historic movement as one of opening themselves and their settings to such young people, to families of new beginnings. When some members of our campground community decide that they really want to try a new start, find a point of entry into the kind of life-affirming history they have seen in *Eyes*, and when they are convinced that they must have an alternative setting in which to begin again, I look for many hands, arms, lives to open wide.

At this point I have no idea where such a vision ends and "reality" begins. Perhaps such things no longer matter. It may be that all we need to know is that there are tremendous healing, transformative powers bound up in *Eyes on the Prize*, waiting to be released into the lives of even those persons we consider most desperately at risk in our society. It may be that all we need to hear now is that there are hidden campgrounds of hope and many creative resources waiting for committed teachers, teachers who are ready to call forth the impossible, from ourselves and everyone else.

Clearly, my rudimentary vision of how all this might happen is only a suggestion, an invitation to thousands of teachers everywhere to create your own settings, your own campgrounds of renewal, to form your own extended family, to take your own risks—to experience great joy.

12

Letters to Teachers in Religious Communities and Institutions

Dear Friends,

Although the essays in this book are addressed to teachers of every kind, located in a broad variety of settings, there was no way that I could complete the work without sharing some very specific expressions of memory, hope, and concern with those of you who are teaching in religious and other spiritually grounded situations.

As I reflect on why I am moved to close out this endeavor with a word to you, it seems to me that at least one of the obvious motivations is firmly embedded in my own most personal history. In addition to my mother, who was constantly teaching and encouraging, the first teachers I remember were in the little Harlem church where so much of my early life, vision, and commitment was nurtured. So my movement toward you in your synagogues and mosques, in your churches, temples, and dharma retreats, in your storefronts and basilicas, is a natural one, shaped by many early habits of the heart.

But far more than the force of habit and the call of memories are at work here, friends. I come naturally to a closing in your company because so many of the seminal issues in this sacred history of African-American transformative struggle are familiar to you, beginning with the idea of a "saving history" itself.

I am drawn to you, because you have been constantly teaching in words and actions the connections between convictions and commitments, the interplay between faith and works, the seamless junction between love of God and love of neighbor. I am here because I believe that no movement that seeks to lift the level of human hope, that calls forth the great creative potentials within us, no history filled with human struggles for justice, truth, and new community can be foreign to your own most faithful agenda. I come to you because the raising of rejected stones, the empowerment of the weak and exploited, the establishment of jubilee generations, the healing of broken human connections are as central to your best religious teachings as they are to the heart of the freedom movement.

Do you see? I come because it seems clear to me that you will receive and recognize as saints, martyrs, gurus, and bodhisattvas those women, men, and children who gave their lives in the cause of human freedom, therefore in the cause of truth. For their examples surely affirm and modernize your ancient teachings concerning the focal power of sacrifice, the necessity of innocent blood, and the inevitability of pain and tears in the creation of new joy, laughter, and hope. In other words, it may be that I come to you now seeking nothing more or less than affirmation for my own fierce conviction that the Afro-American freedom movement at its best and deepest levels has always been a splendid struggle of the soul, both personal and collective.

To say that, of course, is to say nothing original. Rather, it is to join with all the men and women among us who have long recognized the unmistakably religious meanings of our relentless movement through generations of searing pain and unquenchable hope. And here, too, is still another reason for my turning to you. For many of you, dear sisters and brothers, were actually the very solid ground on which the freedom movement was built. Your church buildings provided essential meeting places across the South (where you sometimes paid the price in fire and death). Your congregations were the sinew and substance of the people in struggle. Your songs and spirituality—often shaped long ago in the cauldron of slavery—provided solace and strength for those who marched to meet the modern foes of freedom. You were the human bedrock of this movement, and I come to you recognizing the awesome responsibility for the future that accompanies so powerful a history, so profound a contribution.

In the same way, I turn to you daughters and sons of the churches and synagogues who often sent strong and faithful representatives to the front lines of the freedom movement. (Of course, I know some of you had to steal away from your home congregations to join us, while others were condemned for such "political" involvement. But now we can place all that behind us and go on to claim a new history by committing ourselves to a new future.) You were more than token whites. At your best you were comrades in a holy quest, and the earth still carries the blessing of your companions' blood—watering, witnessing. In those days you recognized the meaning and universal promise of the movement, for it reflected the best scriptures and commitments that had shaped your lives. It gave substance to your own sometimes flagging hopes for democracy, for the communities of faith, for humankind. At times it even resurrected your expiring faith in the constant movement of the divine and loving presence among us.

I saw you on those marching lines of blessing, confrontation, and danger. I recognized you in your surplices and cassocks, with your yarmulkes and in your steadily changing nun's habits. I saw you in robes, bearing banners and crosses, carrying the Torah, and heavy coffins, and other holy objects. Sometimes you were recognizable only by the radiance of your hope. I saw you. (Toward the end of the 1960s I recognized your forever neat and dark suits and bow ties and the covered heads of our sisters as you drew nearer to the marching lines, offering both your loving support and your searing critique, in Malcolm's hallowed spirit. Even you who were then thousands of miles away in Southeast Asia, living under the terror of our military fire and bombs, I heard your bells and gongs and chanted prayers, offered up on our behalf. In the same way I was moved by you who called throughout the day, beseeching the All-Merciful One for truth to prevail, whose prayers ascended like the incense of Egypt. I heard you, and felt the fires of your compassion and your anger.)

I pause here in your camp, with all its varied signs and sounds of faith and hope, because this is also my camp, and because this African-American epic is your story, the particular and universal story of captivity and struggle, of enslavement and deliverance, the account of long wandering and searching for clouds and fiery pillars and holy rivers. This freedom movement history is your story, my story, our story of sacrificed heroes and the call to life instead of murderous revenge. This is your singing of songs of hope and of lives transformed. This is your story of battles lost and won and still contested—both on the streets and in our hearts—but not forgotten. I am here because ultimately this is your own testimony concerning totally unexpected, amazing grace, welling up, pouring in, from sources long considered dead.

In other words, my friends in the religious communities, I stop here to affirm not only our shared and sacred history in this land, but to urge you to consider the destiny that is still ours to create together. For deep within me, I believe that the story of our great Black-led struggle for democracy and wholeness, for justice and truth, for the divinity of our humanity, is not simply an interesting side event to the central narratives of our various faith communities. No, I am convinced that this American odyssey has thrust its way with blood and hope into the central archetypal accounts of humankind's great hunger and thirst for righteousness, justice, and peace. In all of its voices and silences it testifies to the fact that we are forging a common hope, a new story, whose stanzas are still evolving and exploding in people's struggles for democracy, and for our best possible selves, all over the world.

Because we are teachers we must teach. Because this is *our* story we must surely take responsibility for telling it. Because it is written in blood and undergirded by lives of extraordinary dedication it must not be forgotten. Because it speaks to needs that are often deeply hidden but nonetheless ubiquitous in their presence, our healing vocation is clear. Creatively sharing it with the children of our communities, whose hunger for authentic life goes deep, opening it to the adults whose daily experience too often has no transformative meaning—from this base we begin. Nurturing each other, remembering that both our history and our destiny are sealed with sacrifice and hope, we are drawn by the vision of a new land, moving toward the deeper common ground from which we all first came.

Now, remembering how much of our life and hope arises out of our encounters with the personal and the concrete, I take the liberty and the privilege of addressing certain words to each of you in your specific settings of faith.

I. To My Sisters and Brothers in the Black Churches of the United States

As the old folks used to say, the Lord has laid his hands on us — and that is an awesome reality. We have been the primary bearers of this powerful epic, the great, continuing story of struggle, deliverance, harsh challenges, and new hope. In a way that is unique but not exclusive, this is *our* story, continuously rising from the unfathomable depths of our foreparents' struggle for freedom.

How shall we honor them? As one suggestion, can we begin to consider what it might be like to take this story of God's saving acts in our nation's history (in our people's history) and move it firmly toward the center of worship, praise, and commitment in our congregations? What would it be like for faces and scenes from the great transformative freedom struggles of the South and North to begin to appear in our stained glass, at our altars, on our fans, in our Sunday school materials? Perhaps, dear sisters and brothers, it is time to balance our stirring proclamation of God's saving action in long-ago Canaan with words of deliverance from today's Birmingham, Chicago, and Los Angeles.

Indeed, we may even need to experiment with the uses of a liturgical year in ways much richer than most of our African-American churches normally observe. For instance, January might be focused, as it is now, on King's birthday, but February could be much more than a generalized Black History month. It might include our celebration of the rise of the redemptive sit-in movement, or recognize the birthdays of freedom saints like Frederick Douglass or W.E.B. Du Bois. It would help us properly to appreciate the life and mourn the death of our faithful brother, Malcolm X. Such rich materials are available for our use throughout the year. So no matter how such a resource might be utilized, it would be important for congregations, seminaries, or jurisdictions to commission the research and publication of these liturgies. Then, guided into new encounters with our own sacred history, we might sing with new voices and some new words, "Faith of our parents living still, we will be true to thee 'til death."

In the same way, what if our Sunday schools took a resource like the *Eyes on the Prize* television series, used the videos so that they extended over perhaps twenty-six weeks, and at each appropriate point allowed the profoundly religious and often disturbing messages of the series to open new space in the minds and hearts of our students? What vibrations and discussions would that create in the local neighborhood, in the women's missionary society, in the April and September and November and all the other birthday clubs of the congregation? For an example, can we imagine members of the twelve birthday clubs (and other groups like them could use similar strategies) digging deeply into the resources of our revitalized church libraries and discovering those martyrs and heroes of our freedom movement who were born or who died in their club's month? Eventually, at each week's worship service it might be possible to hear a presentation from the clubs, honoring the heroes of our faith. Or we might see a dramatic re-enactment of some significant movement event, with old and new songs bursting out all around us.

By such paths we may discover new ways to act on our stated belief that God still has more light to break forth to us, that the sacred canon of our faith was not closed before we children of Africa in America entered on the modern Christian scene. Through such study and celebration we may say to ourselves and our children that the faithful witnesses who were our fathers, mothers, and grandparents surely pleased God in the twentieth century no less than those women and men included in the powerful list of saints, martyrs, and other beloved witnesses who appear in the Biblical Letter to the Hebrews. Indeed, isn't it time we made some new lists? For unless we nurture the memory of their words and deeds, how else shall we remember the radiant black cloud of witnesses who now sing and shout all

around us, "We'll never turn back . . . until we've all been freed."
What a list! When we have written and spoken their names,
names like Martin King and Fannie Lou Hamer, Amzie Moore,
Malcolm X and Medgar Evers, Ruby Doris Robinson and Clarence Jordan, C. B. and Slater King and Viola Liuzzo, Ella Baker
and Herbert Lee, Mickey Schwerner and Jimmy Lee Jackson,
James Chaney and Jonathan Daniels—when we have folded
such names into our bosoms and into our minds, we will then
have only begun the list. So teachers, preachers, let the names
be read from the pulpits and their deeds be molded into new
songs for the choirs and congregations. Have the children memorize the names and recite the words. Let us create pageants
and plays and local television dramas to tell their story, how
they overcame. Let the pastors and priests hold forth in the
pulpit on the books of their lives. Let their names be engraved
into the cornerstones of the new community centers and clinics
that we will establish in the heart of the most needy neighborhoods of our land. Let our annual revivals carry the spirits of
the faithful heroes out into the streets of our cities so that we
may be helped to proclaim and manifest liberation and real hope
for us all.

How else shall "a new earth rise" among us? How else shall
"another world be born"? Wasn't Margaret Walker, daughter
of a Methodist pastor, talking to us, teachers, believers, when
she declared, "Let a second generation full of courage issue
forth . . . let a people loving freedom come to birth"?[1] Who will
nurture them, who will water the trees, if not us? For whatever
the intentions or the audience of Ms. Walker, we recognize her
good news when we hear it. And at the heart of the Good News
for this historical time is our discovery that there is, indeed, a
courageous, freedom-loving, spirit-filled generation of young
and older Black church folk who are getting prepared to call,
join, and share leadership with their sisters and brothers of every
faith (and hope) and ancestry, as we take on the personal and
structural challenges the twentieth century has produced in the
United States and beyond.

That is why we need the renewed and renewing freedom
church, beginning with the freeing of our spirits, and our vision,
grounded in the freedom we shall win from our fears. Then we

will celebrate the modern saints and their struggles in the coming revival time because we need the witnesses. To do the work of this age we shall need every manifestation of the courageous spirit of the great cloud of witnesses in our lives, every movement of amazing grace, every practice of spiritual disciplines. As we take up our own next stages of the long struggle for a liberating faith and a just society ("Must I be wafted to the skies on flowery beds of ease?"), we shall need these precious memories.

Surrounded by such a host, encouraged by the faith of our foreparents, we can move toward the streets of Philadelphia, the board rooms of New York, the gang-war fronts of Los Angeles and Chicago, the crack-house doors across the land, the classrooms (where we must create and become new, humane scientists, new city planners, well-trained and intuitive healers, compassionate political analysts, creative and fearless teachers, and everything else we need). Inspired by those who fought the battles of hope before us, we can stand in the AIDS clinics, with the abused and battered family members, in the homeless shelters, organizing men and women to challenge any uncaring and uncreative ways of Pentagons, Congresses, and city halls, mobilizing the unemployed, with all the endangered young people in their terrible and beautiful middle passage, working in solidarity with Native Americans and Latinos, with Asians and white friends, with all of our sisters and brothers. In every such setting, and many more, the need is great for women and men who embody the epic story in their lives, who love God and freedom, people and justice, more than they love a private version of "making it" in the nation's meandering and dangerous mainstream. In others words, friends, we need you and your students.

The potential is there in all the people we teach. Please challenge them. Nurture them. Open the way. For all these tasks and these students, young and old, let there be new ecumenical mass meetings, gathering our churches on common, troubled, urban ground to create a united front of struggle for the new justice, the new humanity. Let there be magnificently focused and inspiring sermons, based in our saving history. Let there be new all-night prayer and organizing sessions. Let us help each other open ourselves to new disciplines of the spirit, to new risks and dangers on behalf of "another world" and its birth among us. There is no escape from such a calling (unless we are determined). The Lord has laid strong hands on us. Let us celebrate. Let us petition. Let us prepare ourselves. As our spirituals-quoting brother Martin used to remind us, "The battle is in our hands."

II. To My Sisters and Brothers in the Predominantly White Churches

Because we have learned that our lives are ultimately one, especially because we have jointly purchased that truth through many perilous struggles in the recent movement decades, you know that the epic story of the Black-led struggle for the expansion of democracy and humanity in this country is also your story. So please share as deeply as you wish in the message directed to the African-American churches; and even as you open yourselves to receive it and engage its challenges you may find that your capacities, your abilities to respond, are far greater than you dreamed. (That's what your sisters and brothers discovered when they entered the ranks of the freedom movement in the 1960s. Some of them even found out that they could sing— and shout—and dance—sometimes all at once!)

Not long ago, I sensed such possibilities as I spoke from the pulpit of a predominantly white church where carefully sculpted busts of Martin King and Mahatma Gandhi, among others, occupied places of honor in the pulpit area, silently proclaiming to all who gathered in that place the magnificent movement of God's justice-seeking love in the twentieth century. It felt good to be there, and I anticipated how healing it would be for such saints as Harriet and Fannie Lou and Martin to grace the walls and windows of all our houses of worship—and our homes. They would announce our joint claim and commitment to the great freedom story. They would proclaim the great ability to respond in compassion and courage which inhabits all of our lives.

Against that background of solidarity and hope, there are a few other things that I would say directly and briefly to you:

• Please listen to your women. And, women, please listen to your deepest selves. For the vision, energy, and challenge of committed women may be the closest, broadest-based approximation that the white churches can have to the African-American experience of struggle and hope. The women bring a challenge from within the mainstream that could be saving and healing. And, women of the white churches, if you can modernize your long-held, heartfelt connections to Harriet Tubman, Sojourner Truth, and Ida B. Wells-Barnett, if you can approach Johnetta Cole, Angela Davis, Yvonne Delk, Diane Nash, Zoharah Simmons, Sonia Sanchez, and many, many other Black women of conscience and power as equal partners (and sometimes teachers) in the continuing struggle, then a great redemptive opportunity lies in store for us all.

• Listen to your children. Rosemarie and I spend significant periods of time sharing the story of the American freedom epic with the high school and college students of your congregations. Like the white young people we met in the South in the 1960s, many of these offspring of your communities have a deep hunger and thirst for a just and righteous society, and for personal lives filled with truth and integrity. They need the time and space to express these yearnings, to have them affirmed and encouraged. They long for guidance into lives and actions that can connect them to the long struggle for the expansion and correction of democracy. They are also prepared to consider the great costs that always accompany the quest for new life. In order to keep on moving forward they need structures in home, church, and community which will reinforce their own fundamental intuition that the way of selfish material accumulation and careerism is not the way of discipleship or compassionate humanity. They also need alternatives for the visioning of their lives and their vocations.

They are ready to respond. But they also need pastors, priestess grandmothers and aunts and fathers and mothers and role models who will emerge out of their own congregations and households and call them to the realization of their best and most beautiful human possibilities. Please go with them to the learning trees of the Black freedom movement story. Sit with them in gratitude, awe, and power. Then encourage them to follow the dreams and commitments that always arise out of communion with such powerful places. Go with them as they claim and expand the faith-full story into our own time. Go with them.

• Please move beyond fascination with "the resurgence of racism." Recently I have been asked by many white church-related groups to speak to that topic. In a way the concern is a bit trendy. In a way it is very factually based. (Of course, even the facts have become more complex in light of the significant white votes for Black candidates in the most recent American elections.) But more often it does not go beyond the facts to the truth of our struggle, of all human struggles for revival. For what we are seeing in our nation is not so much a resurgence of racism as a result of what happens when a powerful pro-democracy momentum is slowed, diverted, or temporarily halted in the movement for social transformation. In human society as in other manifestations of nature, there is apparently no real stasis. Either we go forward or we go backward. We cannot stand still. That was surely the reality in Martin King's mind when he ended the triumphal (and costly) march from Selma to Montgomery in 1965 with the call, "We must keep going."

At various points along the way, from the end of the 1960s to the close of the 1970s, many of us in the churches and else-where decided not to keep going in this risky, demanding, and unpredictable movement for the expansion of American democracy. (Or we thought we could put it on "automatic," or "cruise control," and all would be well.) In the white churches there were fears and hurts raised by the call for Black Power and the move toward a new focus on assertiveness and solidarity within the African-American communities. There was also a sense of loss and confusion engendered by the political assassinations of Martin King and Robert Kennedy, within months of each other. Of course, some Christians were never sure how much they wanted democracy expanded, and with which kinds of "worthy" people it should be shared. Perhaps even more significantly, many of us were not prepared for the temporary and sometimes profound disorder that often seems a natural accompani-ment to the transitional movement from a system of unjust, dehumanizing, and exploitative "order" to a new, previously unexplored level of democratic human possibilities and respon-sibilities. The scent of anarchy seemed too close, too sharp, as we forgot that structural injustice is itself the greatest anarchical attack on the compassionate order of divine community.

Now we have learned anew why King was constantly quoting the words so often attributed to Edmund Burke: "The only thing necessary for the triumph of evil is for good men to do nothing." The decision is in our hands. You have seen some of the ways it faces the Black churches. Here, *you* are being asked if you will use your whiteness, your relative economic and physical security, and your access to persons of conventional power to re-engage and deepen the struggle for the expansion of democracy, the quest for justice and truth—or will you try to hide from a storm that is ultimately relentless in its movement, avoiding a powerfully loving justice which seeks only our healing?

You know the continuing frontiers for justice, for community, for the redemption of the soul of our nation. You realize that the issues of militarism, materialism, racism, and poverty did not die when King was assassinated. You have seen sexism, homophobia, and fear of the poor and of the rising tide of color at their worst. You have witnessed our willingness to allow the anti-democratic, bullying military interventions of our government to go unchallenged. I trust you also know that it is only as we decide to keep going toward a more just and humane society (with all the personal, fiscal, and psychic costs involved) that we can build the strength to love, receive the power to carry on the struggle. Only then will we draw each other from behind our barricades and reconstitute a lively, expanding rainbow wedge, a force for the creation of new political, cultural, ecological, and economic realities. A new community of democratic hope and action still awaits its builders.

As you remember, there was a time when we had so allowed our churches to become outposts of anti-democratic privilege, irresponsible piety, and white American nationalism that the cry of "God is dead" seemed very logical to many ears—that is, if mainstream Christians were to be primary evidences of divine existence. Just at that moment the awesome, religiously fueled power of the Black freedom movement broke in and mooted the question of God's life or death. But now, as each generation works out its own salvation, the white churches are offered life and death choices again. You/we can choose to affirm and develop the magnificently perilous story you helped to create, or you can turn away to other pursuits and specialize in sophisticated ways to leave your children "secure," without a story worthy of our faith, without a life worthy of their living. God be with you in your choices, sisters and brothers. And so will I.

III. To My Sisters and Brothers in the Churches of the Other Peoples of Color

One of the great challenges of living through and participating in a period of profound social transformation is facing the special demands that it places upon those of us who think we have been on the side of the angels in the course of the struggle. I faced such a demand as I began to think about these letters. For I had to keep reminding myself that our post–World War II freedom movement had done much to help open a new set of realities in this country that these letters simply could not ignore. For instance, it is more clear than ever before that the old dualistic discussion of racial issues in America, which tended to include only Black and white participants, was inadequate in the 1940s and is unforgivably misleading now. In the same way, the traditional tripartite definition of our religious "pluralism" as Protestant, Catholic, and Jew is also outmoded. Indeed, it had been outmoded when it was first introduced, focusing as it did almost exclusively on white Protestants, white Catholics, and European-derived Jews.

What this meant for me was that letters that were addressed to the white and Black Christian communities did not by any means exhaust the possibilities of the Christian faith in this country, not even the range of the Christian churches. So I want to make sure that we meet each other as directly as possible. Reaching beyond the limited categories of Black and white, I address this letter especially to you sisters and brothers who are members of the churches where people of color (other than African-Americans) are represented in large proportions.

I recognize the great variety of believers this covers, including Native Americans who were on this land before the first Christian churches anywhere were born, and Hispanics/Chicanos/Latinos, who have known a great mix of Protestant and Catholic experiences over the centuries. I also recognize a rich variety of Asians, as well as sisters and brothers from the Pacific Islands and from the African diaspora in the Caribbean and Latin America. I realize, as well, that I am missing too many, but I trust that all those missing on the list will know that you are present in my best intentions.

As you have gathered from the essays in this book, I am very grateful for our coming together on these shores. Both because of and in spite of the often cruel paths we have had to take, I see our assembly as one of the most important and spiritually powerful events of the twentieth century. That is why I sometimes cannot avoid using traditional terms to speak of the movement of God among us, cannot avoid wondering, envisioning, what the great Gatherer has in mind for us. So I am writing to you now not only in a mode of gratitude, but as one who watches on the battlements of the new city for the coming of the morning sun, a coming you have anticipated and in which some of us have participated. Indeed, it is my belief that you have arrived here, you have re-entered this history, you have re-established your ancient claims to our great mother at a time of signal importance for us all.

Our nation, profoundly affected by the post–World War II struggle for freedom, justice, and democracy, is now at a crossroads, and you, and we, are faced with crucial choices, as citizens of the country, as children of God. Moved by our own divinely sparked inner imperatives, responding to the burgeoning worldwide quest for democracy, we citizens of the United States, we church members, may claim the freedom movement as our own and keep going. We may continue exploring, experimenting with those movements for humane social transformation that suffuse our political identity with the compassion and justice of the Kingdom. This path, of course, would be in keeping with some of the best hopes and dreams of the visionaries and activists of our ancestral communities. It would also affirm the words and deeds of the prophets and teachers of our faith communities, including Jesus of Nazareth, who was apparently very clear about his liberating, empowering, and saving ministry.

At the same time, I know that there are sisters and brothers in our churches, and fellow citizens in our nation, who counsel against your joining the struggle for the expansion of democracy, who do not believe that "advanced ideas" concerning democracy and advanced life in the spirit of God go together, who do not remember your own powerful experiences. I am writing to invite you to explore the reviving connections between profound spirituality and courageous social responsibility, connections often deep within your own history. Taste and see, and remember. I am inviting you to wade in the water, suggesting that while the waters of American democracy are surely troubled, it may well be that it is the God of the churches—the God who loves the world—who is troubling them. So there may be no healing for us or our nation unless we step in together, just as there was no ultimate safety for those who refused to risk the terrors of the Red Sea, or who clung to the edges of the pool at Bethsaida, while the great healing spirit moved in the deeps.

Do not be afraid when some people say that you are "newcomers," or that you have not sufficiently established yourselves, or that you may not have adequately found your new voice among the ancient treasures of your people. In a sense, most of us are newcomers to this land, but it now belongs to all of us who will work for its redemption, and as we work our new voice develops. Sisters and brothers, we need workers for the creation of a compassionate democracy—gentle, persistent, courageous warriors of the spirit who apply their disciplined inner strength, who focus their powerful prayers and loving actions on the social, economic, and political needs of their nation and its people. We need you. This is not simply a political or secular task. The work of expanding, developing, empowering women and men to see and believe in their great, divinely given creative powers is a profoundly spiritual and religious vocation. Ultimately, as you know, it is the work of encouraging human beings to discover and give witness to the magnificent transformative presence of God within us and among us. What better work is there?

So when I hear people say that such tasks do not belong to the churches, when they especially encourage people of color to be enthusiastic in our worship but passive and silent in our citizenship, I am strengthened by Pablo Neruda's marvelous statement concerning our vocation, identity, and promise as earth-

hued children of life and light. In "So Is My Life," the Chilean
poet-martyr wrote,

> I exist not if I do not attend to the pain
> of those who suffer: they are my pains.
> For I cannot be without existing for all,
> for all who are silent and oppressed.
> I come from the people and I sing for them:
> my poetry is song and punishment.
> I am told: you belong to darkness.
> Perhaps, perhaps, but I walk toward the light.[2]

From Chicago to Birmingham to Santiago and Soweto, the
experience seems to be very similar to what we found in the
freedom movement. The churches are challenged to their best
life when we hear the cry of the oppressed as a siren deep within
our bones, when we risk our lives to respond, when we discover
that there is no fundamental contradiction between waking up
with our minds stayed on Jesus and stayed on freedom. Both
songs belong to us. Both open us to the morning light.

Of course, many of you, dear sisters and brothers, have
already given witness to that reality with your entire beings,
sometimes at great cost. I am writing now to invite you to continue, to renew your stand with the embattled ones, to pick up
the best strands of your own rich, justice-seeking traditions and
join them with the new history we have created in the Black-led
freedom movement in this land. Perhaps we shall then receive
Neruda as our brother. Perhaps we shall all understand more
deeply than ever the Jesus of his home synagogue, the Jesus of
the Sermon on the Mount, the Jesus of the sheep and the goats.
Without *this* Jesus the cross we promote becomes nothing more
than a tired piece of rhetoric, or, worse, a weapon with which
to defend ourselves against the desperate advances of those who
come to us in search of the compassionate liberator Jesus.
Refusing that deadly sword, abandoning that betrayer's role,
attending to the pain of our people, of all jobless, homeless,
unrealized, and hopeless people, let us bravely walk with them
toward the light.

Finally, dear ones, I wish to suggest an experiment. As you

know, the fact that we exist in so many separated ethnic manifestations within the One Body is both a blessing and a curse.
Now that the parts are gathering from around the world in this
one nation, perhaps we can use our common national base as a
path to deeper unity among us. And it may be that we will locate
and comprehend both our religious and political territory more
fully by trying out a kind of gathering that is still too unfamiliar
among us. Suppose one of your churches in a local setting invited
representatives from other congregations, especially among the
peoples of color, to come and share a pot-luck meal (always a
great pluralist attraction!) and watch together something like
segments of *Eyes on the Prize*. This might be done once or twice
a month, alternating locations, inviting one or more veterans of
the freedom movement to serve as a resource person.

I've participated in enough approximations of such a gathering to know that it can be a rich and mutually beneficial experience, especially when sensitive and committed leadership is
provided. Not only does it allow us to feel our way among the
smoldering coals of racial and class divisions that exist among
us, but it opens to our people a segment of this country's history
that they have often bypassed. Even more important, perhaps,
the leadership, ideology, and settings that we see and feel
through such history suggest a role for the churches that may
be especially helpful for us to consider at this crucial juncture
in the development of the worldwide struggle for political and
economic democracy. (Such pot-luck and video-viewing gatherings might also inspire some of your own gifted filmmakers to
consider sharing the story of your struggles in a more complete
way with us all.) Of course, we cannot predict the outcome of
such an experiment, but if it reminds us of our purpose, if it
echoes Neruda's summons to our destiny, if it opens to us the
possibility of sharing more deeply in both history and future,
then its goals would be well served. Shall we experiment?

IV. *To My Sisters and Brothers of the Jewish Communities*

Once again it is the power of our shared history that calls
me. And here, as everywhere, the most intimate personal details

precede the grand design. For even before the time of my well-remembered formative years at Victory Tabernacle Church in Harlem, I have mostly vague but sometimes powerfully precise memories of an even earlier setting where the life of the spirit was vividly marked by the Hebrew Scriptures and they literally engulfed all else. The place was a three-story brownstone on East 130th Street that had been transformed into a rooming house, and where my mother and I lived in one rented room, sharing a bath and kitchen "privileges," as they were called, with several other renters, including a man everyone knew as Uncle Jimmy, who wore a yarmulke and a beard and called himself a Black Jew.

Even more important for our connections, though, is the fact that on the first floor of the house, occupying a slightly remodeled version of the original, ample-sized living room and dining room, the little congregation known as the Israel of God Seventh-Day Adventist Church held its services each Friday night and Sabbath day. (I'm fairly certain that there was another midweek evening service as well, but all I remember of that are the refrains of songs wafting up through the open door to our room where my mother thought I was asleep, and where sooner or later I was—except for those times when I came out to the top of the wooden staircase to try to look down and make sure that Momma was really there.) So when Sister Mabel Harding later decided to join the somewhat larger (but not much) Victory Tabernacle Seventh-Day Christian Church, her five-year-old son was already prepared for another Black religious community whose worship days and dietary habits were generally modeled on the Jewish experience.

There is much more to that story (including the account of my own painful but necessary decision to take a different path when I was in my twenties), but this is not the place to tell it.[3] Here, I should probably reflect for a moment on the influence of the Jewish teachers who seemed to love and respect me and who certainly did much to nurture me through the New York public school system. (Let Irene Berger of Walton Avenue and Morris High School be especially remembered.) And then, of course, there was the unique experience of the City College of New York, still overwhelmingly Jewish in its student population when I entered in the late 1940s, but enmeshed in struggles over charges of antisemitism leveled against some of its faculty. (My development as a student leader here, as well as in the multi-racial public schools, probably influenced my thinking about the possibilities of American pluralism and the role of African-American leadership in such a society far more than I realize.)

In the light of such peculiar personal history, the formation of deep friendships, and the establishment of still unbroken interior connections, I was not surprised when I met many of you on the frontiers of our freedom struggle in the South. I realized that if you knew your story and its meaning, then you also knew that it was imperative that you find some way to respond to our call. (Indeed, some of your foreparents had heard earlier versions of the call and had responded in a variety of ways even in the pre–World War II years.) So in Albany, Georgia, we laughed together at the consternation you caused the police who had never seen folks in yarmulkes standing in front of city hall. In Meridian, Mississippi, the newly established community center in the Black neighborhood became a fascinating place to meet my fellow New Yorker, Mickey Schwerner, for the first time. Though I was almost ten years older than he, we shared recollections of people and places, and his feisty humor in a very dangerous situation reminded me of friends in many points of my past.

Then, although I wasn't there when it happened, I have always cherished my proxy memory of Rabbi Abraham Heschel introducing Martin Luther King, his marching mate and movement leader, to a gathering of rabbis in upstate New York in March 1968. It was about ten days before King's assassination — in the midst of a very controversial time — that Heschel, with the wisdom of his prophetic forbears, boldly declared to the gathering,

> Martin Luther King is a voice, a vision, and a way. I call upon every Jew to harken to his voice, to share his vision, to follow in his way. The whole future of America will depend on the impact and influence of Dr. King.[4]

For me, my sisters and brothers, much of my own message to you is summed up in that setting, in those words. King had come north. He was challenging the structural elements of American life and values that contributed to poverty, militarism, and political disempowerment, as well as to a paranoid anti-communism. He was attempting to mobilize and organize the poor, and the allies of the poor across racial lines, for a major, much-maligned, nonviolent confrontation with the federal government scheduled to take place that spring in Washington, D.C. Seeking to call the nation from its shameful war in Vietnam and turn it toward an authentic and costly commitment to the eradication of poverty in the United States, King was experimenting with the possibilities of revolutionary nonviolence. As you may remember, these issues and actions, set against the fiery background of urban rebellions and burgeoning Black consciousness, were much more difficult for the Jewish community—like the rest of white America—to deal with than the relatively unambiguous and apparently distant confrontations in the South. Heschel knew all this, but he insisted nevertheless that these important leaders of his/your community face the truth as he saw it: "The whole future of America will depend upon the impact and influence of Dr. King."

Heschel was, and is, correct. For those who have participated so often and so deeply in the story of the twentieth-century Black freedom movement, it is imperative for you to remember that much more than Black people, or Jews, are involved in what we are building. For the energies of the freedom movement helped bring us to a powerful moment in the continuing re-creation of this nation, and we are all imperiled if we do not go forward together. Indeed, it appears to me that much of the pain inherent in our current stage of Black-Jewish relationships grows out of our high expectations for each other, out of our disappointment with the failures of our memories and of our nerve. For instance, just as our African-American foreparents chose to identify with the Biblical children of Israel, with their captivity, suffering, and redemption, so we expected that the anguish of your own more recent blood-soaked history would bring you into a special relationship with our story. But even as I have gratefully recognized your presence, often sacrificial, among us, I also sense the great temptation among many of you to lose yourself in the protective coloration of mainstream

America's whiteness and to imbibe too much of its success orientation, as well as its racist paternalism—thereby betraying your own best religious and spiritual traditions. (And we Black people have too readily absorbed the mainstream's antisemitism and forgotten our healing times together in collective struggle and hope.)

Over the millennia you have been called many times to stand up for the unpopular causes of justice and righteous social orders. You have been admonished to refuse to accept the comforts and rewards offered by the powerful established forces in exchange for your acquiescence in the crushing of the poor. You know all that far better than I do. You also know that the same unrelenting challenge now extends from Brooklyn to the West Bank to South Africa. (So we have much to discuss, as mutually respectful sisters and brothers, as veterans and co-workers in the struggle for the expansion of democracy in the United States.) What I know is that we have experienced our deepest levels of unity, trust, and fulfillment when we have both remembered the full statement of that early call to freedom: "Let my people go, that they may serve me in the wilderness."

I think both Heschel and King understood that our histories have been linked in grand and terrible ways (including the histories of unspeakable holocausts), in ways that call us to become again fellow travelers, co-workers, servants together in the wilderness. There are, as well, a thousand writings on the walls of this nation which tell us that there is no real safety or integrity here for you or me, for Jews or Black people, unless we open ourselves to King and to Heschel, together, again. Let us study them again, by ourselves and in concert. Let us deepen the meaning of their message for these times, and then let us take the call from them, and from Schwerner and Goodman and Chaney, and from Moses' burning bush, with utmost seriousness. Our true vocation as persons and as peoples is to use our freedom to give our whole selves to the continuing task of turning this wilderness nation into a land of promise for all its people, especially its most needy and forgotten ones. ("We, the people, must redeem our land . . .")

Please tell that to your children and grandchildren, to your sisters and brothers, and I will tell it to mine. And when they ask us to show them what we mean, to demonstrate how we walk our talk, let us gather at the rendezvous of struggle and hope, telling our stories and our one great story, continuing to create the next stages of its powerful unfolding. Moving as wounded, obedient servants into the wilderness, rejecting the false comforts of the status quo, rejoicing in the wonderful breakdown of the destructive Cold War order, we may yet discover together the meaning of our pasts and the purpose of our future.

V. To My Sisters and Brothers in Other Life-Giving Communities of Hope

For you the message must be much more brief, but the appreciation of your presence is no less deep. For example, I gladly acknowledge that one could never tell the story of these last fifty years without a sense of awe and gratitude for what Malcolm X, more deeply known as El-Hajj Malik El-Shabazz, gave to us all. Here was a model of a life totally submitted to the will of the All-Merciful One. Here was powerful testimony to the reality of personal resurrection, of life transformed and renewed. Malcolm was our image of the unrelenting search for truth, a search that never strayed far from the streets he knew so well, from the people he loved so deeply. For him the quest for personal truth and the struggle for social justice became one inseparable "straight path." And even though I recognize that there are many varieties of Moslem experience and manifestation, it will always be Malcolm who brings me to the tents of Allah, the Compassionate.

As I understand it, my sisters and brothers of the Islamic communities, Malcolm's implacable quest for the will of Allah was leading him ever more deeply into the center of this great story of the Black-led struggle for justice, truth, and redemption in the United States. Indeed, less than three weeks before his assassination our brother responded to the call of the southern-based freedom movement and went to Selma, Alabama. There he declared, "I'm for a society of human beings that can practice brotherhood." And as he faced the young people of the movement who were risking their lives for such a society, Malcolm said,

I pray that God will bless you in everything that you do. I
pray that you will grow intellectually, so that you can
understand the problems of the world and where you fit
into that world picture. And I pray that all the fear that is
evident in your heart will be taken out.[5]

He was speaking to the youth. He was speaking to himself. He
was speaking to us. He prayed that they might find the way,
might exorcise their fears. So for himself. So for us all. And now
I pray that we, too, will enter this story together, will claim it as
our own, learning it, teaching it, bringing new life to it, offering
prayers of silence and action. For even though many of us have
come only recently to share in this common country, I trust that
we, like Malcolm, will explore the vision of a transformed nation,
"a society of human beings." Like him, I hope you will emblazon
it on the consciousness of your children, that you will bring the
great strengths of your faith, of our faith, into the continuing
creation of a land where we can "practice brotherhood—and
sisterhood."

I speak in the same voice to my Buddhist sisters and brothers,
again expressing great joy in your presence here. For even
though I understand some of the terrible paradoxes of history
and the brutal misdeeds of my own country which brought many
Asians here, I am convinced that even the wings of anguish can
carry healing ointments in their flight. So I remember that some
of my own earliest introductions to the ways of Buddhism came
as a result of contact with your great teacher, peace worker, and
Bodhisattva, the Venerable Thich Nhat Hanh, a contact made
possible by the war in his native Vietnam. In his early commu-
nications with Martin Luther King, Jr., through his long and
dangerous struggle for peace and justice, against the terrorism
of the United States government's presence in Vietnam, and in
his continuing work of social service, he represents for me much
of the beauty and power of Buddhist traditions. And I am very
glad that he continues in his retreats and publications to teach
us how to build our inner resources for the demanding work of
personal and social transformation to which we are called.

Over the years, His Holiness, the Dalai Lama, the Buddhist
Peace Fellowship, and teachers such as sister Chiu-Nan Lai,

guides into Vipassana meditation, and Professor Don Swearer of Swarthmore have opened additional paths of study and practice to my family and me. So I know something of the gifts you have for us all in this land, beginning perhaps with the disciplines of the spirit. Since I am convinced that the next stages of our work for the transformation and humanizing of our nation will demand that we heed Thich Nhat Hanh's call to "struggle with patience," I am glad that you are here. Certainly your concern for the unity of all life will also strengthen our Native American and African ecological visions and provide continuing power to our commitment to redeem the earth itself.

Yes, dear sisters and brothers of the Buddha, this is now our land together. All our ancient and modern gifts will be required for the expansion of our part of the great human story. Together we will search out the paths of truth for our time and our place. I look forward to our continuing struggle and hope, for ourselves, for our children, for all living beings.

My Hindu sisters and brothers, at the outset I confess a strong bias in your favor. There are two reasons for this, and one is named Gandhi. Now, I realize that there are significant variations of opinion and feelings among you concerning the Mahatma and his continuing relevance for our lives, but I also know that it was your traditions which nurtured him, your *Gita* which inspired him, your freedom struggles which opened his own best possibilities to himself and to the world. So when I see you—whether from India or not—I see not only you, for I cannot escape his presence.

For me, that presence is powerful. My earliest memories of it are connected with Victory Tabernacle Church, where my very well-read and largely self-educated pastor knew all about Gandhi's movement in the 1930s and 1940s and often called our attention to "that little brown man who has challenged the British Empire." Since those days I have come to meet Gandhi at deeper levels and to recognize not only his profound contributions to our own African-American struggles, but his great gift to all men and women who seek to hold together the unity of the quest for justice, peace, and human community. (When at the close of the 1980s I hear a Russian Communist Party member saying, "Sacharov was our Gandhi," I rejoice.)

As you settle into the benefits and perils of this land, as you build new temples and societies here, I trust you will remember your own story, both its ancient verses and its Gandhian truths, for if you are faithful to those memories, you will also recognize our story, identify with our Black American pilgrimage, exercise your great gift for absorbing new religious experiences. Then, refusing to allow the racism and color (and caste?) consciousness of East or West to distance you from us, you will discover with us a magnificent common ground, and we will claim new sisters and brothers in the continuing quest for social transformation, in the search for the God within us all.

Friends, I know that this meeting of the hearts, minds, and spirits is both possible and deeply rewarding. Indeed, I have experienced it on very personal grounds—and that brings me to my second reason for bias in your favor. Over the past decade my family and I have been granted the gift of entry into some small but powerful corner of your world through the loving invitation and initiation of my brother Sudarshan Kapur and his family. Steeped in the experience of grassroots rural organizing and development work in India, in quest of ever-deepening commitments to the way of nonviolent social change, planning and yet not planning to meet us, he came here from India with his wife and two children. We met in 1979, and since that time I have seen and felt true bonding on both personal and more than personal levels. For Sudarshan has immersed himself in the story of the Afro-American freedom movement in this country. Indeed, in the course of a most valuable doctoral dissertation he has given us an account of the ways in which the Black American community and the Indian independence movement met each other in the years between World Wars I and II, long before the rise of Martin King.[6]

But none of this has been confined to intellectual activity. Rather, the quest for the joining point of our stories grew out of the search for common ground in our lives. (As a matter of fact, Sudarshan's mother says she is convinced that I knew her son in another life. It feels that way.) So I write to you out of the regions of my heart. I welcome you to a nation that is still in its infancy compared to your own ancient kingdoms. I challenge you to discover with the Hardings and the Kapurs, and others who have risked and ventured themselves, to expand the frontiers of our continuing movement toward American democracy—"the land that never has been yet, and yet must be."

We need your spirit, your vision, and your history. We need Kali and Krishna. We need Ganesha and Gandhi. We can only begin to imagine the visions and the songs, the hopes and the inner disciplines that are possible when our stories and our lives are deeply joined. What power, what new manifestations of compassionate, justice-seeking, musically saturated power are awaiting us? Sisters and brothers, let us find out. Let us begin.

And, of course, my dear Bahais, you know this call is also to you, from you. We need your truth. Please share it, in all its living power. Let the new race be born.

VI. To My Brothers and Sisters in the Native American/Indian Communities

Both the call for new beginnings and our need to close out these letters remind us that we are drawn by our origins as well as our destiny in this country to seek out some real communion with you, our oldest ancestors on this land, Native Americans, Indians, the People. So, teachers of the plains, the mountains, the cities and the lakefronts, please accept this last, brief note as more of a response than a letter to you. For you are unique among us, partly because of the millennia of your tenure here, the power of your teaching in words and deeds, the ancient wisdom which assists our own search, and because of your truth which reminds us that "our first Teacher is our own heart."[7]

Now, called to begin our movement toward democracy again, embracing the life and truth you share with us, we all must pause, in gratitude, repentance, and hope. Listening to the teacher within, we recognize that no amount of time and space is adequate for the recollection that will draw us into deepest harmony with our Indian sisters and brothers, with our ancestors of this earth, with you, with our hearts. We know, too, that you who have cared for this land so long cannot be pressed into any one community of faith, cannot be captured by the languages and structures of religious belief that others have created for you. That is why the first person singular voice with which I

began these letters now joins all other voices, recognizing our
special debt and relationship to you on this continent. That is
why you are not last among the addressees, but first on the
frontier of our new beginnings. For we take seriously the words
of one of your most thoughtful spokespersons, Vine Deloria,
who predicted two decades ago that we are approaching "the
beginning of a new world religion on this continent that will
create its own mythology and symbolism and sweep the world
with its vision."[8]

Meanwhile, sisters and brothers, Chippewas and Utes, Hopi
and Ojibwa, Blackfoot and Apalachee, we pause with you before
ending, before beginning, simply because our integrity allows
nothing else. We pause to remember in profound gratitude all
of you who taught us and still teach us so much about the art
of living with this rich and native land, about its needs and
generous possibilities, about its precious fruits and divine spirits.
We thank you for reminding us about "our first Teacher"; we
pause to listen and to learn. We dare to seek forgiveness from
you, from ourselves, for the greed and madness which led (and
still leads) to our participation in the decimation and impris-
onment of your ancestors, our ancestors, the Creeks and Osage,
your ancestors, the Seminoles and Kiowas, our ancestors, the
Crows, Lakotas, and Navahos—your ancestors, our ancestors,
whose names are now remembered only by the winds (but that
is a mighty remembering).

In many urgent ways you were our first instructors in physical
survival, our first teachers in democracy on these shores. So you
are close to our hearts. We pause to thank you, rejoin you in
hope and solidarity. We promise to stand with you in your continuing quest for justice. As we rebuild this nation, as we seek
to begin again, we need you, all of you, to be teachers and vision
seekers with us. We need Chief Seattle to promise us again that
in every new beginning "these shores will swarm with the invisible dead of my tribe." We need him to remind, call, warn, and
inspire us to "be just and deal kindly with [Indian] people, for
the dead are not powerless. Dead did I say? There is no death,
only a change of worlds."[9]

My sisters and brothers of every communion and community,
of every household of faith, of the one family, clearly the word

has been given. The worlds are now changing. This is our time to teach, to learn, to open the way for the seventh generation.

This is our time to dance, to fly, to see visions of life beyond the old boundaries, to search out the new common ground. The story and the stories are within our hearts. Let us begin.

Your brother,

Vincent

Acknowledgments

At various points along the way I have tried to call attention to the humanizing power that a sense of gratitude can bring into our lives. Now I am pleased to participate in that spirit myself, acknowledging and celebrating a few of the debts I have incurred in the development of this work.

Of course, some aspects of my appreciation have already been expressed, beginning with the Introduction and its remembrances of the teachers in my life. However there is more to say, and contrary to the usual practice in such a setting, I choose to begin with the profound sense of gratitude I bear for my immediate family of Rosemarie, Rachel and Jonathan Harding, and the essential role they have played in this creative process. Their compassionate and critical readings, their essential research assistance, and their unfailing gifts of loving support were foundational components of the book's development. (In addition, my daughter Rachel Harding's important work on the accompanying teacher's resource guide will soon be available as part of a separate publication.)

I am also very grateful to the diverse company of students and other fellow-seekers who have helped to focus and deepen my own appreciation for the many meanings of the freedom movement, especially through our shared reflections on the *Eyes on the Prize* video series. My family and I have experienced the power of this story and these films in the company of men, women and children in settings as apparently disparate as Scotland's Island of Iona, the Canyon City (Colorado) prisons, St. Leo's monastery in Florida, Spelman and Swarthmore Colleges, Hampton and Denver Universities, and in public and independent schools in this city. Moreover, the story and the films have elicited exciting and engaging discussions in churches and

229

retreat centers, in classes at the Iliff School of Theology, and even at the Denver Museum of Natural History—where we explored "The Natural History of Democracy in America." For all the persons who arranged these visits and experiments, for all the participants who shared so much of their learning and teaching with me (including the six-year-old boy who saw Rabbi Abraham Heschel marching with Dr. King and said, "That's me! My name is Abraham"; the teenager who proudly announced that her parents had named her after Angela Davis, and the gifted Rock quartet at Colorado Academy's upper school who responded to the films with an original musical composition— "Keep Your Eyes on the Prize"), I am forever indebted.

Of course, I cannot exhaust the categories of gratitude when I think of the courageous, gifted and indomitable teams who actually made the two *Eyes* series. These women and men— under the genuinely wise leadership of Henry Hampton—are a gift to us all. As I watched Henry guide his feisty, multiracial working community through the demanding years of the project, I realized that their film-making process itself was an experiment in a certain kind of pluralistic democracy, aided by a leadership at once flexible, visionary and firm. In a profound sense, as I indicated in the Introduction, Henry and the Blackside community of teacher/filmmakers are the most immediate inspiration for this book.

While working on the writing project I have had consistently helpful cooperation and encouragement from Robert Lavelle, Blackside's Vice-president for publishing, and from my conscientious and appropriately demanding editor, Sarah Flynn. I am grateful as well for the kind assistance given the manuscript by Blackside's Nicole Keating. I am also very pleased that it was possible for us to team up with a publishing house I have long respected, Orbis Books. In addition, all of us were really happy to have the Foreword written by Lerone Bennett, Executive Editor of *Ebony* magazine, and magnificent teacher/historian. (All of this, of course, has taken place under the amazingly patient eye of Drenka Willen, my editor at Harcourt Brace Jovanovich, who continues to wait for the manuscript of the second volume of *There is a River*.)

The gestation time for *Hope and History* extended longer than any of us had expected (even though my previous record should have warned me), and it could not have been completed without the solid financial support and moral encouragement of Ms. Jacqui Burton of the Lilly Endowment, as well as the fullest cooperation of Dean Jane Smith and President Donald Messer at Iliff. In addition, I am grateful for the generous support that the Charles H. Revson Foundation and the Rockefeller Foundation gave toward the development of educational materials based on *Eyes on the Prize*. Of course, it was a secretarial genius like Ms. Margaret Manion and a conscientious assistant like Vivek Pinto who really brought it off in the final accounting, and it was research assistants like Mike Hofkamp and Palmer (Don) Palmerdon who did so much to keep us all honest along the path. I am grateful to them and to all my students and colleagues at Iliff.

But I need to return for a moment to this matter of inspiration. Taking the word in its most literal sense, I have often felt the encouraging breath of some persons being shared with me, enlivening me, all along the way. Although many such persons could be named, I think especially of some of my friends (and relatives) who are among the living veterans of the modern freedom movement and who continue to work in a variety of ways for the expansion of democracy in the United States. They include Bob and Janet Moses, James and Dorothy Lawson, Octavia and C.T. Vivian, Katherine Dunham, Bill Strickland, Alice and Staughton Lynd, Diane Nash, Jim Wallis, Sonia Sanchez, James and Grace Boggs, Andrew and Jean Young, George Ofori-Atta Thomas, Dorothy Cotton, Charles Freeney and Coretta King. Though some of them may not know what they have given me, I am grateful for such lively sources of renewal and hope.

Finally, as many of us can affirm, it is good to have some hidden space for work and solitude. With this project, as with others, such help has been generously available. I appreciate the flexibility of Dotty Creager, Iliff's housing coordinator, and I am glad that our friends, Bill and Ava Brackett, were able to share their home at an important moment in the process. I have the same sense of gratitude for Thomas Mikelson and Patricia Sheppard who so gently committed their living room to the project for a while. Most of all, though, I have literally been gifted by the quiet, undemanding and gracious space that has been opened to me at St. Thomas Seminary here in Denver. The school's president, Father John Rybolt, and the housing director, Ms. Ruth Gonzalez, made the gift seem almost effortless. But I knew it wasn't and am even more thankful as a result.

On a closing note, let me respond to a probing question raised by several persons who read the manuscript. Because it is a question I appreciate I place it here among the acknowledgments. These readers wanted me to explain the use of an upper case B when writing about Black people and my use of a lower case w when referring to white people. Although I am not absolutely certain, I think this practice may be partly a cultural lag from the days of the 1960s and early 1970s when many of us fought long and hard battles for the right of Black people to create a freedom which would empower us to affirm our Blackness as an act of self-definition, self-affirmation, and self-determination.

Though it may be difficult for some persons to imagine now (especially as we gather around the important current term, African-American), the energies demanded by the earlier struggle were often protean. It was a movement to transform Blackness from a negative usage to a positive affirmation. Deeply grounded in culture, psychology, religion and politics, it seemed to require a very large B for its adequate expression. Besides, our foreparents had fought an equally demanding battle for the capitalization of the word Negro — the progressive term in *their* time — in American public life, and so we often kept the spirit and the large letter of that history. Somehow, in my mind (and at levels deeper than the mind) white and whiteness did not have the same kind of history, the same energies connected to them.

So while I understand the logic of a capital W, or can force myself, whenever necessary, to see the equal justice behind the use of small b and small w, I cannot easily escape the power of the history of the struggle for Blackness and all the meaning it has carried. It was, and is, sometimes beyond logic. But at no time have I ever intended to demean our Anglo/EuroAmerican sisters and brothers who are not called Black, and who live within the arena that the world calls whiteness. Rather than demean, I recognize with them the inadequacies of all the terms we use to try to describe the uniqueness of our varied historical and genetic pilgrimages. For I am deeply convinced that our ultimate origin and destiny are one—and so is our name.

Meanwhile, I respond to the queries of this interim time, offering a very condensed account of my own pilgrimage, reflecting on the larger African-American experiments with the world's substitutes for our true name. At the same moment, I gladly affirm the righteous power of the search for Blackness in a world that has so long derided both the color and the people. But I know that the greatest power of all, the power of our true name is here waiting for us, and is yet to come. So I continue to listen to the questions of my friends concerning upper and lower cases, and I continue to share with them whatever responses seem consistent with the integrity of my memory, with our unique and common history and with the undying power of our necessary hope, our one love. This is the final acknowledgment, the source of deepest praise.

Notes

Introduction

1. "Re-visioning Education," in *ReVISION*, vol. 2, no. 2 (Fall 1988), pp. 27–30.

2. "Reflections: After the Cold War," *The New Yorker* (January 1, 1990), p. 65.

3. Henry David Thoreau, *A Week on the Concord and Merrimack Rivers* (Princeton: Princeton University Press, 1980), p. 155.

4. The nineteenth-century version is in Henry Wadsworth Longfellow's poem "A Psalm of Life": "Lives of great men remind us/We can make our lives sublime,/And, departing, leave behind us/Footprints on the sands of time." *Favorite Poems of Henry Wadsworth Longfellow* (New York: Doubleday, 1947), p. 302.

5. Herbert Aptheker, ed., *The Autobiography of W.E.B. Du Bois* (New York: International Publishers, 1968), p. 422.

1. Signs . . . Signs . . . Turn Visible Again

1. This assessment was conducted in 1986 and reported in Diane Ravitch and Chester Finn, Jr., *What Do Our Seventeen-Year-Olds Know?* (New York: Harper & Row, 1987). See especially pp. 1–5, 61, 76.

2. June Jordan, *Naming Our Destiny* (New York: Thunder's Mouth Press, 1989).

3. *Rolling Stone* (April 7, 1988), p. 63.

4. From Robert Hayden's poem "El-Hajj Malik El-Shabazz" in *For Malcolm*, ed. Dudley Randall and Margaret G. Burroughs (Detroit: Broadside Press, 1967), p. 16.

5. Quoted in Harvey Sitkoff, *The Struggle for Equality* (New York: Hill & Wang, 1981), pp. 74–75.

2. Advanced Ideas about Democracy

1. "Mother, I'm not in the Wrong," *China Talk Newsletter*, vol. 14, no. 4 (June 1989), p. 10.

2. For example, two sharply focused expressions of concern about failures of the American press to serve its essential, unmanipulated, "watchdog" role in our nation's most recent history appeared almost simultaneously in disparate settings: the *Wall Street Journal* (Hodding Carter III, "A Confederacy of Liars, Guarded by a Yawning Watchdog," January 25, 1990, p. A15) and *The Nation* (Alexander Cockburn, "Beneath a Peak in Darien: The Conquest of Panama," vol. 250, no. 4 [January 29, 1990], pp. 114–15).

3. Richard Kluger, *Simple Justice: The History of Brown v. Board of Education and Black America's Struggle for Equality* (New York: Vintage Books, 1977).

4. Shortly after the massacre in Beijing, we are told of a "legend spreading widely in China, of the 100 students who, when the tanks entered Tiananmen Square, locked arms and stood together singing the Internationale while the bullets sprayed into their bodies. And then another 100 took their place and met the same fate." The reporter then added, "It makes no difference, really, whether this happened or not. Beijing simply believes that it occurred and the legend is spreading all over the country." *New York Times*, June 6, 1989, p. 27. A similar powerful story was spread by creative use of videotape in Czechoslovakia's pro-democratic revolution.

5. While he was spending time in a local jail, along with a dozen other Mississippi freedom organizers, Bob Moses smuggled out a letter that included these words: "This is Mississippi, the middle of the iceberg. Hollis [Watkins] is leading off with his tenor, 'Michael, row the boat ashore . . . Mississippi's next to go, Alleluia.' This is a tremor in the middle of the iceberg—from a stone that the builders rejected." Joanne Grant, ed., *Black Protest: History, Documents and Analysis, 1619 to the Present*, 2d ed. (New York: Fawcett Premier, 1968), p. 303.

6. Fortunately, Doug Harris, the gifted photographer and filmmaker who served in the 1960s as a SNCC organizer, is now working with Bob Moses and Professor Ronald Bailey (of Northeastern University in Boston) to create an invaluable set of documentary film resources based on the memories and reflections of hundreds of Mississippians and others who labored long and hard in that dangerous state. Obviously, similar historical restoration needs to be done on the organizing experiences of at least half a dozen other southern states — to say nothing of the many stories still hidden in scores of urban settings across the nation.

7. At some point we might want to compare the Chicago experience with similar paradoxes elsewhere—from Mississippi to Mexico. In the latter situation the poet Octavio Paz reports, "I grew up/ Fostered alike by beauty and by fear."

8. I am not aware of any book-length historical study of this powerful phenomenon, which combined the search for educational, cultural, and political democracy in fascinating ways and which is still alive in the nation's current (often weak) attempts to create a multiracial educational system. The best contemporary, ongoing accounts of the struggle can be found in the pages of Johnson Publications' *Negro Digest/Black World* for the 1965-72 period, and in some issues of *Ebony* magazine over the same years. For instance, see my "Black Students and the Impossible Revolution" in *Ebony* (August/September 1969).

9. Frantz Fanon, *The Wretched of the Earth* (New York: Grove Press, 1965).

10. Walter Rodney, *How Europe Underdeveloped Africa* (Washington, D.C.: Howard University Press, 1974).

11. Kenneth O'Reilly, *Racial Matters: The FBI's Secret File on Black America, 1960-72* (New York: Free Press, 1989).

12. We will probably need help from our students, and from many other sources of wisdom, to know how to receive the latest news concerning William O'Neal, the admitted FBI informant who was placed in the Chicago Black Panther organization, and whose disclosures led directly to the police murders of Fred Hampton and Mark Clark in 1969. On January 15, 1990, while much of the nation remembered Martin Luther King, Jr., and the freedom movement, O'Neal ran out on a Chicago freeway and was killed by an oncoming car. The police labeled his death a suicide. What shall we say? What silent vigils shall we keep?

13. National Black Political Agenda (Greensboro: National Black Political Convention, 1972), pp. 1–4.

14. In the more recent set of 1989 elections the "prize" was taken to even more symbolic heights, and the related questions were deepened. The victory of a Black gubernatorial candidate in the once profoundly Confederate bastion of Virginia—the first African-American governor anywhere in the nation—and of a Black mayor in New York City were landmark events. However, it is still important to try to understand what happens to our focus on "advanced ideas" of democracy when the appeal to the mainstream seems to be a central element in such campaigns.

15. Michael Crozier, Samuel P. Huntington, Joji Watanuki, eds., *The Crisis of Democracy* (New York: NYU Press, 1975), pp. 114–15.

16. Martin Luther King, Jr., *Stride Toward Freedom: The Montgomery Story* (New York: Harper & Brothers, 1958), p. 197.

5. More Power Than We Know

1. Henry Hampton and Steve Fayer with Sarah Flynn, *Voices of Freedom: An Oral History of the Civil Rights Movement from the 1950s*

through the 1980s (New York: Bantam, 1990), p. 359.

2. Huey P. Newton with the assistance of J. Herman Blake, *Revolutionary Suicide* (New York: Harcourt Brace Jovanovich, 1973), p. 127.

3. Peter Geismar, *Fanon* (New York: Dial Press, 1971), p. 185.

4. Howard Zinn, *SNCC: The New Abolitionists* (Boston: Beacon, 1964).

5. Clayborne Carson, *In Struggle: SNCC and the Black Awakening of the 1960s* (Cambridge: Harvard University Press, 1981).

6. One of the marvelous gifts inherent in this country's multicultural potential is the ability it offers us to choose our ancestors. Just as members of religious groups are free to claim spiritual ancestors who may have no direct genetic connection to them, so, too, persons committed to the expansion of American democracy are able to claim forebears on the basis of common commitment and common vision. So white students may consider Sojourner Truth, John Lewis, and Diane Nash as their ancestors and Black students may freely choose Dorothy Day and Tom Paine. And all of us may graft ourselves to the extended family trees of Cesar Chavez, Chief Seattle and Toyohiko Kagawa. (Wasn't this what Jesus was opening to us in his audacious questions: Who is my mother? Who is my family?) All of which ultimately reminds us that it is not only in our country but across the globe in the post–World War II period that young people played a crucial role in the struggle for freedom, independence, and hope, even before Soweto and Beijing.

7. Martin Luther King, Jr., *The Trumpet of Conscience* (New York: Harper & Row, 1968), p. 46.

8. Ibid.

9. *Never Turn Back: The Life of Fanny Lou Hamer*, 1983. 16mm film. 60 minutes, color. Rediscovery Production Inc. Directed by Bill Buckley.

4. Fighting for Freedom with Church Fans

1. Quoted in Eknath Easwaran, *Gandhi the Man* (Petaluma, CA.: Nilgiri, 1978), 2d ed., p. 60.

2. "Trend Gaining in Public Schools to Add Teaching About Religion," Peter Steinfels, *New York Times*, March 19, 1989, p. 1.

3. Mohandas Gandhi, *All Religions Are True*, ed. Anand T. Hingorani (Bombay, India: Bharatiya Vida Bhavan, 1962), pp. 83–84.

4. Gayraud S. Wilmore, *Black Religion and Black Radicalism* (New York: Anchor Press, 1973), pp. 177–78.

5. Langston Hughes, *Selected Poems* (New York: Knopf, 1959), p.

88. Apparently this was one of Hughes's favorite poems. It is found in many published collections, edited by Hughes and by others.

5. "God's Appeal to This Age"

1. A condensed account of the visit with the U.S. military forces appears in Vincent and Rosemarie Harding, *Mobilizing the Forces of Hope*, a booklet published in Germany but available in the United States from the Peace Section, Mennonite Central Committee, Akron, PA 17501.
2. King, *Stride Toward Freedom: The Montgomery Story*, p. 224.
3. Carson, p. 23.
4. King, *The Trumpet of Conscience*, p. 15.

6. Gifts of the Black Movement

1. From "A Testament of Hope," in *A Testament of Hope: The Essential Writings of Martin Luther King, Jr.*, ed. James M. Washington (San Francisco: Harper & Row, 1986), p. 315.
2. Upon reading the preceding paragraph, my daughter, Rachel, a graduate student at Brown University, with a history of deep involvement in Third World organizations and actions, noted that we must not forget the many persons of color in the U.S.A. who do recognize a common cause with and a debt to the African-American freedom movement. Among the most important examples of the insightful responses from other people of color are two works by the Native American scholar-activist Vine Deloria, Jr.: *Custer Died for Your Sins* (New York: Avon, 1969) and *We Talk, You Listen* (New York: Delta Books, 1970).
3. It would be helpful if we introduced our students to the instructive and fascinating anthology, *Vietnam and Black America*, ed. Clyde Taylor (New York: Anchor Press, 1973).
4. From June Jordan and Terri Bush, eds., *The Voice of the Children* (New York: Washington Square Press, 1974), p. 63.
5. Paraphrase of a story told to the author by Howard Thurman.
6. Vine Deloria's comments are especially helpful in exploring the connections between the rise of Black consciousness and the search for a culturally-rooted education among Native Americans and other peoples of color at that time. See Deloria, *We Talk, You Listen*, pp. 38–44, 100–13.
7. Eric Foner, *Reconstruction: America's Unfinished Revolution, 1863-1867* (New York: Harper & Row, 1988), p. 29.

7. Poets, Musicians, and Magicians

1. Floyd Stovall, ed., *Walt Whitman* (New York: Hill & Wang, 1961), p. 379.

2. From "Let America Be America Again," *The Poetry of the Negro 1746-1970*, ed. Langston Hughes and Arna Bontemps (Garden City, NY: Doubleday, 1970), pp. 193–95.

3. Rolland Snellings, "Sunrise!!" in *Black Fire: An Anthology of Afro-American Writing*, ed. LeRoi Jones and Larry Neal (New York: William Morrow, 1968), pp. 322–23.

4. LeRoi Jones/Amiri Baraka, "Black Art," in Jones and Neal, pp. 302–3.

5. Margaret Walker, "For My People," in *Black Voices: An Anthology of Afro-American Literature*, ed. Abraham Chapman (New York: New American Library, 1968), p. 460.

6. Mari Evans, "I Am a Black Woman," *I Am a Black Woman* (New York: William Morrow, 1970).

7. Sonia Sanchez, "Malcolm," in *For Malcolm*, ed. Dudley Randall and Margaret Burroughs (Detroit: Broadside Press, 1969), p. 32.

8. Sonia Sanchez, "poem at thirty," in *The Black Poets*, ed. Dudley Randall (New York: Bantam, 1971), p. 232.

9. Mari Evans, "Speak the Truth to the People," in *I Am a Black Woman*, pp. 91–92.

10. As a beginning point, see the poetry discographies in Randall, *The Black Poets*, pp. 343–49.

11. Rainer Maria Rilke, cited in Kimberly Benston, "Late Coltrane, A Re-membering of Orpheus," in *Chant of Saints*, ed. Michael S. Harper and Robert B. Stepto (Urbana: University of Illinois Press, 1979), p. 413.

12. Indeed, the poet-musician relationship was formalized in the late 1960s by the gifted writer-singer Gil Scott-Heron and the (first) Last Poets ensemble, led by David Nelson, who took the poet-rapper tradition, joined themselves with musicians, and became a ́powerful presence of the time. And among the publishing poets no one represented this reality more faithfully than Michael Harper and a work like *Dear John, Dear Coltrane* (Pittsburgh: University of Pittsburgh Press, 1970).

13. Robert F. Thompson, *Flash of the Spirit* (New York: Random House, 1983).

14. Stovall, pp. 379–80.

15. Don L. Lee, "A Message All Blackpeople Can Dig," *Don't Cry, Scream* (Detroit: Broadside Press, 1969), p. 64.

16. The song appeared in an earlier version by the Isley Brothers.

17. From "Keep on Pushin'," quoted in *Black Nationalism in America*, ed. John H. Bracey, Jr., et al. (Indianapolis: Bobbs-Merrill, 1970), p. 447.

18. This and previous quotations from Simone from Phyl Garland, *The Sound of Soul* (New York: Pocket Books, 1971), pp. 151–52.

19. Benston, "Late Coltrane," in Harper and Stepto, eds., *Chant of Saints*, p. 415.

20. Langston Hughes, quoted in Arnold Rampersad, *The Life of Langston Hughes*, vol. 2 (New York: Oxford University Press, 1989), p. 153.

21. Barry Kernfeld, ed., *New Grove Dictionary of Jazz* (New York: Grove's Dictionaries of Music, 1988).

22. Benston, in Harper and Stepto, p. 417.

23. These and the following quotations are from Garland, p. 182.

24. Benston, in Harper and Stepto, p. 420.

25. Ibid., p. 424.

26. Garland, p. 186.

27. Ibid., p. 190.

28. James Baldwin, *The Fire Next Time* (New York: Dial Press, 1963).

29. James Baldwin, *Nobody Knows My Name: More Notes of a Native Son* (New York: Dial Press, 1961).

30. Quincey Troupe, "The Spiritual Victory of Muhammed Ali," *Black World* (January 1975), p. 44.

31. Ibid., pp. 36–37.

32. Larry Neal, "An Afterword: And Shine Swam On," in Jones and Neal, pp. 655–56.

33. *Black World*, v. 20, no. 1, September 1971, p. 69.

34. In Jordan and Bush, pp. 36, 56.

35. Ibid., p. 31.

36. *China Talk Newsletter*, vol. 14, no. 4 (June 1989), p. 10.

37. Ed Bullins, "Creation Spells," *The Journal of Black Poetry*, Summer/Fall 1969, Vol. I, No. 12, p. 58.

8. Doing the Right Thing in Mississippi and Brooklyn

1. Jesse Kornbluth, "The Struggle Continues," *New York Times Magazine*, July 23, 1989, pp. 47–48.

2. *Never Turn Back: The Life of Fanny Lou Hamer*, 1983. 16mm film. 60 minutes, color. Rediscovery Productions, Inc. Directed by Bill Buckley.

3. Spike Lee with Lisa Jones, *Do the Right Thing: A Spike Lee Joint*

(New York: Fireside/Simon & Schuster, 1989), pp. 62, 58. This companion volume to the film includes Lee's journal and production notes as well as the screenplay.

4. Ibid., p. 282.

5. Interestingly enough, Lee tells us in his journal that he employed some twenty members of the Fruit of Islam as a security force for the filming project. Early in the course of their work, a crack house on the block being used as the set was closed down.

6. Ibid., p. 68.

9. In Search of the World

1. Dunham and Primus no longer perform as dancers, but they continue to be profound, exciting, and stimulating teachers and lecturers.

2. King, *The Trumpet of Conscience*, p. 17.

3. Martin Luther King, Jr., *Strength to Love* (New York: Harper & Row, 1963).

4. I have taken a slight liberty with Césaire's original text, which was, "The work of man has just begun. . . . There is room for all at the rendezvous of conquest." Aimé Césaire, *Return to My Native Land*, trans. John Berger and Anna Bostock (Baltimore: Penguin Books, 1969), p. 85.

10. Is America Possible?

1. Henry Etzkowitz, ed., *Is America Possible? Social Problems from Conservative, Liberal, and Socialist Perspectives* (St. Paul: West Publishing, 1980).

2. *New York Times*, August 23, 1989, p. A15.

3. Langston Hughes, *The Dream Keeper* (New York: Alfred A. Knopf, 1946), p. 7.

4. This and subsequent quotations from "Let America Be America Again," in Hughes and Bontemps.

5. Adam Clayton Powell, Jr., "Seek Audacious Power," *Negro Digest* (August 1966), p. 8.

11. One Final, Soaring Hope

1. Hayden, in Randall and Burroughs, p. 16.

12. Letters to Teachers

1. From "For My People" in Abraham Chapman, ed., *Black Voices: An Anthology of Afro-American Literature* (New York: New American Library, 1968), p. 460.

2. Pablo Neruda, in *Song of Protest: Poems by Pablo Neruda*, trans. Miguel Algarín (New York: William Morrow, 1976), p. 68.

3. One of the places I have discussed the early years is in an interview that appears in a book edited and produced by MARHO (Mid-Atlantic Radical Historians' Association), *Visions of History* (New York: Pantheon, 1983), pp. 219–44.

4. Stephen B. Oates, *Let the Trumpet Sound: The Life of Martin Luther King, Jr.* (New York: Harper & Row, 1982; New American Library/Mentor, 1985), p. 455.

5. Malcolm X, *By Any Means Necessary*, ed. by George Breitman (New York: Pathfinder Press, 1970).

6. Sudarshan K. Kapur, *Gandhi and the Afro-American Community, 1919–1955: A Study of the Image and Influence of the Gandhian Movement in the Black Communities of America Before the Coming of Martin Luther King, Jr.*, doctoral diss., The Iliff School of Theology and the University of Denver, 1989.

7. Hyemeyohsts Storm, *Seven Arrows* (New York: Harper & Row, 1972), p. 21.

8. Deloria, *We Talk, You Listen*, p. 207.

9. Frederick W. Turner III, ed., *The Portable North American Indian Reader* (New York: Viking, 1974), p. 253.

Index of Names and Titles

About the Author

VINCENT HARDING is a native of New York City and holds an M.A. and a Ph.D. in History from the University of Chicago. From 1961 to 1964, he and his wife, Rosemarie Freeney Harding, worked in various capacities as full-time teachers, activists, and negotiators in the southern freedom movement. They were friends and co-workers with Martin Luther King, Jr., and many other movement leaders. In 1968, after several years as Chairman of the History and Sociology Department at Spelman College in Atlanta, Georgia, he became the Director of the Martin Luther King Memorial Center, and Chairman of the nationally televised *Black Heritage* series. Harding was one of the organizers and first director of the Institute of the Black World founded in 1969 in Atlanta. After several research positions and visiting professorships, Harding has been Professor of Religion and Social Transformation at the Iliff School of Theology on the University of Denver campus since 1981. He has lectured widely in this country and overseas on history, literature, and contemporary issues.

With his family, he has been active in various movements for peace and justice. He and Rosemarie conduct workshops and lead retreats on the connections between personal spirituality and social responsibility. Recently he has served as senior adviser to the PBS television series, *Eyes on the Prize: America's Civil Rights Years*.

Harding's essays, articles, and poetry have been published in books, journals, and newspapers. Two of his most recent books are: *The Other American Revolution*, and *There is a River* (the first in a three-volume history on the struggle for Black freedom in the United States). The Hardings have two children, Rachel and Jonathan DuBois.